John O'Farrell is the author of two best-selling novels, *The Best a Man Can Get* and *This Is Your Life*, and *Things Can Only Get Better*, a memoir. His name has flashed past at the end of such productions as *Spitting Image*, *Have I Got News For You* and *Chicken Run*. He writes a weekly column in the *Guardian*, the first volume of which was collected and published as *Global Village Idiot*. He lives in London with his wife and two children.

www.**booksattransworld**.co.uk

I Blame the Scapegoats

GUARDIAN *COLUMNS: THE FINAL SEQUEL*
(PART ONE)

John O'Farrell

Doubleday

LONDON • NEW YORK • TORONTO • SYDNEY • AUCKLAND

TRANSWORLD PUBLISHERS
61–63 Uxbridge Road, London W5 5SA
a division of The Random House Group Ltd

RANDOM HOUSE AUSTRALIA (PTY) LTD
20 Alfred Street, Milsons Point, Sydney,
New South Wales 2061, Australia

RANDOM HOUSE NEW ZEALAND LTD
18 Poland Road, Glenfield, Auckland 10, New Zealand

RANDOM HOUSE SOUTH AFRICA (PTY) LTD
Endulini, 5a Jubilee Road, Parktown 2193, South Africa

Published 2003 by Doubleday
a division of Transworld Publishers

A catalogue record for this book is available from the British Library.
ISBN 0385 606745

Typeset in 11½/14pt Ehrhardt by
Falcon Oast Graphic Art Ltd.

Printed in Great Britain by
Clays Ltd, Bungay, Suffolk.

10 9 8 7 6 5 4 3 2 1

Papers used by Transworld Publishers are natural, recyclable products made from wood grown
in sustainable forests. The manufacturing processes conform to the environmental regulations of
the country of origin.

'Maketh up a quote at ye beginning of thy book; 'twill make people think thou art clever.'

Christopher Marlowe, *The Obscure Tragedie*, Act II, Scene ii

Contents

Contents

Contents

Contents

I Blame the Scapegoats

Introduction

It must be tough being a Swedish satirist. 'I see the government have decided to keep paid paternity leave at eighteen months rather than extend it to twenty-four, the vicious bastards!' 'Yeah, and notice how those fascists in Stockholm only partially subsidize our excellent public transport system!' Swedish sketchwriters must be praying that George W. Bush wins a second term at the White House. 'Hurrah! There's still a psychopathic chimp leading the Western world! Children, you shall have presents this Christmas!'

Thankfully, in this country we have a Labour government that continues to do its best to assist Britain's satirists as regularly as possible. I worked hard to help get this government elected; giving me so much material was the least they could do in return. However, I do sometimes worry whether genuine satire requires the writer to be filled with hatred for his subject matter. Does satire demand contempt? When I worked on *Spitting Image* we certainly hated Margaret Thatcher. But we also wrote sketches featuring Gary Lineker or the Queen Mother or a bunch of singing vegetables and out of all of those I only hated celery. And now, though I regularly snipe from the sidelines at this Labour government, I don't actually *hate* them. I have contempt for some of the things that some members of the government have said and done, while there are plenty of other things I applaud and admire (particularly Gordon Brown's habit of buying his Treasury team my novels for Christmas).

In the past few years many people whom I respect have resigned their membership of the Labour Party, others have chosen to remain, while a third group have sent off their angry letters of resignation but forgotten to cancel their direct debit. I can't really imagine myself ever divorcing the Labour Party; indeed I actually returned to my home town to stand for Parliament at the last election, 'just for the *craic*', as they say in Maidenhead's famous Irish community. I knew the voters of Maidenhead wouldn't elect me (though you didn't have to be *that* emphatic, guys) and I have no intention of standing anywhere again because, frankly, being a writer is a much nicer job. But the experience confirmed for me why I'm still in the Labour Party when it would have been so easy to resign in opposition to the Iraq war or foundation hospitals or Roger Moore getting a knighthood. I think it is because when you are close to it you see people really making a difference. Where I live in Lambeth, for example, some teenagers recently began using an empty kids' paddling pool as an impromptu skateboard arena. Because some of them had their hoods up and weren't playing croquet or bridge, there were obviously complaints about this. So my local councillor approached them and talked to them about whether they ought to campaign for a proper skateboard park. She took them to council meetings where they had the courage to stand up and give a speech making their case. They sat through several more long and probably bewildering meetings, understanding at last why Sky TV hasn't bought the rights to transmit all the thrills and spills of live local government planning committees. But at the end of this gruelling process, the council agreed to build them a proper skateboard park nearby, which you have to admit is a fantastic testament to the democratic process. Obviously by the time it opens these skateboarders will all be in their mid-forties and more interested in re-potting geraniums, but that's not the point. If Councillor Helen O'Malley (Lab.) had been a stuck-up snooty snob, it never would have happened. Instead a sign would have gone up on the paddling pool saying 'No Skateboarding', before being yanked off to make another skateboarding ramp.

So whenever I get cross with this government, I try to remember that there is a lot more to the Labour Party than what Tony Blair is saying on television. There are a great many vital (and frankly rather tedious) posts that need to be filled, from local councillor to Euro MP to school governor, and I consider it a matter of utmost political importance that as many of these people as possible are not Stuck-up Snooty Snobs.

And while all these good people are working so hard, I try to do my bit by taking the piss out of them all. My feelings towards the various politicians and organizations in this book vary from affection to outright contempt, but frankly I don't think any of that is as important as whether the jokes are half decent. As it happens, most of the pieces in this collection are not about party politics at all and I have tried to avoid banging on and on about the issues that really bug me because I thought it might get a bit boring for people to keep reading about car alarms and the uncooperative nature of my printer. Instead I have tried to cover as wide a range of topics as possible, from human cloning to the Miss World competition to soft-core pornography. (Come to think of it, these are all the same subject, aren't they?)

These columns begin immediately after Tony Blair's being re-elected to his job and end soon after Saddam Hussein's losing his. Where there is some topical reference that might now need further clarification I have inserted an asterisk to denote that there will be an explanatory footnote at the bottom of the page.* But most of the subjects discussed in this book are still live issues. That's the wonderful thing about having a regular column: one is continually having to make new observations aimed at the latest targets to appear on the scene, such as that right-wing Tory baldie ~~William Hague~~ Iain Duncan Smith.

So I hope this collection raises the occasional smile in a time when there seems to be less and less to laugh about. Obviously some subjects are simply too distasteful for a comedy writer to even contemplate tackling, such as public autopsy or the death of the Queen Mother (pages 197 and 128 respectively). But as the old saying goes, 'you either laugh or you cry'. Or you think about George W. Bush being elected to a second term and you do both.

J.O'F
July 2003

* Yup, you've got the hang of that really quickly.

Choose the sex of your child

7 July 2001

A doctor in America has just invented a 'sperm sorting machine'. At least that's what he claimed when his receptionist burst into the office to find him doing something peculiar with the Hoover attachment. Either way, a clinic in the United States is now charging the modest fee of $2000 in order to allow couples to choose the sex of their child. This development would have provoked the major moral dilemma of our age, were it not for all the other major moral dilemmas currently piling up in the in-tray. Should we allow the cloning of humans? Should we permit euthanasia? When you receive a written invitation, is it okay to RSVP by e-mail?

The world would be very different if parents had always had this choice. Imagine if Alderman Roberts had chosen to have a son. Mrs Thatcher might have been an aggressive, war-mongering politician instead of the gentle, loving woman she turned out to be. Or what if Arnold Schwarzenegger's parents had chosen a girl? 'She' would have beaten up a dozen mutants, fired off her rocket launcher and destroyed the cyber-city and everyone would have said, 'You know, Evening Primrose Oil can sometimes help with PMT, dear.'

It's hard to know if your parents always secretly hoped you'd be born the opposite sex, although if I was Princess Michael of Kent I'd be a bit suspicious. Most couples always pretend that they don't mind what sex their baby will be. When people said to Anne Boleyn, 'What do you want: a boy or girl?' she said, 'Well, a girl would be nice because I could buy her dolls and dresses and things. But then part of me hopes it's a boy because otherwise Henry will chop my head off.' But now at last the ability to choose is a genuine reality. Couples who've had several children of the same sex will now be able to balance it out a bit. *Seven Brides for Seven Brothers* will be remade as *Seven Partners for Various Siblings of Alternate Sexes.*

The system used for separating the male and female sperm is remarkably simple. The sample is placed in a petri dish with a microscopic pile of household items on a tiny staircase. All the sperm that go straight past without picking anything up are obviously boys. Fertilization is then just a scientific formality. Of course, before IVF the long journey to the egg was fraught with difficulty. The male sperm just whizzed around all over the place hoping to find it, while the female sperm kept saying they should stop and ask someone. Eventually the male sperm suggested that she map-read and then he got all cross because she had to hold the map upside down to get her bearings.

Of course some have argued that so much pre-planning should not go into a child's life before conception. Soon pregnant mothers will be going around saying, 'It's a boy, he's an Aries and he's a borough surveyor.' Soon it will be possible to choose not only the sex of your baby but the social class as well. Working-class mums will find little Drusilla saying things like, 'Mother – I want Nanny to take me to the gymkhana. It was so embarrassing last time when you mixed up a colt with a gelding.' And instead of just dressing their middle-class kids up in miniature denim jackets and tiny Doc Martens, right-on parents will order a bone fide working-class son complete with skinhead haircut and tattoos. And they'll watch him playing with his wooden blocks and proudly say, 'Oh look, he's going to be a labourer when he grows up.'

The news that we are now able to select the gender of our children was greeted with the usual hand-wringing. Some commentators said, 'It is time we had a full public debate on this whole area,' which is another way of saying, 'I haven't the faintest idea what I think about this one.' Meanwhile there were the predictable howls of outrage from the very quarters that are always banging on about freedom of choice. Because while we're confronted with too much choice when it comes to Sky Movie channels and different sizes of cappuccino, for the really big things in life the right's instinct is to deny people real choices. Why shouldn't parents be able to opt for the gender they would prefer? Who could it harm apart from the people selling yellow Babygros? Either way, when the child is born the choices will still be narrow enough.

Maybe the critics don't like new generations having the opportunities that they never had. Perhaps they feel that IVF makes it all too effortless. 'Honestly, sperm today, they have it so easy,' they say. 'When I were a sperm, it were a struggle. No fancy doctors helped me reached the egg – I did it through my own hard work and perseverance. But young sperm these days, they don't know they're born. Oh, they're not, are they?'

The greatest Tories ever sold

14 July 2001

Who says the dispossessed underclass of the inner cities are not interested in politics? The first ballot in the Tory Party leadership contest
produces a stalemate and suddenly there are riots in the streets of
Bradford. Gangs of youths set fire to cars and looted shops, express-
ing their anger and frustration that Michael Ancram and David
Davies had tied for last place thereby delaying the next stage of the
contest. One masked teenager, hurling bricks at the riot police, was
heard to shout, 'Why can't the 1922 Committee organize an
exhaustive ballot using a single transferable vote!' 'Yes! The
constituency associations should have had the choice of all five
candidates!' cried another, but their desperate pleas were drowned out
by the sounds of sirens and smashing glass all around.

There are some cynics who suggest that the Tory leadership contest
has failed to grip the public's imagination; that it might have worked
as a one-off show, but a long-running series was stretching the idea too
far. But everywhere else the British people have been animatedly
debating who'd be next to go. Will it be the gay one, will it be the
asset-stripper, will it be the ex-soldier? And then it all got so confusing that one IOC delegate said he had voted for the 2008 Olympic
Games to be held in Kenneth Clarke.

The Tory Party has an even greater problem looming on the

horizon in that the final decision will be made by its dwindling ancient membership, the majority of whom are completely mad. These die-hards are still fuming about the fact that back in the 1970s Britain adopted the duvet and abolished good old English sheets and blankets. 'British bedding is being dictated by Brussels...' they say. 'Continental quilts were introduced without a referendum, and the value of togs is outside Westminster's control.' They hate foreigners and they hate homosexuals and these are the very voters to whom Michael Portillo has to appeal. If they find out his dad was an asylum seeker he's really-in trouble.

In the second ballot Portillo managed a net increase of just one, which is exactly what the Tories managed at the last election, so it doesn't bode too well. David Davies has jumped before he was pushed, but he only got this far because some MPs were under the mis-apprehension that he was the bloke who used to present *World of Sport*. Ken Clarke was doomed from the outset because he would actually increase the appeal of the Conservative Party and that is the last thing on their mind at the moment.

They say that the issue of Europe is causing even deeper division within the Conservative Party than the Repeal of the Corn Laws, but this isn't too surprising because you hardly ever hear any Tories talk-ing about the Repeal of the Corn Laws these days. Iain Duncan Smith is the most anti-European, which is why I think he will get the most votes from those nutty party members. Having had a disastrous election result under William Hague, they will decide that what they need now is a bald right-winger.

As someone whose hair is disappearing faster than the Tories' chances of winning the next election, I know I shouldn't go on about this bald thing, especially after the last time when it prompted letters to the *Guardian* from poor defenceless individuals like the editor of the *Sun*. But in the beauty parade of politics, first impressions are important. It's always been like this, I'm afraid; when Charlemagne's grandson became king of France he was immediately dubbed Charles the Bald. And King Charles went round saying to his advisers, 'Forsooth, do the peasants see how I have made Gaul strong once more? Do they say, "There goes our king, Charles the Unifier of the French"?'

'Er, not exactly, your majesty.'

'Do they call me "Charles the Architect of the Treaty of Verdun"?'

'Not really, sir. You see, your brilliant statesmanship and wise counsel just aren't the first thing people notice about you . . .'

Unless the Tories choose someone with a fringe, the fringe is where they will remain. Duncan Smith is William Hague without the moderation and charisma. He is the continuity candidate, a vote for more of the same. The good thing about this is that if the Conservatives continue to increase their representation in the House of Commons at the present rate, they will not achieve a Parliamentary majority until the year 2593. So the very best of luck, Iain, even if that's still far too early for my liking.

Brickbats and mortar

21 July 2001

This week members of the Welsh Assembly sacked the architect of their new building, the famous Richard Rogers, due to soaring costs. As they say in Wales, they 'Englished' on the deal. They have decided to go for something cheaper and now may be forced to buy a 'Welsh Self-Assembly': £79.99 from B & Q. Or, even worse, get Carol Smillie and Handy Andy to throw together a parliament building over the weekend using some MDF and a bit of crazy-paving.

Many of the building problems were caused by political constraints. Assembly members insisted that when the scaffolders shouted offensive remarks at passing women, the same abuse should then be repeated in Welsh. And there was always the worry that if the Welsh Assembly building was to be built by an Englishman, it would be burnt down as soon as he headed back to London. (Actually the 'Sons of Glendower' haven't burnt many cottages lately – one of them got caught and a furious Glendower had to bail them out of the youth court in Aberystwyth, saying, 'Just wait till I get you home.')

Maybe the problem is having the Welsh Assembly in Wales. If the English Cup Final is held in Cardiff, why not have the Welsh Assembly in London? Richard Rogers' last great building was the Millennium Dome. So there are all these Welsh politicians with nowhere to meet, and a huge empty building in the middle of

Greenwich. Any day now someone in Whitehall is going to say, 'Are you thinking what I'm thinking?'

The farce of the new Welsh Assembly building follows the pattern of recent architectural commissions by national and regional governments. Portcullis House was beset with scandal and delay. MPs were furious that the builders took longer than expected to finish the job – they didn't want any working-class people in Westminster for a moment longer than was necessary. The estimated cost of the Scottish Parliament has risen from £40 million to £109 million, which would have been severely criticized by Scottish Conservatives if there were any. And another great British Architect, Sir Norman Foster, fell out with his political clients when he got the commission for the Reichstag in Berlin. Personally, I was surprised to discover that it had taken the Germans so long to rebuild the Reichstag after that fire. I suppose it took ages sorting out the insurance claim. Apparently under 'Cause of Fire' the claimant, a Mr A. Hitler, had written 'International conspiracy of Bolsheviks and Jewish bankers', when most people had thought it was just down to some dodgy wiring. In any case, Nazi Mutual Insurance Ltd must have finally paid up because Sir Norman finished the job a couple of years ago, only to have the Germans withhold the final payment till the builders came round and removed that pile of sand from the drive and finished the little wall at the front.

Every time a new major government building is commissioned, we end up with a political scandal. It must be a really hard issue for the tabloids to call. Imagine the extended editorial conferences at the *Sun* as they agonize over which side of the fence they should come down on: 'So – politicians spending millions of pounds of taxpayers' money on their own offices employing the latest modern architecture. Hmmm, are we for or against this?' and they all scratch their chins and wonder.

When we are constructing new centres of government we have to be clear what these buildings are actually for. The word 'parliament' comes of course from the French 'parler' which means 'to ask sycophantic planted questions in a desperate bid for eventual promotion'. The building of great debating chambers is a throwback to the days when the debates changed things. These days most decisions are quietly fixed by a couple of civil servants who happen to bump into each other at the urinals. Maybe in recognition of this fact the centrepiece of a new parliament building should indeed be the urinals; great marble bowls could majestically sweep down from the wall containing beautiful hand-carved, scented disinfectant bars. There could even be the televising of the urinals so we could hear the crucial discussions of the day.

Of course by sacking Richard Rogers and showing so little ambition for the new Assembly, the cheaper new building in Cardiff will probably be a bit of a toilet anyway. We're lucky to have great architects in this country, and our centres of government should be exciting and bold statements about the type of country we are. But the members of the Welsh Assembly are still reeling from the fact that, shock, horror, a major architectural project has gone up in cost during construction! Yet this happens every time. And the angry politicians round on the builders and scream, 'You said you'd be finished by now. You said it wouldn't cost so much. I can't believe it – you haven't kept any of your promises.'

And the builders just shrug and say, 'Well, you started it . . .'

After you with the trough

28 July 2001

This week a survey revealed that the average British chief executive now takes home half a million a year, not including bonuses, share options and those Post-it notes that he nicked from the office stationery cupboard. Defenders of the very rich say that the criticism of these enormous boardroom salaries is based on envy and class hatred. And they say it as if this is a bad thing.

Boardroom salaries first soared after the famous Company Directors' Strike back in 1982. Who can forget those dramatic scenes as an angry mob of pin-striped businessmen fought pitched battles outside the Stock Exchange? Food convoys were organized to bring them four-course lunches from L'Escargot. Violence erupted as they got their chauffeurs to overturn cars. Mounted policeman rushed up to the strikers, saying, 'Are you all right there, sir?' After months of bitter struggle a complex pay settlement was agreed and executive salaries are now decided on the following criteria: the chairmen say to themselves, 'What's the most outrageous and exorbitant pay rise I can give myself? Right, I'll have that much then.'

Even companies that are laying off staff still seem to find the money to pay huge bonuses to the board. A director of Marks and Spencer's just decided his bonus was the wrong size, so he took it back and got a bigger one. Last year the chairman of Vodafone took an award of

£13 million. I know it sounds like a lot, but really by the time you've paid the accountants and the tax man it's actually only around £12 million. And now the only good causes that are getting more money from Camelot are the directors' own bank accounts. It leaves you wondering why these greedy people need so much money. If I was a multi-millionaire, I wouldn't want much more than I have now. All I'd buy is a nice house with a bigger garden and that would be it. And I suppose if I've got all that garden I might as well have a swimming pool in it. And a tennis court, and there could be, like, a little stream with a bridge and a path that leads down to the orchard. But apart from that – oh and the cars, and the flat in town and the villa in Tuscany – my needs would be modest.

There is an unhealthy fascination with the lifestyles of the super-rich that needs to be countered with some positive publicity for the people at the other end of the pay scale. As well as *Hello!*, there should be a magazine called *Wotcha!* in which skint ex-squaddies invite the cameras in to see their cockroach-infested bed-sit. And the colour supplements should publish a 'Sunday Times Poor List' – 'this week we list Britain's 100 most impoverished plebs. At number 57 is Fat Degsy of Urine Towers, Rotherham, whose assets include half an ounce of Old Holborn and a beard. Total value: 34 pence. But he's still much richer than the couple who've just gone straight in at number one: congratulations to Neil and Christine Hamilton.'

Just as Britain's poorest have formed an underclass, so the very rich are excluded from society as an 'overclass'. They do not use the schools, hospitals, trains or anything else which might involve the horrors of mixing with ordinary people or, even worse, queuing. These poor people are outcasts from society; they need all the help and support we can give them so that they can start to live normal lives once again.

What is needed is a new windfall tax to be levied on Britain's fat cats. This suggestion is based purely on economic grounds and is certainly not prompted by any sort of left-wing bitterness. Anyway, the so-called 'Rich Bastard Tax' would involve a £10,000 tariff on anything that the newly appointed 'Toff Tsar' deemed to be 'vulgar, ostentatious or just annoyingly wealthy'. Personalized number plates would be a good place to start – I don't see why these don't just all say

'2 MUCH MONEY'. There'd be a surcharge for anyone driving a Porsche with a sticker in the back saying 'My other car's a Porsche'. Second homes would be another good target, and the tax would be doubled if the owners were overheard referring to them as 'just a little bolt-hole in the country'. Rolex watches, automatic garage doors, Moschino handbags, or any clothes bought from a shop where you have to ring a bell to be let in – all sorts of things would warrant the extra duty. I'd like to put in a personal plea to surcharge the owner of that £100,000 cabin cruiser I saw on the Thames that was called *Just A Whim*.

'Ah, but it's not that simple . . .' say the government. 'Tackling these fat cats is a very tough job indeed. It's going to need the very best people to see it through, a cabinet of the highest calibre, who won't be tempted to get better-paid jobs elsewhere. So we're all agreed then, ministers: we'll just award ourselves a massive pay increase before we get started . . .'

Product placemeNt sIcKEns me

4 August 2001

This week saw the biggest row in Hollywood since ET quit the movie business claiming he was always being typecast as a lovable alien.'I am a serious actor! I can do Shakespeare, look: "To be, or not beee goood, Damn! Damn!"'

The latest scandal to rock Tinseltown is over a product placement deal for the film *American Pie 2*. You may have been unfortunate enough to catch the original that is endlessly reshown on the Sky Godawful Movies Channel, which was famous for a scene in which an adolescent boy has sex with an apple pie. Obviously this is not something any normal person should ever attempt, as I said to that doctor at the burns clinic next door to McDonald's.

In the sequel, the teenagers actually graduate to having sex with each other and, to the film-makers' credit, the sex is safe. No condoms were featured in the original film, which led to criticism that the boy could have been infected by one of the apple pie's previous lovers. This time round the money men at Universal Studios thought they'd spotted the chance for some lucrative product placement, and struck a deal with the manufacturers of Lifestyle condoms which would feature prominently in the movie (presumably before they were put on, or that PG certificate would have been a real long-shot). The studio also undertook to promote the Lifestyle brand in the adverts for

American Pie 2, but instead of honouring the deal, Universal pulled out prematurely which, as we all know, is no substitute for using a condom.

It turns out that American regulations prevent condoms featuring in any commercials that might be seen by a general audience. Car chases, shoot-outs and robberies are fine, but mention contraception and you have crossed the boundary of good taste. Which is bizarre because sex has always been used to sell films. Although at least in *Last Tango in Paris* they didn't feel the need to establish what brand of butter it was.

The controversy has highlighted the whole issue of product placement: the prominent featuring of brand names as a form of oblique advertising. Somehow you sense that the great films of the past would not have had quite the same impact if directors like David Lean had depended on covert advertising. When Alec Guinness staggers out of that baking little cell in *Bridge on the River Kwai* he does not say: 'Well, thank goodness I had my Right Guard double protection.'

'Why "double" protection, sir?'

'Because it protects your noses and your clothes-es.'

'Yes, and I should add, sir, that this prison camp is much better since it got taken over by Club Mark Warner.'

'Indeed, the men's morale has been greatly lifted by the pedalo race down the River Kwai.'

Some might argue that the opening of Bergman's 1957 classic *The Seventh Seal*, in which Antonius Block encounters the figure of Death, might have been improved if instead of embarking on a game of chess they had played with the free plastic toys now being given out with McDonald's Happy Meals.

'If your little clockwork turtle goes across the table quicker than mine, I shall release you.'

'And if I lose?'

'Then . . .' says Death, 'you'll have to let me finish your Chocolate McMilkshake.'

Or what about the moment in *Casablanca* when Ilsa walks into Rick's place. All the agony of Bogart's broken heart is written on his face when suddenly the silence is broken by a waitress saying to Ilsa, 'Hello, have you been to a Harvester before?' And only Sam knows who this beautiful woman is, but he acts normally, saying, 'Do help yourself to as much as you'd like from the salad cart.'

The trouble is that some films are easier to get sponsors for than others. Few were surprised when P&O ferries decided not to have their name splashed all over *Titanic*. Of course art needs financial backing – this has been going on ever since the cigar manufacturers persuaded Shakespeare to rename his latest hero Hamlet – but product placement can only diminish the integrity and quality of a film. Furthermore, if a studio has been paid millions of dollars to show the hero drinking Budweiser, then the editor is duty bound to leave in that scene however bad it is and however it affects the rest of the movie.

So now you go to the cinema and you are jolted out of your enjoyment of the film every time a global brand is shoved in your face; every time the star pointedly pulls on his Gap sweatshirt and Nike trainers or the camera lingers on his bottle of Miller Draft or his new Nokia communicator. But there's a reason that the corporations have to promote their wares so crassly within the body of the main feature. It's because before the film proper you have to sit through a dozen arty, pretentious commercials and at the end of each one you turn to your friends and say, 'What was that an advert for?' And they reply, 'I haven't the faintest bloody idea.'

Send in the clones

11 August 2001

The Bible says that God made man in His own image, but really this is just not specific enough. Does God look like Leonardo DiCaprio or like David Mellor? If God made John Prescott in His own image then frankly you'd have to question His judgement. There are certain personalities that make you want to rush through a bill preventing there being any more of them. One Donald Rumsfeld is already more than enough.

And yet it seems likely that at some point next year the first ever human clone will be born. All the visitors will gather around the hospital bed and say, 'Aaaah – he looks just like his dad.'

'Yes, that's because he *is* his dad.'

And the poor woman who has just given birth to a baby version of her husband will say, 'What about the eyes? They're a bit like mine, aren't they?'

'Er – not really – I'd say he had his dad's eyes, ears, nose – well, everything really.'

It was earlier this year that an Italian couple announced they planned to have a baby that was a clone of the 'father', and this week the maverick doctor Severino Antinori confirmed the first human clone was only months away. It has always been part of the human experience to gradually realize that you are turning into your parents, but this poor child will never stand a chance. Every time he slurps his drink his mother will say, 'Well, you get that from your father. And mixing your peas up with your mash, you get that from him as well. And picking your nose and hunching your shoulders and, of course, you'll never buy your wife flowers or take her on a luxury cruise like she always wanted.'

And Dad'll say, 'Leave him alone, he's a good lad. He just never got the breaks in life.'

'Well, he's only five.'

Then when the child becomes a teenager the problems will really start. The boy will look at his dad, and filled with anger and disgust will shout, 'I'm never going to be like you,' and the parents will glance at each other and say, 'Do you want to tell him or shall I?' Then he'll learn that one day he too will wear cardigans and want to look inside churches on holiday. And the poor boy will explode and shout, 'I hate you!'

'No, darling, you can't hate me because I love you, and since I am you, *you* must love you too, so in fact you love me, don't I?'

That should keep him quiet for a while.

The imminence of a human clone this week prompted the French health minister to say that we cannot permit 'the photocopying of human beings'. It is indeed a terrifying thought. Just imagine it – you'd be queuing up at the cloning machine all ready to make a hundred copies and the girl behind you would say, 'Do you mind if I just pop in front of you, I'm only doing one clone.'

So you let her in, and isn't it always the way – the machine jams.

'Oh dear, what's happened? The fault code is flashing "J8" – does anybody know what "J8" means?'

'Is that "Stem cells jammed in copier"?'

'Er – "Copier out of DNA"?'

'It can't be – I put in a new amino proteins cartridge this morning.'

'Oh no – I've got a hundred clones to do before lunch. Now I'm going to have to pop down to Pronto-clone to do them.'

The advances in stem cell technology have until now been rightly justified on the grounds that they are helping prevent diseases. Similarly, everything should be done to help childless couples have babies. But to create a human being who was already someone else is an abuse of the human rights of that newborn individual. It is one thing to clone a sheep, because the life choices facing sheep are pretty limited. Most lambs come out of their careers interview at school and say to their anxious parents, 'Brilliant news! He thinks he might be able to get me into the wool business!' And mum and dad jump up and down with delight that all the hopes they had for their clever offspring will be realized: she's going to stand around in a wet field for a few years and then be served up as Mutton Pasanda with pilau rice.

But how is any person supposed to live a normal life with the knowledge that they are a duplicate of someone, possibly a 'parent'? How are they supposed to become an individual in their own right? It must be hard enough joining the family business without having 'Johnson and Clone' on the side of the van. World leaders should act now to prevent human cloning. I cannot understand why they are dragging their feet. Do they imagine they could use this power and clone themselves so that they can govern for ever and ever? George Bush is doing little to prevent it, as did his father George Bush. Oh no, I've just had a terrifying realization . . .

The scientists are making it all up

18 August 2001

As news stories go, this item has taken slightly longer to reach the front pages than most, but the scientific journal *Nature* has just published an exclusive that four million years ago the Earth was involved in an enormous interplanetary collision. The story was immediately picked up by all the papers, who each put their own particular spin on it. The *Daily Mail*: 'Earth in cosmic collision; Blair failed to heed warnings.' The *Sun*: 'Planets collide to create Earth, Moon and Helen from Big Brother.' The *Maidenhead Advertiser*: 'Interplanetary crash created solar system. No one from Maidenhead involved.'

The revelation that a proto-planet the size of Mars crashed into the Earth, tilting the Earth's polar axis and accelerating our orbit, has caused great excitement in the scientific world and given insurance companies another excuse to put up their premiums. It turns out that before the collision, Earth had a day that was only five hours long. So you'd stay up for two days and two nights and then sleep straight through for a couple of days – it was like being on holiday in Ibiza. The collision sent billions of tonnes of molten rock into the atmosphere, which typically the weather forecasters of the time failed to spot: 'A lady rang in to say that molten gravel and flaming rocks will be raining down for the next million years – don't worry, they won't be; though do look out for a little light drizzle over East Anglia over the weekend,' said Ian McCaskill's predecessor, as lumps of molten lava landed all around him. Some of the debris from the collision flew up into space and eventually coalesced to form the satellite we know as the moon, later joined by other satellites sent into orbit by a powerful force known as Rupert Murdoch.

It was previously believed that the moon was created by a white-haired man called God on a Tuesday, but as cosmology has become more advanced, this theory has failed to withstand rigorous scientific scrutiny. The collision theory is not an entirely new one, but now there are detailed computations which have apparently proved it. On page 709 of this week's *Nature*, the scientists explain how they made their calculations: 'We use a beta spine kernel,' they say. Oh yeah, right, a beta spine kernel. Pull the other one. There are then two full pages of mathematical calculations and equations involving lots of Greek letters and squiggly symbols which they knew the sub-editor would take one look at and say, 'Er, yup, that all looks fine!'

Clearly what has happened is that the scientists are making this all up. They have spent the last two years sending each other silly e-mails and playing Minesweeper, and when their deadline suddenly came along they were forced to throw together a scientific theory and some calculations so they didn't get into trouble.

'Okay, quick, quick; when shall we say this happened?'

'I dunno – five hundred million years ago?'

'No, no – bigger numbers are more impressive. Say four and a half billion.'

'Okay, and say it was really, really hot – that always sounds good.'

'Yeah, and make sure we use the words "atoms", "gravity", "unstable" and, er, "beta spine kernel".'

'What's beta spine kernel?'

'Three random words from the dictionary. Don't worry – no one will question it.'

Making things up about space has been a huge industry ever since Richard Nixon decided that the moon landings were a complete waste of money and that the same images could be produced far more cheaply in a Hollywood back lot. The account of what really happened back in 1969 is only just coming out, but it was not much different to any other film set.

'Okay, Neil darling, you step off your ladder and you say your line about the giant leap for mankind . . . and action!'

'But what's my motivation for going down the ladder? What's the back-story here?'

'Cut! Oh no, not this again. Neil, love, you're playing an astronaut. You're landing on the moon. It's a big day for your character.'

'Maybe I should drive around the moon in a big car?'

'No, darling – that's in the sequel, *Apollo 12.*'

'Or lose radio contact and nearly die.'

'*Apollo 13.*'

And the guys from NASA were sulking in the wings saying, 'It can't be that difficult to do this for real. After all, we've put a man on the moon.'

'No we haven't.'

'Well, no, but it's not rocket science.'

'Yes it is.'

Before science accounted for the creation of the Earth and the moon, it was explained in the first chapter of the Bible. It didn't sound very believable but their get-out clause was that you had to have faith. Now religion has been replaced with science and we just have to take someone else's word for it instead. The comforting thing is that at least we no longer live in fear of flaming thunderbolts coming out of the sky if we question the word of the Almighty. Well, not until they've got the Star Wars project up and running anyway.

What's so bloody great about the private sector?

31 August 2001

In twenty-first-century Britain there is a new super-hero that will apparently come dashing to the rescue in any crisis. 'Is it a bird? Is it a plane? No, it's private sector finance! Hurrah, we're all saved!' 'Look over there, a hospital is collapsing; send for private sector finance man! And a tube train is hurtling off the rails; only he can bring it under control. Thank you, private sector finance man! And the best thing is that all you want in return is to know that people are safe and well.' Apart from a generous dividend on your investment, obviously, and a cut-price stake in a new market, and a guarantee to be bailed out by the Treasury should profits dip slightly . . . but apart from that you only think of serving others.

Since the dark days when British Leyland gave nationalized industries a bad name by losing money, having strikes and producing the Austin Allegro, it has been the generally shared presumption that the private sector does most things better than the public. But this is a simplistic fallacy that has no right to be accepted as fact. Do we blame the entire concept of private enterprise when the garage mechanic shakes his head and says it's hardly worth his while? Imagine if the banks were a nationalized industry; we'd blame state ownership every time we were overcharged, patronized by our manager or made to wait on the phone listening to a tinny version of the *Four Seasons*. When the holiday company dumps families at Majorca airport knowing their flights are delayed for fourteen hours, are there calls for this private company to be taken into the public sector? When privatized water companies pump raw sewage into the sea, do we hear news reports of the unacceptable faeces of capitalism?

And yet despite all our experience, we are blithely assuming that the private sector will definitely improve the delivery of our public services. How will this work in the Health Service, for example? To start with you'd find that A1 mini-cabs were now handling the ambulance calls.

'Hello – I've think I've had a heart attack!! I've called three times in twenty minutes and they just keep saying the ambulance is on its way.'

'Oh yeah – well he pulled up outside and tooted his horn but you never came out.'

'But please, I'm desperate – get me to St Thomas's Hospital.'

'Nah – we're not going south of the river this time of night . . .'

If this patient survives and gets a heart transplant, his problems don't end there. Because the job of delivering organs for transplant has been contracted out to the pizza delivery drivers. 'If we don't deliver your new body part in thirty minutes, you get a free bottle of Coca-Cola.' The trouble is that the little organ delivery moped spends two hours buzzing up and down the road trying to find the hospital and when it finally does arrive the surgeon discovers they've brought the wrong order by mistake.

'Um . . . Mr Jenkins, I know you wanted a heart transplant and everything, but they've brought us a pancreas – would you mind having a pancreas in there instead?'

'Yes I would!'

'Okay, what about a bit of garlic bread?'

I call him a surgeon; in fact, he was until recently working in the private sector as well, in the building trade to be precise – another famous bastion of excellent service and efficiency.

'Oooh, well, I can do you a new heart if that's what you really want, but you see, for a job like that, well, oooh, you'd need an anaesthetist an' all and my one's on another job this week . . .'

'But if you don't put a heart in soon I'll die.'

'Tell you what, I can tie up the ventricles in the short term, stick in a central heating pump I've got in the van, that should keep you alive until October. It's just that I'm going out to Spain tomorrow to do up my new villa and this afternoon I'm finishing off a kidney transplant that I've been promising to stitch up since Christmas . . .'

What you don't get in the private sector is goodwill, but no one ever includes this in the equation when they're working out how much money they think can be saved by bringing in British American Tobacco to run the local infant school. In fact, the amount of cash being saved is relatively tiny – and it's simply not worth the demoralization that it is causing to workers in the public sector. There really ought to be a public inquiry about the whole issue; the trouble is, you couldn't have a public inquiry any more – it would have to be a public-private inquiry, and the first two years would be spent finding a suitable sponsor from the business community. Finally they would announce that, with private investment from Foto-Kwik, 'the happy snaps people', the public-private inquiry has at last been delivered.

'What does it say? What does it say?'

'Oh no, this isn't our inquiry – they've sent us someone else's by mistake.'

Welcome to England: smacking area – 200 yards

8 September 2001

Under proposals unveiled this week, Scotland is set to make the smacking of young children illegal for the first time in the UK. Dinner time in East Lothian will never be the same.

'I'm not eating my vegetables – they've got black bits on.'

'DO YOU WANT ME TO DRIVE YOU OVER THE BORDER AND GIVE YOU A SMACK?'

They'll have to build a special lay-by on the outskirts of Berwick-upon-Tweed with a sign saying 'Welcome to England: smacking area – 200 yards'. Little stalls will spring up selling Brussels sprouts and broccoli and stationery for writing thank-you letters for Auntie's birthday present.

The plan is to ban the smacking of children under three, so now instead of saying, 'Wait till your father gets home,' toddlers will be told, 'Just you wait until your third birthday.' But the proposals have received a surprisingly positive response in the tough estates of Glasgow. In response to the question, 'Do you think parents should be allowed to give their kids a little smack?' most people answered, 'No, maybe just a bit of crack cocaine every now and then.'

Of course smacking has only been the symptom of a historical problem – this ruling will do nothing to prevent the recurrent breakdown of negotiations between adults and their offspring. If the

Scottish government is ruling out the use of force, then clearly more efforts will have to be made on the diplomatic front. The first step should be sporting sanctions. Parents will continue to play football with their children but they will no longer be prepared to let their kids always win. 'And the final score here from Jamie's back garden: Dad twenty-seven, little Jamie nil! And the six-year-old must surely be wishing now that he hadn't been rude to grandma back when he was four.' Games of hide and seek will be much quicker as parents find their children in under three seconds. 'It's no good crying, Ellie; you've hidden behind that curtain four times in a row – of course I was going to look there first.' Because if punishment is not to be physical then it will have to be psychological. 'Night night, Rosie. And darling, you know you were scared that there was a great big bear that lived behind the cupboard on the landing? Well, you're right, there is: a huge fierce one with big sharp teeth and long claws! Anyway, sweet dreams, darling.' Other sanctions will include seizure of all comfort blankets and being honest about how crap their drawings are.

Eventually the civilized example of Scotland will spread to the rest of the country, if only because government ministers find it impossible to negotiate with children's representatives. 'At Downing Street today, talks have broken down between the pre-school children and the government. A draft proposal was put before the toddlers, but they reacted by scribbling on it and then putting it in and out of the water jug. When ministers objected, the two-year-olds lay on the floor kicking and screaming and then fell asleep on the rug.'

Before Westminster is prepared to follow the Scottish example, more concessions must be made by young children. If no violence is to be used against toddlers, then they must undertake not to climb into bed at two in the morning and kick their dads in the bollocks. And it is no good them merely promising not to strike their little sisters with the plastic sword; their arms must be put permanently beyond use. Super-soakers, spud guns, sharp bits of Lego left beside the bed – all these weapons must be decommissioned before the peace process can really proceed. But eventually it will be illegal to give a child a light slap on the back of the hand (unless they are Iraqi kids of course; you'll still be allowed to drop bombs on them).

In the meantime, if you are tempted to strike a child in anger, they say you should make yourself count to ten first. This either prevents you from using violence or results in your child growing up into a neurotic adult with an irrational fear of double figures. All parents will know that there are times when it feels as if smacking your child is the only possible response – like when your seven-year-old son announces that he supports Manchester United. But even if a quick slap seems to work in the short term, there has to be a better way of punishing them. Wait till they're teenagers and meet them at school in purple checked golfing trousers. Visit them at university wearing a fur coat and a tiara. Wait till they have kids of their own and give your grandchildren a slush-puppy and a king-size Mars bar before they go on the big dipper. And keep endlessly telling your kids, 'We never smacked you as a child, and that's why you're not a violent person.' And then our grown-up children will say, 'I know I shouldn't really hit my parents, but sometimes it's the only thing that works.'

They've run out of IDS

22 September 2001

There's a sign on the wall of Broadmoor Prison workshop that says 'You don't have to be mad to work here, but it helps'. So it is with membership of today's Conservative Party. What the election of Iain Duncan Smith has proved is that 61 per cent of the Tory membership are completely insane. Ken Clarke knew he'd lost when he saw that a majority of the envelopes to Central Office were addressed in green ink. Suddenly it was official: three out of five Tory members believe that the Earth is flat, that Elvis was abducted by aliens and that Iain Duncan Smith has the best chance of leading them to victory.

Yet people were still surprised by the new leader's choice of shadow cabinet. When lunatics take over the asylum, they don't reassure everyone by announcing a bi-annual audit and getting the photocopier serviced. They make the bloke who thinks he's Napoleon head of carpet-chewing and abolish Tuesdays. So wearing his big badge that says 'Lose Votes Now, Ask Me How', Iain Duncan Smith has appointed a shadow cabinet that is the logical extension of the collective madness that has seized the Tory Party. Electoral appeal and political effectiveness do not matter – Europe is the only issue. With the final rejection of Ken Clarke, the Tories have ceased to be a political party and are now a single-issue pressure group. 'I'm going to lobby my MP night and day. Now – who is my MP? Oh it's me, isn't it.' For IDS, all roads lead to the Treaty of Rome. Expecting him to put Europhiles in prominent positions would be like asking the RSPB to have a couple of cats on the executive to even things up. 'Do we have to have Kitty on the committee? She keeps dragging half-dead pigeons into meetings.'

Ken Clarke was always fighting an uphill battle in a party whose average age was 117. Conservative organizers took this into account and so the wording on the ballot paper said in extra large print: 'WHO DO YOU WANT AS TORY LEADER, DEAR? I SAID, WHO DO YOU WANT TO VOTE FOR AS TORY LEADER? NO, YOU CAN'T HAVE WINSTON; HE'S DEAD, DEAR.' But amazingly, Clarke still made it to the final two in what had become the most thrilling political contest for days. For one of them it would mean a future in the wilderness, disappearing from public life for ever. But for Ken, it would mean going back to working for British American Tobacco. 'I look forward to working with Ken,' said IDS in his victory speech, so I suppose we can expect to see the new Tory leader flogging fags out in Vietnam as well. IDS is the first Tory leader not to have served as a minister and looks set to keep it that way. The result was only the second decision the Tory rank and file has ever had to make, the first one being when they chose Jeffrey Archer as their candidate for Mayor of London.

One week later IDS has assembled a Tory front bench that perfectly reflects the outdated reactionary views of the people who elected him. Normally we only get to hear these sorts of opinion when the grand-parents come to stay at Christmas. 'I don't know why they have to have all these queers in showbusiness nowadays. In my day we had proper gentlemen like Rock Hudson and Noel Coward.' And you half choke on your turkey but stop yourself saying anything because there's really no point. Now it'll be like that in the House of Commons – everyone will sit there patiently, silently smiling to one another until the shadow minister has finished his little rant about the foreigners and then they'll just carry on as if they hadn't heard him. 'Well, it's not worth getting into an argument – it's only the opposition.'

It seems to be the received opinion that a weak Conservative Party is bad for democracy, but excuse me if I don't shed too many tears. I agree that we have to have an opposition, but the present government needs to be pulled to the left, not the right. The Scottish Assembly's decisions on tuition fees and care for the elderly offer a visible working alternative – that's a real opposition. What is required is sustained pressure to push the Conservative Party even further off the political map. So now it's competition time once more. The challenge is to write a letter to a local or national paper saying that you are resigning from the Conservative Party because Iain Duncan Smith is proving to be insufficiently anti-European. The best letter published and forwarded to me will win £25 worth of book vouchers. Your letter must contain a reference to the Second World War, your made-up name should be double-barrelled and please include your former military rank. Best of luck, although given the insanity of today's Tory Party, I have this terrifying feeling that the funniest entry will be from Iain Duncan Smith.

Rather gratifyingly, I did receive a sack of brilliantly nutty letters that were published in local papers across the country. The only problem was that lots of people sent me the entire letters page and much of the other correspondence on other issues was no less rabid than the parodies.

Edward – stalker laureate

29 September 2001

The media should leave Prince William alone. His arrival at university should barely be reported. Obviously, intelligent critiques on media intrusion are excepted; it's important for commentators such as myself to examine the conflict between private life and public duty, but that is the only valid reason for even mentioning Prince William in the newspapers right now. Anyway, doesn't he look like his mum? Aaah bless him, I hope he settles in all right. I wonder if he'll get a girl-friend? More pictures, pages 7, 8 and 9.

Prince Edward's production company has managed the impossible: now we have the bizarre reversal of Andrew Neil (the rector of St Andrews) lecturing a member of the royal family about media intrusion. Edward has clearly forgotten the words of Diana's brother at her funeral. Maybe this was because he was secretly filming it for release on Ardent Royal Videos, a great Christmas gift at only £12.99. It's one thing for the paparazzi to be caught trying to film Prince William, but for a modern-day royal to attempt to cash in on his royal connections – it would be like Vlad the Impaler buying shares in Stakes 'R' Us.

Apparently Prince Charles is beside oneself with anger. Personally I don't think he should attack members of the royal family because they can't answer back. It is in fact possible that Prince Edward has unwittingly ensured that his nephew's university life will remain private for the time being. Which if we're really honest is a bit of a shame because it would have been quite entertaining to watch the everyday life of a royal undergraduate.

'Now listen, young man, if you don't work hard and get a good degree, you'll never get a decent job, will you?'

'Yes I will. I'm going to be king.'

'Er, well yes, but er, you'll still need to earn a living before then.'

'No I won't.'

'Er, well no, but that aside, we're going to treat you like any other student. So here's your first essay: two thousand words, please, answering the question "So what do you really think of Camilla?"'

William is studying History of Art, but his comments in his first tutorial apparently showed he was a little confused. 'It's amazing how Van Dyke managed to do that picture of Charles I while balancing on a stepladder peering over the palace wall. And Holbein's eyesight must have been fantastic – the picture of Anne of Cleeves has amazing detail considering he didn't have a telephoto lens.'

If Ardent's cameras had never been spotted, we could have seen William in the student production of *Waiting for Godot*, with that memorable scene where the tramp wanders out alone on to the bare stage followed by seven Special Branch security officers. We could have watched him break the college record on the rugby pitch as the opposing players decide against jumping on him whilst all those police marksmen are taking aim up in the trees. We could have seen him get up to all the usual undergraduate high jinks: sneaking into his friend's bedroom and getting his equerry to make them an apple pie bed; the late nights sitting on the floor and talking about life, as the butler brings in a silver tray with mugs of blobby coffee; all of this will take place in private. Or perhaps the real reason Charles doesn't want William filmed is that he doesn't want everyone witnessing the embarrassing period when his undergraduate son goes all left wing, arguing for the abolition of the monarchy and desperately trying to play down his privileged background.

'Actually my family aren't that well off – we got Windsor Castle when property prices were much lower. And we had to do loads of work to it, especially after the Wars of the Roses.'

And he'll cringe when dad phones to say he's coming to visit. 'Well, don't all arrive in the big ostentatious Sikorsky. Come in the little helicopter. And tell granny not to wear her crown.'

Poor William is as desperate to be a normal student as Edward is to run a normal production company. In the old days there were pretenders to the throne. Now the royals pretend to be commoners. But Uncle Edward can't remain a royal and monopolize broadcast access to the royals. Since his company has always struggled, Edward should now return to state duties. A new position in the royal household needs to be created – Edward should be appointed the 'Stalker Laureate', official harasser and invader of the royal family's privacy. 'The strange man who got inside the royal apartments today turned out to be the Queen's youngest son. Police found pictures of the Countess of Wessex in his wallet and said he had regularly been filmed trying to get into royal residences.' Edward might even find his celebrity status back up with the rest of them. Then the only problem would be stopping him making a documentary about himself.

Lack of identity cards

6 October 2001

When identity cards were brought in by the BBC, a comedy producer I knew decided to test the system by making a few changes to his pass. For a while he was waved through without question. Then one eagle-eyed security officer called him back. The guard took a good look at the photo on the card, which featured a shady man wearing sunglasses and a headscarf. He then checked the name on the pass which read 'Abu Nidal'. Now completely satisfied, he said, 'All right, sir! In you go . . .'

It still seems possible that compulsory identity cards will be the response to the heightened state of world tension. Because the great thing about ID cards is, of course, that they will prevent terrorism. Yup, after years of plotting, encrypted messages, international co-ordination, secret training and smuggling weapons, the terrorists will be asked for their ID cards and they'll go 'Drat! Foiled at the last minute! All those years of planning and I forgot to forge an identity card!'

ID cards would of course represent an outrageous infringement of basic human rights. Because they'd mean regularly presenting strangers with a deeply embarrassing photo of yourself. And to make sure the authorities recognized you from the picture, you'd feel the need to pull the same gawky expression that was momentarily caught in the photo booth at the back of Woolworth's. Perhaps to set an example our politicians will agree that their own identity cards should feature excruciating pictures of themselves from their younger days. A long-haired Tony Blair with huge round collars and sideburns; a young John Prescott with a big quiff in his Teddy boy gear; Estelle Morris with a perm and huge Deirdre Barlow glasses; and then Robin Cook – well, he's fine as he is.

Whether it means the end of historic freedoms cherished since the Magna Carta I somehow doubt, but I'm against them for other reasons. They've got all the information they want about us already; the trouble is that most of it is wrong. There's probably a computer database somewhere that thinks that 'Mr Duke Edinburgh of Buckingham Place, London' might be interested in subscribing to *Reader's Digest* prize draw. Because the real oppression of identity cards would not be some Big Brother surveillance nightmare – it will be the more mundane tyranny of having to endure yet another crappy piece of technology that doesn't work properly.

Imagine what fun students will have by drawing an extra couple of lines on each other's bar codes. 'I'm afraid, young man, you are not entitled to a student discount because according to this scanner you are a Müller twin-pot yoghurt.'

'No, I am a student, really, ask my friend here.'

'Well there's no point in talking to him – he's a small tin of Pokémon pasta shapes.'

Those in favour of ID cards talk in glowing terms about the wonders of modern technology. Identity cards would do more than just prove who you are. All the information that can possibly be needed about you could be stored on one handy smart card replacing all the others in your wallet. A quick swipe will establish that you are prepared to donate your kidneys in the event of an accident, that you are due a free cappuccino at Caffé Nero and that eleven months ago you paid a lot of money to join the local gym but have only been there twice.

Then police officers will be able to swipe the cards through their machines and say, 'Look, Sarge, we've got him now. It says here that *Barney's Big Adventure* was due back at Blockbuster Video yesterday before eleven p.m.'

'Oh yeah – and look at this – two thousand Sainsbury's reward points accumulated. Been doing a lot of shopping recently, haven't we, sonny?'

Because there is, of course, a civil liberties issue. As a middle-class white male I don't suffer much aggravation from the police. Whenever my car is pulled over, I utter a few words and they are suddenly very polite.

'Is this your own accent, sir?'

'Yes it is.'

'That's fine, sir, thank you. We're just doing a random check of accents in the area. Sorry to have troubled you.'

But for young black men, failure to produce an identity card on demand could be used as a reason for further harassment. Asylum seekers, stigmatized enough already, will be made to feel even more like non-persons without an official ID card.

The opposition should not be so obvious as to come out against ID cards altogether. Instead they should insist that the processing is done by DVLA Swansea. That should hold things up for the next couple of decades. And then just when they're getting on top of it all, the shadow cabinet could send in their own forms. That'll really put a spanner in the works.

'Oh no, the Conservative front bench have just blown the whole ID cards scheme out of the water.'

'How come?'

'We should have thought of this. They've got no identities to put on the cards.'

The wrong sort of shares

13 October 2001

Occasionally one reads about the tragic plight of a desperate group of people in our society and one is moved to tears by the terrible injustice they've had to endure. Such a group is Railtrack shareholders. After years of receiving healthy dividends on their investment, they are suddenly to be denied any more free money from the taxpayer. Where is Michael Buerk's moving report about the anguish of these poor victims? Where are the old ladies rattling tins in the High Street? Where is the Band Aid-type charity record featuring Bob Geldof and Ginger Spice singing 'All Aboard the Love Train – Oh no, it's just been de-railed outside Ealing Broadway.'

When I was eight my brother and I had a small train set but we could never get it to work properly. The little bits of track wouldn't fit together and whatever you did the trains kept stopping and starting and then they'd simply refuse to budge altogether. I now realize that this is the most futuristic train set ever developed – it was just preparing us for the real thing later on. Railtrack has been an unmitigated disaster, and anyone who was stupid enough not to have sold their shares ages ago has no right to complain now the company's been taken into administration. You've heard of 'the wrong sort of snow'; well they bought 'the wrong sort of shares'. I don't remember a disclaimer on the advert saying 'Remember – the value of shares will only go up and up.'

In the years since it was created, money has poured out of Railtrack into the pockets of shareholders almost as fast as the taxpayer has been paying it in. The week after the Hatfield rail crash they all got massively increased dividends as a reward for opting to invest in such an efficient and well-run company. But now that the government is no longer prepared to keep throwing bad money after bad, the shareholders' indignation is beyond belief. Crispin Oddey, founder of Oddey Asset Management, said, 'There is very little difference between what Robert Mugabe has just done to white farmers in Zimbabwe and what Byers has done to Railtrack's shareholders.' Yeah, fair comment I suppose: Robert Mugabe and Stephen Byers, I'm always getting those two mixed up. So look out for thousands of Stephen Byers supporters storming into the Railtrack offices wielding machetes and torching the stables.

Now Railtrack shareholders will have to try to make a quick buck somewhere else. I can't wait to see them approaching the pay-out desk at Ladbroke's after their horse has come in last.

'Hello – yes, I popped in yesterday and put fifty pounds on Lively Lad, running in the three o'clock at Kempton.'

'Yeah, well, he lost, mate.'

'Now look here, I invested a lot of money on that bet, and through no fault of mine the horse fell at the third fence, so I must insist that you give me my winnings.'

'Listen, pal, there's no winnings if your horse doesn't win.'

'What? But that's ridiculous. Surely the government steps in and pays up for me?'

It is a measure of how appalling Railtrack has been that it's actually made us nostalgic for British Rail. Yes, who can forget those happy days of BR when charming guards would help you aboard before dashing to the buffet to make a few more rounds of delicious cheese sandwiches. In reality the railways have always been a disaster area. If the classic film *The Railway Children* had been a bit more accurate, Bernard Cribbins would have been a grumpy old stationmaster who's only line would have been to tell the kids to piss off, before Jenny Agutter and her siblings disappeared to amuse themselves by chucking stones at passing trains and leaving dead birds on the line to watch them get squashed. In fact, at the very first passenger railway trip in 1830 the train ran over and killed the former cabinet minister William Huskisson. The inquiry into this event is due to report next month. (The incident prompted the first ever railway apology: 'We would like to apologize for the delayed arrival of the 11.04 from Liverpool. This is due to a former colonial secretary on the line.') Okay, so the British government has waited a very long time to get revenge on the railways, but Railtrack shareholders have no case for complaint. They got the shares for a fraction of their real value, and we have been subsidizing them ever since. For years they have been riding in the first-class carriage without a ticket, but the gravy train stops here.

Such is their fury that they have announced they are taking the government to court. I can't wait. And when they lose and are ordered to pay the government's costs, no doubt they will look confused and say, 'Yes, I understand that we lost the case. But, erm, we still get a huge pay-out, don't we?'

Shop for victory!

20 October 2001

Last week I was in a pub with some friends and after two pints realized I ought to be heading home. But then I thought about how tourism has been damaged by the current crisis, how the recession is starting to affect the leisure and catering sectors, and I thought, 'No – by not spending any more money in this pub I'd be doing exactly what those extremists wanted.' So I resolved to defy terrorism and have another pint. In fact I defied terrorism several more times after that, and then we all defied terrorism some more by going for a curry and eventually sharing a mini-cab home. It was expensive and time-consuming, but these are the sorts of sacrifices we should all be prepared to make in times of national crisis.

In the United States, Weight Watchers have reported significant weight gains among its members as patriotic US citizens do their utmost to help the economy by trying every single pudding on the dessert trolley. Some analysts have attributed the increase to a renewed sense of perspective and a grim fatalism that makes counting calories seem irrelevant. But the reality is that people are always looking for an excuse to have whatever they want and if September 11th is the nearest justification to hand, then that'll do fine. In the Second World War people could not help but lose weight, but as we slide into the sequel, Mayor Giuliani is calling for more people to go to restaurants.

It's time to loosen our belts. With a recession looming it has become our patriotic duty to spend as much we can on consumer goods and Tony Blair has been leading the way as he flies around the Middle East.

'President Musharraf, the British Prime Minister just called. He's coming to see you again and asked if you wanted him to pick up any more duty free at the airport.'

'Oh yes, two hundred Marlboro Lights please.'

'Oh, but no more ciggies – he's used up his allocation getting a load of B&H for Sheik Said of Oman. How about a big Toblerone?'

In fact, it's only Tony Blair's shuttle diplomacy that's keeping the airline companies afloat at the moment. Too many people remain anxious about flying, which is quite ridiculous. Statistics show that you are still far more likely to die at home following a terrorist chemical weapon attack. You've got less chance of being killed in an aeroplane than you have of being wiped out by the anthrax virus, so there's really nothing to worry about.

Osama Bin Laden wanted this recession, so now we must all contribute to the war against terrorism by buying loads of stuff we don't need. 'Once more unto the Arndale Centre, dear friends, once more!' Carpet manufacturers would like us to do our bit by buying more carpets. Or maybe you could stand shoulder to shoulder with the Americans by having a conservatory built onto the back of the house. If there is any capital outlay which you've been putting off, now's the time for getting yourself into debt and splashing out. 'That's one in the eye for the Al-Qaida network,' you can say to yourself as you unpack your new DVD player from Dixons.

But although we must spend more, it is also our duty to expect less in our wage packet. One business group last month called for a cut in the minimum wage in order to stave off recession. And can you believe it, the unions were against this idea! How can these lefties be so insensitive at this hour as to break the prevailing sense of peace and unity by opposing this patriotic suggestion from our company directors? You'd think low-paid workers would be delighted to do their bit by slipping back below the poverty line, but no, even after all the suffering that we have seen, they are selfishly clinging on to their £4.10 an hour. Okay, so the recession started before September 11th, but anyone who claims it's the fault of anyone except Bin Laden must be on his side.

The businessmen who try to use the current crisis to increase their profits are the corporate equivalent of those bereaved relatives who rush back from granny's funeral to be first to grab all the silver. 'It's what she would have wanted,' they say, as they flog off her best stuff at the car boot sale. In America, this syndrome has been dubbed 'hitch-hiking'; major corporations have been using the September 11th tragedy as an argument for lifting restrictions that were placed upon them by previous Democrat administrations. 'I think as a mark of respect we should be allowed to drill for oil in the National Park' or 'In order to send out a clear message about freedom we are asking for federal health and safety regulations to be abolished'. 'Business as usual' was the slogan that appeared outside bombed corner shops in the last war. 'Big business even more appalling than usual' is the axiom of this one.

Pentagon seeks part-time helpers – no terrorists please

27 October 2001

On September 11th, soon after two jets were crashed into the World Trade Center causing the twin towers to collapse to the ground, an internet poll was set up by one of America's leading search engines. It said, 'This time have the terrorists gone too far?' Hmmm – a tricky one to call, but apparently most people voted 'yes'. Perhaps this was an elaborate surveillance scam by the CIA. They were waiting for someone to click on the little 'no' button, and then the marines could dash round in the hope that they'd finally located Osama Bin Laden.

In fact the reality is not that different. This week the Pentagon publicly appealed for help in 'defeating difficult targets' – announcing a competition for ordinary Americans to come up with snappy ideas on ways of thwarting the terrorists. 'We're open to ideas from just about everybody,' said Pentagon spokesman Glenn Flood as the guys in the mail room went 'Oh terrific – another million strangely addressed envelopes to check out.'

So far the only entrant to this competition is a man called G. W. Bush from Washington whose idea was to blow up the whole of Afghanistan. To be fair to the US military, they're doing their best to give due consideration to Afghan civilians. All the American planes have little stickers on the back saying 'How's my bombing?' and then there's an 0800 number that you can call if you think the US Air

Force are blowing up any cities in a discourteous or aggressive manner.

It doesn't exactly fill you with confidence that the moment the world's only superpower is faced with a military foe, they call a press conference and say to the world's media, 'Er – I don't suppose you guys have any ideas, do you?' In 1940 when France had fallen and Churchill broadcast to the nation to stiffen British resolve, he didn't say, 'Er – well, frankly we're a bit stuck about what to do at this end, so we thought we'd have a little competition. Answers on a postcard please. Send your entries to "Defeat the Nazis Competition, Ministry of War, Whitehall", and remember the lucky winner gets some book tokens and a seat at the Yalta conference to help decide the post-war settlement.'

Our current Prime Minister may have got wind of the Pentagon's novelty competition for lateral ideas because I'm sure I heard him saying that Britain will be contributing our very own Ground Force. So the Americans are sending in thousands of highly armed marines and we're contributing a Channel 4 gardening programme. Mind you, once the senior clerics in the Taliban are confronted with the bra-less Charlie Dimmock jumping about, the regime will probably cave in overnight.

Washington are so desperate for ideas that they have said that the contest is open to anyone and that the winner could be offered a Pentagon contract. The trouble is that there are housewives in the Midlands who make a living out of repeatedly winning competitions from *Take a Break* magazine and the back of cereal packets; they're bound to have a head start on the rest of us. When the invasion of Kabul goes horribly wrong we'll find out that this is because the assault was planned by a retired dinner lady from Droitwich.

Meanwhile American defence chiefs are continuing their research into military operations in Afghanistan by watching *Carry On Up the Khyber* and they are gradually developing some sort of strategy. There was a setback when they found that their precision bombing was not quite as accurate as had been hoped. When the White House announced that they'd be using their famous smart bombs in Afghanistan, workers rebuilding the Chinese Embassy in Belgrade three thousand miles away said, 'Oh no – but we'd nearly finished it,' before dashing off to the bomb shelter. So then the Americans had the idea of dropping food supplies to the victims of the Taliban, the logic being that if these were aimed really carefully at the fleeing refugees they would miss so comprehensively that you could be sure they'd land right on top of Osama Bin Laden, instantly crushing him to death. Okay, so it's an outside chance, but the Pentagon policy competition has only been going a few days.

PC Plod goes to PC World

3 November 2001

This week it was announced that Britain's police officers are to be issued with portable computers to help protect the public against crime. The thought is that so many people have been mugged for their laptops that now the police are going to walk round with them as well to try to spread it about a bit. As a whole string of technological accessories was announced for our law enforcers, the futuristic fantasy of *Robocop* finally came true. Or maybe it's more *Dixon of Dock Green* with a pager.

PC Plod is being taken to PC World to save him having to spend hours back at the police station filling out endless forms and statements. So as the armed gang screech away from the bank heist, police officers will now rush to the scene and, instead of producing a little black notebook, will whip out their laptop computers.

'So you say you saw the getaway car?'

'Yes, I memorized the number plate and everything. Quick, get it down before I forget it.'

'Okay, hold on . . . Press "file", then "open", then "enter". Hmmm . . . "Windows file path invalid . . ." '

'It was a red Nissan, registration X148 . . .'

'Hang on, hang on – "File not configured . . ." Look, you don't know anything about computers, do you?'

'Registration X418, no – erm, try pressing "Help". I think it's F1.'

'Ah yes, let's see . . . "Specify font when converting files" – hmmm. Can we borrow your computer, sir?'

'Sorry – it's just been stolen.'

Even if the police computers crash as often as their cars, I suppose they'll still have their uses. To protect all that complex micro-technology, laptops now have a tough titanium alloy casing – so they could always use them to whack someone over the head when they've forgotten their truncheons.

The introduction of pagers is another clever New Labour step forward. At the last Police Federation conference, Jack Straw was nearly booed off the stage. Next time the Home Secretary speaks, all the officers in the audience will get messages on their pagers saying 'Applaud now!' 'Cheer!' and 'Standing Ovation!' Another innovation will see video identity parades replacing the traditional police station line-up. For the witness, this will remove the fear of coming face to face with your assailant, making it just like watching an ordinary video. So before you get to the main feature there will be an endless string of over-long trailers: 'Coming soon from Scotland Yard Pictures,' says the deep American voice-over, 'a story of six men, and the criminal who lurked among them. From the director of *Identity Parade 5* – a thrilling story of one man's search for justice.' And then there'll probably be a trailer for *The Perfect Storm* and *Meet the Parents* because there always is, and the witness will shout, 'That's him! That's the one who did it . . . I'd recognize him anywhere!' 'No, madam, that's Robert De Niro.' All this is presuming that the officer in charge didn't record over the tape by mistake, replacing essential footage of the chief suspects with last night's edition of *Top Gear*.

However, giving policemen camcorders also brings new risks of facilitating miscarriages of justice. Will all participants in the identity parade be filmed in the same neutral manner? Or when they get to the bloke they want to see banged up, will they zoom violently in and out and then use the caption facility to type in 'GUILTY!' in big letters across the screen? Maybe the best judicial cock-ups could appear on their own video clips TV show called *You've Been Framed*.

Like all tools in the fight against crime, modern technology can be used for good or ill. There's always a civil liberties issue, but no point would be served by holding the police back and saying that they were only allowed to use blue phone boxes and whistles. The use of modern technology really took off with the spread of CCTV cameras, which, though they helped reduce crime, also had a down side as we were forced to endure endless newspaper articles about the realization of Orwell's nightmarish vision. I used to be against CCTV, but earlier this year my wife's handbag was stolen in a coffee shop and there was the culprit caught red-handed on camera. Then he tried to buy petrol with her credit card and there he was again, number plate and all. Fantastic! Obviously nothing was ever done to follow any of this up, trace his car or bring any charges, but you can't expect everything.

So we should welcome any technology that assists the police in their vital work and it is clearly much easier to alter a defendant's statement on a computer than it is on a handwritten sheet of A4. And we should not be deterred from proceeding to the next stage by the expense of buying our policemen new laptops, pagers, palmtops and camcorders. As it happens, the fight against crime will not cost as much as you might expect. Apparently there's a bloke down the pub who can get all this stuff for them half price, no questions asked.

Goal not dole

10 November 2001

Over the past few weeks, Britain's footballers have been voting on whether they should take industrial action. Fabien Barthez was handed his ballot paper and then dropped it. Andy Cole went to pop his voting slip into the ballot box, but at the last minute lost his footing and missed completely. Paul Gascoigne walked across to the polling booth but pulled a calf muscle and was led away in tears. But for those players who did manage to put a cross into the box (which was a first for Leicester's midfield this season), a huge majority voted in favour and now we can expect to see the first ever industrial action in the history of league football.

Strikers' support groups are already springing up around the country, shaking buckets outside the factory gates to try to collect the £20,000 a week that the average Premiership player needs to make sure he has a DVD player in every car. Food convoys are ferrying lager and kebabs to impoverished strikers. Shop stewards wearing badges saying 'Goal Not Dole' are asking other sports workers to come out in sympathy. The England cricket team are expected to be out in no time.

Under Britain's draconian industrial law, it would be illegal for England's Premiership players actually to refuse to turn out onto the football pitch, although a small picket would be permitted on the edge of the penalty area. So Michael Owen will rush up towards the goal-mouth with the ball at his feet only to be met by five footballers in duffel coats and flat caps standing around a brazier.

'This is an official strike by the PFA and we're asking you not to cross this picket line.'

'Look, I dunno anything about no strike. I've just been told to deliver this football into that net over there.'

'Listen, lad, I've got striking players on this picket line who don't know where their next mansion in Essex is coming from . . .'

'But if I don't make sure this ball gets over that goal-line, my boss says I won't get my ten grand bonus this week . . .'

It's heart-breaking stuff. Of course, if they argue for too long, the referee then moves the picket line back ten yards. At this point tempers become frayed and the police step in to calm things down. An officer puts a gentle hand on Ginola's shoulder and he falls to the floor in agony, rolling about clutching his injury.

Highlights of all this would have appeared on the Sky Sports Strike Action Channel except that it's the televising of football that has caused this dispute. The PFA want a modest 5 per cent of the money that comes from transmitting the beautiful game to fund its various welfare schemes and to assist ex-players who've fallen on hard times. 'We want to benefit from the enormous popularity of televised football,' they say, as ITV moves its Premiership programme to a later slot due to lack of viewers. Obviously the Premiership chairmen believe there are more important things to do with all that money, like spending £10 million on a midfielder and then selling him for half the price the following season. But the players' union is right to ask for this money and the players are right to vote for a strike. Footballers are always being criticized for being poor role models, but here they are setting a great example: the greatest ever turn-out in a strike ballot, and the greatest majority prepared to take strike action. They are prepared to risk confrontation with their own clubs in order to help players less fortunate than themselves. At last England might have some decent left-wingers.

The next stage looks set to be fought out in the courts, which could take several years while the judge is having the offside law repeatedly explained to him. With all their millions, the Premier League will have an unfair advantage in the law courts, even if the public gallery is packed out with fans singing 'Who's the bastard in the wig?' This is one dispute where there is already a much clearer mechanism for finding a winner. The PFA should challenge all the club chairmen to a game of footy. What a match that would be. Mohamed Al Fayed as captain of the Chairmen's XI would lose the toss and claim this was the result of a conspiracy by MI5 and the Duke of Edinburgh. Elton John would spend £50,000 on his outfit, thereby seriously under-cutting the Manchester United club shop. Instead of half-time oranges, Delia Smith from the board of Norwich FC would serve up Roasted Summer Vegetables, and Ken Bates would be made to sit on the subs bench (tickets start at £75). Finally, Mohamed Al Fayed would score and in the celebration whip off his shirt, revealing his naked torso right in front of the TV cameras. And at a stroke the dispute would be completely irrelevant. Nobody would watch televised football ever again.

Hey, Mr Taliban Man

17 November 2001

The hills are alive with the sound of music! Like Baron von Trapp, the Taliban had banned all singing, but now Julie Andrews (in the guise of the Northern Alliance backed up by B52s) has brought the sound of music back to the hills of Afghanistan. Now in Kabul's west end they are singing the old tunes once more: 'I Have Confidence In George Bush', 'Bomb Every Mountain', and 'How Do You Solve The Problem Of Osama?'

Even the greatest cynics and anti-war campaigners should celebrate the fall of the most hated tyrants since the advent of car-clamping. Suddenly thousands of Afghan children are experiencing the joy of flying kites once more. And then two minutes later saying, 'Actually, this is quite boring. You haven't got a Playstation Two by any chance, have you?'

The Taliban was a regime made up of former religious students. Afghanistan is what happens when you hand the government over to those kids at school who actually wanted to do RE. And yet back in Britain we are increasing the role of religion in our schools. As church and state are being separated in Kabul, we are proposing that the next generation of Britons be educated in a more religious environment. Let us be in no doubt of the terrible fate that lies at the end of the faith schools road. The Middle East will come to Middle England; militant

Christians will seize power in a religious revolution that will see Britain become the first ever fundamentalist Church of England state (or second, after the Isle of Man).

After declaring the Archbishop of Canterbury the new head of state, the religious students will impose an austere regime based on the harsh strictures of their own extreme brand of English Christianity. Women will be forced to observe a strict dress code and made to wear long floral dresses with puffy sleeves. Men will wear Arran sweaters and sandals and be too cheerful. A Christian mob clutching tambourines and chanting 'Kumbaya' will surround Tesco Metro, forcing them to close their doors on the sabbath. The only shopping permitted on Sunday will be at the bring-and-buy sale at the vicarage, where the local populace will be coerced into purchasing little spider plants and home-made jam. Where Afghan kids shouted 'Allah is great!', English schoolchildren will chant the central tenet of Church of England doctrine: 'There probably is a god, though perhaps not in the literal sense, more as a sort of spiritual concept maybe.' There will be no music except Cliff Richard, so there will be no music. An exception will be made for the singing of hymns; it will be compulsory for everyone to go to church and self-consciously mumble their way through the second verse of 'To Be A Pilgrim', and then sing out the last line loud and clear to make up for not knowing the rest of it. It will be an offence to get out of bed in the morning only because *Thought for the Day* has just come on the radio. School nativity plays will not be permitted to edit the original biblical text and so will go on for several days. Loose adaptations will also be forbidden, so having the Virgin Mary clutching a plastic Baby Annabel from Toys 'R' Us and then singing Spice Girls hits is definitely out. Anyone breaking any of these strict Christian laws will face instant forgiveness.

Of course, all this is a ridiculous fantasy. Nothing so foolish could ever come to pass. Future schoolchildren will learn about the dawn of a lasting world peace when they study this period of history in their new faith schools. For what could be more conducive to world peace than having all the Christian kids in one school and all the Muslim kids in a different school down the road? Why not stick a Jewish school in the middle and have an inter-schools jihad on sports day? Creating new faith secondary schools now seems about as sensible as a Taliban version of *Pop Idol*. 'Well, we don't know what she looks like and we're not allowed to hear her sing, so we'll just have to hope for the best.' You'd think the government would have enough problems on its hands deciding what to do with all these Taliban leaders, without setting up new faith schools back home that'll be needing religious heads to run them all. Oh no, they wouldn't, would they? Suddenly it all fits together . . .

Between a rock and a hard place

24 November 2001

It has been decided that the time is right for the Foreign Secretary to begin talks on Gibraltar. The weather's suddenly turned cold here and it's still quite sunny in southern Spain. All sorts of wider discussions have been put on the agenda.

'Look, we'll give you back Gibraltar – as long as you take Northern Ireland as well.'

'No thanks – we were hoping you might like the Basque Country . . .'

Meanwhile Gibraltar's chief minister was outraged that these talks were even taking place and gave it to Jack Straw straight: 'You have talks with Spain if you want. But I'm boycotting them.'

'All right. See you about.'

'I mean it! Either the Spanish minister goes, or I go.'

'Okay, bye then.'

In trying to sort out this post-colonial hangover now, the government is brazenly flying in the face of years of established Foreign Office policy, which is to wait until a territory is the focus of a major international crisis involving hundreds of British troops, with billions of pounds needing to be spent to defend a place we'd forgotten we had in the first place. Maggie Thatcher would never have dreamed of negotiating over Gibraltar. She would have wanted to use it as a base for getting back the American colonies.

These old bits of empire are like embarrassing LPs that ended up in your record collection after some long-forgotten college romance.

'The Falkland Islands?' says your incredulous wife. 'How long have you had these?'

And you blush and stutter: 'Oh yeah, er, they were Victoria's and somehow I've still got them.'

'And what's this? The Chagos Archipelago?'

'Oh well, um, when me and India split up, I was all upset so I refused to give it back . . .'

Gibraltar was gained during the War of Spanish Succession, which was fought in order to bore people doing History A-level three hundred years later. Invasions of Spanish territory by the British have always taken the same form. Eyewitness accounts of the occupation describe how hundreds of sunburnt English lads in Union Jack shorts, clutching Stoke City scarves and copies of *Loaded*, stormed the local tavernas at dawn shouting, 'Oi, Manuel! Ten pints of lager pronto.' And the Spanish fled in horror as the victorious English struck up a chorus of 'Ere we go! Ere we go! Ere we go!' During that war Britain also gained the island of Minorca, and quickly went about establishing another vital naval staging post by building the Benny Hill Bar, providing Premiership highlights on satellite TV and paella and chips with Yorkshire pudding.

Minorca was handed back, but Gibraltar remains an embarrassment. Imagine if a 300-year-old war had meant that Clacton-on-Sea was still a Spanish colony today. Would we demand the return of that Essex coastal resort? Okay, bad example. Opponents of surrendering sovereignty insist that Britain has a right to Gibraltar under the terms of the Treaty of Utrecht. The same treaty handed Sardinia to the Austro-Hungarian Empire and ceded the island of Sicily to Savoy. This week the government of Savoy was saying nothing. The settlement in 1713 also ensured that British companies had a monopoly of the transportation of African slaves to the Spanish colonies. Only a handful of Tory MPs still argue that these rights should be upheld today.

If people want to remain British, I know an excellent place they could live. It's called Britain. I have never understood why the Union

Jack-waving expats living thousands of miles away from the mother country are always so self-consciously more British than the people who live here. If they really want to be like everyone back in England they should wear NYC baseball caps and eat Big Macs while watching *Friends* and *Sex and the City*. Gibraltarians have no more right to perpetuate the anachronism of the British Empire than the descendants of Jewish settlers in the West Bank should have a right to veto a settlement in the Middle East.

Till now it's always been presumed that sovereignty might possibly be shared at some vague point in the future – a sort of '*mañana* split'. But the brave way to deal with this problem would be to set a definite date for Gibraltar's return to Spain. It should be far enough away that the Gibraltarians can't really imagine it ever coming round, but soon enough for the Spanish to think it's not worth making a fuss between now and then. How about 2029 – the two hundredth anniversary of the Treaty of Seville when Spain renounced its claim to the Rock after its failed invasion? But the government must make this announcement soon before the Gibraltarians realize that they have one very persuasive negotiating ploy left up their sleeve. What if they were to ally themselves with other Britons living further up the Spanish coast? Suddenly they might find their wishes being respected. Round the conference table would be the Spanish Minister, Jack Straw and Mad Mick from Romford who moved to Marbella in a hurry after the Brinks Mat heist.

'Well, Mr Straw, you can overrule the Brits living in Spain if you like. But I'm afraid it means I will have to saw your legs off and have them buried in the concrete of the Stratford East Rail Link.'

'Um . . . yeah, well, maybe we shouldn't rush into any decision just yet . . .'

And the Spanish will say, 'Oh no – it's just like negotiating with Maggie Thatcher all over again.'

I blame the scapegoats

1 December 2001

It's a mistake any of us could have made – spending three years studying cows instead of sheep. I'm always getting those two mixed up. All right, so they are the Institute of Animal Health, but it doesn't mean they can be expected to spot all the subtle variations between every single species; to know the difference between, say, a bank vole and a short-tailed vole, or a wood warbler and a sedge warbler. Or a sheep and a cow.

The latest twist in the BSE saga is even more farcical than anything that has gone before. In the quest to establish whether British sheep have contracted the disease, scientists spent the last three years studying sheep tissue and reached a distressing conclusion: the British flock did indeed have BSE. Except the animal samples they'd been studying for three years were the wrong ones. The creatures which they had diagnosed with mad cow disease were cows. The clue is in the name. We shouldn't be too hard on them – this sheep/cow mix-up happens all the time. Thousands of sheep farmers have recently realized why they've been finding it so hard to make a living: they've been shearing cows all this time. Last year in a packed Spanish arena, one bullfight had been going for about half an hour, with the nervous woolly bull running away from the matador and bleating occasionally, before someone in the crowd said, 'Are you absolutely sure that is a bull? Because I can't help thinking it looks a little bit like a sheep.'

For future reference, sheep are small, with thick white fleeces and go 'Baaa!', whereas cows are much bigger and go 'Mooo!' I know it can be confusing, but they are professional biologists. If it's not in any of their scientific manuals, there are some pre-school picture books which set it out quite clearly.

This week's report into the fiasco points the finger at a laboratory in Edinburgh, although no one seems very sure. What seems even more incredible is that nobody noticed for so long. Lots of us have days at work when we feel we're wasting our time, but three whole years down the drain must make you a little bit depressed. And all because someone got the wrong bottle out of the fridge. That's the last time he'll be making the tea.

'Are you sure you put milk in the mug, cos it tastes a bit strange . . .'

'Oh sorry, I must have used the liquidized cows' brains by mistake. It's not my fault, they've both got pictures of cows on the side . . .'

When BSE was discovered in the samples, ministers seriously considered destroying the entire British sheep flock. Fortunately they didn't have to take this drastic step, because all the sheep had already been slaughtered during the foot-and-mouth epidemic a few months earlier. The scientists' error was discovered only after a last-minute DNA test on the samples. Well, they claim they tested the DNA – for all we know it might have been a jar of sundried tomatoes. And now the report into the fiasco has concluded that the standards of labelling and storage were well below international standards. You don't say. Perhaps the description of the animal samples was done by people who write posh menus. You could never write anything as straight-forward as 'Liquidized sheep's brains' – you'd have to write '*Cerveaux de mouton pressé à la formaldehyde*'. One theory is that somebody got confused about the words 'bovine' and 'ovine'. Often scientists use the Latin names for different species, but since the Latin for sheep is 'ovis', we should just be grateful that they didn't spend three years studying a brand of sliced bread from Yorkshire.

Who knows what other similar slips have occurred in other government departments? For all we know, British jets might have been bombing Uzbekistan for the past few weeks . . . Intelligence assessments of Taliban positions are being carried out by MFI. Right now all sorts of frantic calls are being made from Downing Street. 'You did what?' says Tony in disbelief. 'Nationalize Railtrack?! I said "rationalize", you idiot. God, I hope Gordon heard me last night. We were trying to get a cab and I said this country needed more taxis.'

Meanwhile the work of the Institute of Animal Health was defended by Elliot Morley MP, who apparently has the misfortune to be the 'Animal Health Minister' (although this post was obviously invented last week to save any proper ministers the embarrassment of defending it). He called their work 'world class'. Sounds like someone's got their labels mixed up again. This was in fact a catastrophic series of errors, which nearly caused the extermination of all British sheep and has left us still ignorant as to whether BSE exists in our sheep. Heads should roll, except they'd probably only fire the wrong person by mistake. 'Don't worry, minister – we've found the person responsible for this animal mix-up and sacked him. It won't happen again, we promise: he's definitely not a token scapecow.'

Hotel health service

8 December 2001

The decision was taken by a handful of ministers, late one night in Downing Street. Thousands of NHS patients still waiting for operations . . . hundreds of private hospital beds lying empty . . . there had to be a solution in there somewhere.

'So what do you think, Tony? Shall we nationalize BUPA and seize all private health companies in the name of the workers?'

'Hmm, no, it doesn't feel right . . .'

'Raise more cash for the NHS by putting a super-tax on all those toffs who always go private?'

'No . . . How about we work in partnership with the private sector, and pay BUPA a load of money to treat NHS patients?'

And there was an excited gasp of breath around the room and they spontaneously leapt to their feet and sang 'The Red Flag'.

The announcement that the government is signing a deal with BUPA to fill up one of its hospitals with NHS patients was heavily criticized by union leaders this week. No one on the left likes private health companies – what could be more symbolic of uncaring capitalism than profiting from the sick and the dying? 'Why should our money go to line the pockets of BUPA shareholders?' we say angrily, and then get even more irritated when we are informed that BUPA doesn't actually have any shareholders – it is a provident association.

'Yeah, well, er, exactly!'

Various schemes were considered. One idea that went out of the window quite early was for Alan Milburn personally to take out private health insurance and then see if they could get 12,000 people who were on the waiting lists to go into a BUPA hospital and pretend they were Alan Milburn. The long-term solution is, of course, to increase the capacity of the NHS and, to the government's credit, they are actually spending a fortune building new hospitals and doing up old ones. But these refurbishments take ages; when the builders are trying to swing the steel girder into position, they have to keep being extra careful not to whack that bedridden pensioner on the head.

Meanwhile the waiting lists remain and the government has been gazing across longingly at the plush private hospitals that were sitting there half empty. BUPA hospitals are basically just very expensive hotels where you can get a bit of medical treatment as an optional extra. Sometimes they even host two-day conferences of sales executives and after the discussions the delegates try the jacuzzi, have a massage and then decide to get themselves a plastic hip joint before they head home. Now one of these BUPA hospitals will be used to treat only NHS patients. The government are not saying 'The lists are so long you should pay to go private', they are saying 'The lists are too long, so we'll pay for you to go private.' Health care remains free to all at the point of delivery. That is the Rubicon that must never be crossed.

There is a lot of confusion about how a hospital can be part private and part NHS. Let's take mealtimes as an example of how it will work. For their entrée the patients will be served honeydew melon balls with seedless grapes in an elegant cut-glass bowl. Then the main course will be a big dollop of mince with a crumbling over-boiled potato on a big metal plate, and then for the dessert it's back to the posh menu, zabaglione with langue de chat biscuits. They used to serve 'Death by Chocolate', but one of the elderly residents died half way through eating it and they were worried about a law suit. Every private room will have its own television, but in order to make you feel as if you're still in the TV room of an NHS ward, the telly will be much too loud and will be tuned to *Shafted* with Robert Kilroy-Silk when there's something really good on the other side.

There will, of course, also be a clash of cultures. When a health service has been created with a profit motive, as in America, expensive things like tests and exploratory operations can be considered a waste of money.

'Woman over fifty, you say? Right, give her a hysterectomy.'

'But she only came in with a verruca.'

What the NHS may lack in menus and décor it more than makes up for in the minor matter of health care. The best doctors and nurses are working in the state sector – paying to go private may save six months' waiting, but it won't buy you better treatment.

So eventually the clash between the private and public sector will be too much and the cabinet will be forced to hold another emergency session.

'You were right, guys . . .' says the PM. 'This isn't working at all. There's only one way forward. We're going to nationalize BUPA!'

Now I realize why Tony Blair never made this announcement in the first place. Imagine the strain it would have put on the health service, everyone in Whitehall having a heart attack all at the same time.

Defective defector

15 December 2001

Poor, poor Paul Marsden. Before he was forced to join the Liberals it sounds as if he had a terrible time. Who could help but shed a tear as we read about how those tyrannical Labour whips talked to him in a cross voice? Who knows what brutal intimidation lay ahead: no Christmas cards and someone sneaking into his office to open all the windows on his advent calendar? Parliamentary whips have always been vicious bully boys. In the last Tory government, Gyles Brandreth was a whip. 'Support the government,' he would snarl, 'or I'll give you a teddy bear and make you wear one of my jumpers.'

Or could it be that Paul Marsden is just an unprincipled attention-seeker, desperate for his fifteen minutes of fame? Any politician can grab the cheap temporary celebrity that comes from crossing the floor. But real eminence in politics comes from years of hard work and skilful manoeuvring; that's what has earned the deserved celebrity status of the party leaders, Tony Blair, Charles Kennedy and the other one, er – what's-his-face.

Imagine if other professionals did what Marsden did as soon as someone raised their voice.

'So, David Beckham, could you explain why you came out for the second half wearing a blue shirt and then got a hat trick for Chelsea?'

'Simple, really – Sir Alex Ferguson was a bit mean to me at half time so I thought I'd start playing for the other side.'

Football players do of course switch teams, but only in between games and usually for large amounts of money. Perhaps the transfer system could be the way forward for unhappy politicians. 'Tony Blair held a press conference today to show off his new signing, Alan Howarth, who joins New Labour from the Tories for a fee of twenty million pounds. Blues manager Willy Hague said he was sad to have to let the promising right-winger go, while Howarth said it was a dream come true, as he'd supported Labour since he was a lad, especially when he was a Tory minister.'

We vote for a party and their programme, not for personalities and their individual whims. Of course MPs have the right to a conscience, especially on an issue such as the bombing of another country. Opposition to the war in Afghanistan is a perfectly respectable position held by many MPs (mostly in the party Paul Marsden just left). So why has Marsden defected to a party whose leader also supports the war? It would be far more honest if he defected to a genuine anti-war party – and much more fun when the Socialist Workers Party got their first MP.

Every morning the policeman could wave him through security with a friendly 'Good morning, sir' and he could scream in anger at being the victim of such vicious police brutality. As MPs filed into the chamber he could sell papers outside the Members' Lobby wearing a donkey jacket and fingerless gloves, shouting 'Socialist Worker! Kick out the MPs – oh, that's me, isn't it?' He could try to persuade Tony Blair to join with other workers in a general strike to get rid of Tony Blair. He could be party leader and chief whip, and have furious rows with himself when he broke the party line.

If whips weren't bending the ears of our elected representatives, then other lobbyists would be doing so instead. In America politicians are not whipped in the same way, and big business steps into the vacuum. 'During the election my party said it was against Exxon drilling for oil in our national parks. However, following a meeting with several local voters (a man from the oil company and my accountant), I have resolved to make a principled stand for the independence of senators from the party machine.'

Back in the summer, the voters of Shrewsbury elected a Labour MP. The Labour agent would have worked day and night to see him safely returned. Dozens of activists delivered leaflets and canvassed and gave up their evenings and weekends to explain to voters why they should have Paul Marsden as their Labour MP. And just six months later he has stabbed all those loyal party workers in the back and appointed himself MP for the party that came third in his constituency with just 12 per cent of the vote. The opinion of those 22,253 constituents who wanted a Labour MP counts for nothing. Politicians who swap sides always claim they are forced to do so out of principle. This is the biggest lie since the non-drop Christmas tree. If Paul Marsden has any integrity he should resign and stand for election under the banner of his new party, just as Shaun Woodward should have done when he joined Labour. If there's one thing I can't stand it's a turncoat; some of us have higher principles than to switch sides whenever it suits us. A point I think I made when I had a column in the *Independent*.

Immunizing children against the tabloid press

21 December 2001

The press have always been too intrusive about the private affairs of important babies. Two thousand years ago the tabloid journos from the *Bethlehem Mail* went to extreme lengths to get the inside story on the new baby Jesus . . .

'Look,' said Joseph, 'I know he's the son of God and the saviour of all mankind, but we would rather you respected his privacy if that's all right. So take off that stupid donkey costume and get out of the stable.'

'Tell us about the conception, Mary,' shouted another hack, who was taking notes for a no-holds-barred biography he was calling 'The New Testament'.

'Now listen . . .' said Joseph. 'The conception of this baby is a private matter between myself, God and the Virgin Mary.'

'The "*Virgin* Mary," you say? I think we have a story, lads . . .'

Of course, unless you're a particularly toady Labour MP, Leo Blair is not the son of God, but two millennia later the press are still as hungry for any detail about celebrity babes. This week's bit of snooping (masquerading as an important social debate about immunization) has been the demand to know whether or not the youngest Blair has had his MMR injection. As *Guardian* readers will have observed from seeing all the newspapers read by the builders doing their kitchen extension, the tabloids have been hammering on about this story all week. The Blairs have refused to say one way or the other. Cue a hundred articles on Cherie's duty to be a model mother and provide definitive answers to all the complex parenting questions of the day. Does Cherie use disposable Pampers or are there dozens of re-usable nappies hanging out to dry in the cabinet room? Is it right to breast-feed a baby in the workplace, or would that distract the jury? The fact that both Leo's parents are lawyers is one of the reasons that they are refusing to budge on this. They understand the concept of precedent – once you start responding to personal questions posed by the tabloids you are always going to regret it. Because the inquisition wouldn't just stop with the infant. 'Prime Minister, when you were away in the Middle East, did the boys have a teenage party at Number Ten and trash the place? What did Kathryn's teacher say at parents' evening apart from "Can I have more money?" Is Leo walking yet, or does he have another toddler to drive him about in a little plastic car?' Or what about 'Has Euan ever tasted alcohol?' Sadly these are questions to which we will never know the answer.

The key to the Blairs' apparently obsessive protection of their children's privacy is to understand that Cherie has had first-hand experience of media intrusion from the child's point of view. When she was growing up in Liverpool her father was not just a national celebrity; on Merseyside he was a virtual folk hero. 'Mr Booth, Mr Booth,' the papers would say, 'if your daughter was to grow up and be the wife of the Prime Minister, do you think she should get her baby immunized?' It was very hard for young Cherie; every week she would see her father on the telly espousing radical left-wing views. Though some might say that her husband has gone slightly too far to ensure her kids never have to endure this experience.

Or is there another reason why the Blairs are particularly sensitive about hacks getting too close to baby Leo? It is typical of the British press that they have failed to spot the real story in the middle of all this. There is no Leo Blair. The baby idea was thought up by Alastair Campbell when the Prime Minister's personal rating started to slip a couple of years ago. Since then a variety of infants from a baby modelling agency have been used, but now the casting problem is getting harder and harder. At some point in the New Year they'll come clean and admit that they have only three children, claiming that the fourth child was only an 'aspiration', it was never an actual manifesto commitment. And the Fleet Street editors will kick themselves for their stupidity and promise never to be so gullible again. And then finally Tony and Cherie will be able to turn to little Leo and say, 'Ha ha! Can you believe they bought it, darling? Now the tabloids will definitely leave you alone.'

Osama's Christmas message

29 December 2001

Well, by now we have all seen that infamous video message and listened to all the experts analysing every detail: those staring eyes, the grey hair, the lined face, that religious fervour. But still the question remains: what was the Queen's Christmas message designed to achieve? Many experts believe that the address may have actually been recorded some time ago at one of her secret hideouts – possibly in the mountains surrounding Bal'mor'al. But why did she choose to release her Christmas message over the Christmas period? Perhaps the recording was an attempt to prove that she is still alive, or perhaps a coded message to her supporters. But why did she not move her left hand? Was it tired from a whole year of waving?

Sadly, any attempt by the Queen to get her message across was completely upstaged by another millionaire religious leader – Osama Bin Laden. This Christmas the Arabic satellite news channel Al-Jazeera pipped BBC1 and ITV to top the holiday ratings with their Osama Bin Laden Christmas Special. What is amazing is that Bin Laden managed to talk for thirty-three minutes (or an hour, once the Americans had put in the commercial breaks) without answering any of the questions that the West is desperate to know. Where is he hiding? What is he planning next? Why doesn't 'Al-Qaida' have a letter 'u' after the 'q'? And how is it that a parcel containing the video sent from Pakistan a week ago can arrive more quickly than a Christmas card sent a couple of miles across London? In fact, the video really only tells us one thing: Osama got a camcorder for Christmas. (The FBI are questioning Dixons to see if he sent back his guarantee card.) Now Bin Laden's made a video of himself, which is exactly the sort of cry for attention you'd expect from the middle child of a family of fifty-four children. Next week the offices of *You've Been Framed* will receive a video of a contrived 'accident' of Osama walking past a swimming pool and falling in fully clothed as the Al-Qaida network desperately tries to raise a bit more cash. The delay between the tape's recording and transmission is easily explained. Imagine the scene in the cave: 'Right, we have made the recording, Osama. Now to transfer it onto this VHS tape.'

'No, not that one – I just recorded the Christmas *Only Fools and Horses* on that one.'

'Oh all right, what about this one?'

'No – that's got the Christmas *EastEnders* on it.'

'Oh come on – you're never going to watch that now.'

'I am, I am. Look, what's on this one? Honestly, why can't you label your bloody videos?'

'Um, I think that's *Before They Were Famous*. I wanted to see if they've dug up that clip of you on *Junior Showtime* in 1973.'

In his video address Bin Laden discusses the American action in Afghanistan, although his exact words depend on whose translation you read. For example, the Pentagon version has him saying, 'I now see that American foreign policy is totally benign and justified, oh yes. The United States is truly a wonderful country and I never miss *Ally McBeal* or *Sex and the City*. Oooh I really fancy an Egg McMuffin and vanilla shake and no mistake.' If you put this version to one side, along with the translation in the *Sun* in which Bin Laden claims that the best Christmas telly was all on Sky One, there was very little in the half-hour monologue of any great surprise. He criticizes the Allied Carpet Bombing, which raised a few eyebrows (I knew the missiles were inaccurate but I didn't know they'd hit Allied Carpets). He reads a poem and his eyes go all watery, but frankly it's just all too static, too much 'talking heads'. The producers of *The Two Ronnies* used to get round this problem by having Ronnie Corbett say, 'And now the Young

Generation,' and we'd cut to some dancers in T-shirts and flares prancing around Studio One at TV Centre. Or maybe Osama should have put in some sketches to break it up a bit. Either way, his style is too wooden and the content too thin for this unsolicited pilot to get its own series. So a letter has gone back to the Tora Bora mountains thanking Osama for his tape but explaining that BBC Talent get a lot of videos from people wanting to be on television but competition is extremely fierce, etc., etc. – although his details have been sent to Carol Smillie for her new series, *Celebrity Cave Make-Over*. In fact, the production values on Osama's home video are so poor that it nearly didn't get broadcast at all, but the channel controllers watched it and decided they had no choice. 'No, put it out at peak time,' they said; 'we've got to have at least one programme this Christmas which doesn't feature Neil and Christine Hamilton.'

Top dog collar

10 January 2002

This week George Carey announced that he would be stepping down as Archbishop of Canterbury in order to spend more time with his tambourines and immediately the race was on to become the new top dog collar. Traditionally the Archbishop of Canterbury was one of those jobs that you wouldn't get if you were too obvious about seeking it. It's like the leadership of the Tory Party, or being boyfriend of the most beautiful girl at school. It should seem as if you just happened to be standing nearby looking cool when the vacancy came up.

But this time round the shameless battle for press attention began only minutes after Carey announced he was hanging up his cassock. Senior bishops desperate for a bit of coverage trampled all over each other in the rush to come up with the story most likely to get them splashed across the newspapers. 'Harry Potter is my bastard love-child claims Have-a-Go Bishop', 'Cheeky Cleric streaks at Old Trafford', 'I was dumped by *EastEnders* love-rat says Booze-Hell Bishop'. That worthy 3000-word piece in the *Church Times* entitled 'Whither the General Synod?' never stood a chance.

Incredibly, the post is still not open to women and a couple of the front-runners have grown beards just in case anyone wasn't sure. The bookies already have the Bishop of Rochester as favourite at 3–1, with the Bishop of London at 4–1 and the Muslim terrorist leader Osama Bin Laden looking very much a long-shot at 5000–1. Sven-Goran Eriksson has made it plain that he does not want the job, while a suggestion that it might help end religious divisions if we gave the job to the Pope was only broadcast in order to wind up Ian Paisley. One rogue application has been received from a local parent who wants to become the 104th Archbishop of Canterbury in one last desperate attempt to get his kids into the local Church of England primary school. Another pitch was made by a leading property company hoping to convert Lambeth Palace into luxury riverside apartments.

When St Augustine became the first Archbishop of Canterbury back in 597 it was a very different job, as many of today's churchgoers will probably remember. Evensong would often be disturbed by hordes of Viking heathens charging into the churches, shouting and tipping over the tables and smashing priceless artefacts – an atmosphere not dissimilar to Midnight Mass on Christmas Eve after the pubs have just closed. Most Britons were not Christian; more people believed in the mystical power of the stars, magic crystals and the energy fields around Stonehenge – so in fact there's not been much change there either.

Of course, back in the sixth century the service was given in Latin; no one could understand a word the Bishop was saying, so the clergy generally busked it with what little Latin they could remember from school: 'Amo amas amat, Caesar adsum jam forte, habeas corpus, nota bene, status quo et procul harum.' The Latin versus English debate continued to split the church for hundreds of years after the great Synod of Whitby of 664 settled on the messy compromise that the Bible would still be published in Latin, but they'd put the answers in English at the back.

But of course the relevance of language is still an issue today and any new candidate to lead the Anglican church should now declare himself in favour of an even more modern version of the Bible, that would express the good book in today's inner-city street slang: 'And yo man, that bro' Herod; him was one bad-ass mother chillin' big time with the Judea Massive.'

Even if the Church of England does not go this far, the appointment of a new Archbishop is its big chance to get back in touch with ordinary people. Frankly, leaving the decision to the Crown Appointments Commissions is unlikely to get the great British public caught up in the excitement and heartache of today's ecumenical hopefuls. A nationwide phone-vote should follow a twelve-part fly-on-the-wall TV show in the manner of every other show on telly at the moment. Various clerics should have to audition live on air and then stand there trying not to look embarrassed while their efforts are ripped to shreds by the industry experts.

'So, Bishop of London, you've done really well to get this far,' Pete Waterman will say. 'I think you chose a hymn that was not great for your voice – "When I Survey The Wondrous Cross" is not the catchiest tune in Tin Pan Alley. I loved that little twirl you gave us on the lines "Did e'er such love and sorrow meet, or thorns compose so rich a crown?" Okay, it was a shame your mitre fell off, but you recovered well, so congratulations, you're coming back next week on *Pick a Prelate!*' But of course in the end none of them would win, because if it was a straightforward popularity poll there could only be one contender. 'The Archbishop of Dibley' – it has a ring to it, doesn't it?

Working-class students

19 January 2002

There is still too much elitism in British universities. For example, how come it is always Oxford and Cambridge who get through to the final of the Boat Race? Apparently only 9 per cent of the students currently admitted to Oxbridge are from working-class backgrounds. The Vice Chancellors were said to be shocked at this figure – it's far too many. Critics have suggested that the Oxbridge entrance examinations are still biased towards the upper middle classes and a look at the paper would seem to back this up. NAME: (please put all surnames; you may use a separate sheet if there is not enough room here). Question 1: What team's rugger jersey are you wearing today? Question 2: How many girls do you know whose nicknames are characters from *Winnie the Pooh*? Question 3: When a waiter invites you to taste the wine, can you confirm that you do not feel the slightest bit embarrassed?

This week the National Audit Office has revealed that many youngsters from poorer backgrounds are not going to university because of money worries. The government will miss its target of getting 50 per cent of under-30s into university by 2010 without more help for lower-income students, they warn.

Perhaps this problem is being approached the wrong way round. If not enough young people are going on to further education, then the solution is to reclassify as universities the places where school leavers can currently be found. A few years back the government patted itself on the back for creating lots of universities at minimal expense by taking down all the signs that said 'Polytechnic' and renaming the buildings 'University of Olde Towne Nearby'. This process should now be extended so that young people find themselves at college wherever they are. So the bus shelter by the chip shop where teenagers gather to smoke and give each other love bites will become the University of Bus Shelter.

'There's nothing to do in this crappy town,' says the first teenager, unaware that she is now in a philosophy tutorial. The man with the beard and leather patches on his elbows, who they thought was just waiting for a 137, will suddenly reply, 'But what is "nothing" - indeed is "nothingness" possible? If we can be conscious of such a concept we must therefore exist and in doing so thereby negate the existence of the very concept we have just imagined.' And then the kids stare at each other nervously and slink off to try to nick some cider bottles from the crates behind the University of the Red Lion Car Park.

Another way of getting more working-class graduates is a project which has been going for some time now. Under this scheme students arrive on campus as angelic middle-class eighteen-year-olds, and then rapidly metamorphose into snarling working-class street urchins. The first Christmas holidays back from college can be very distressing for their parents.

'Jocasta, darling, I thought we might go to the gymkhana in the village after church. I thought you'd love to see Drusilla's new pony . . .'

'Shove it, bitch! I is gettin' my eyelids pierced and my tongue tattooed innit?'

'Oh. That's nice, dear . . .'

Some of the most privileged kids entering this scheme struggle to disguise how posh they really are. They have stickers in the back of their Porsche saying 'My other car's a white van'. Their accents veer wildly between upper-class toff and cockney wide boy, leaving them useless for anything other than a career as a stand-up comic.

Many working-class parents worry that their children will go off to university and will be led astray by bad influences, especially if they end up at the same college as Prince Harry.* But, of course, the biggest worry is debt. Since the abolition of student grants, students from poorer backgrounds have been put off from going on to further education because they are anxious about the sum of money they will owe after three years. This is really about confidence. To a middle-class graduate, £3000 a year may not seem such a worrying sum to owe, especially when they have seen their parents regularly spend that much on a few tins of organic cat food from Waitrose. But many working-class kids would be terrified by the prospect of leaving university owing thousands. That's nearly as much as their dad spends on chunky gold jewellery.

Our students have to be adequately funded; those *Lord of the Rings* posters are not cheap, you know. The review of student funding should bring back student grants so that all social classes can enjoy the three-year cushy holiday at the taxpayers' expense that we had. It's great that more people are going to university, but it must go further. People moan about dumbing down, but more British people are well educated today than ever before. We're not dumbing down, we're um . . . doing the opposite thing, up. Damn, I might know what the phrase was if I was better educated.

* There had recently been some negative press coverage about Prince Harry's getting drunk at school one afternoon. Journalists were appalled that anyone should start drinking so late in the day.

Tyson bites yer legs

26 January 2002

Mike Tyson said in his defence this week that he is not Mr Politically Correct. Self-knowledge is a wonderful thing. I'd say the convicted rapist, who once assaulted elderly car drivers in a road-rage incident, attacked journalists and photographers, spends much of his time in hostess bars making obscene crotch-grabbing gestures and is wanted on further sexual charges, is indeed probably a bit of a longshot for the post of Head of Gender Awareness at the Hackney Women's Unit.

Yet Mike Tyson remains a role model for thousands. Where I live in South London far more young working-class men have named their pet Rottweilers 'Tyson' than, say, 'Melvyn Bragg', for example. You never see these blokes standing on the common shouting, 'Yoko, come here!' or 'Germaine! Get down!'

But this week their hero sank to another new low. In a staged press conference with Lennox Lewis, he proved unable to wait until the fight proper and attacked Lewis after just ten seconds, even biting his intended opponent in the foot. The event was intended to generate publicity but it was far too successful. It was the ugliest mêlée since that drinks party at Downing Street when Noel Gallagher bumped into John Prescott.

Mike Tyson is supposed to be on medication to control his temper.

They said to him, 'Mike, you know you're a professional boxer – well, we're giving you these drugs to stop you being so aggressive.' No wonder he's so cross. The visits to the doctor were always a tense affair; last time his physician gave him a gentle tap on the knee with a little rubber hammer. That doctor gets out of hospital next month some time.

Tyson became world heavyweight champion at the age of twenty back in 1986. But things started to go wrong fairly quickly. Soon after, he was knocked unconscious when he crashed his car into a tree, with the result that for a brief period the WBO heavyweight title was held by a large horse chestnut. The tree then had lots of gold teeth fitted and was photographed dating Miss Wyoming and pretty soon, well, he just went to seed. Tyson regained the world title, but has since been to prison, been fined for punching a referee and been banned for biting off an opponent's ear. Still, it's better than bottling it all up. Onlookers were particularly shocked when they saw him spit out Evander Holyfield's ear. He could at least have popped it discreetly into a little napkin.

Maybe Tyson should redirect his energies towards a sport less likely to bring out his violent side. Figure skating, for example, or synchronized swimming. Because this week's ugly scenes probably won't be the last, and every time the moral commentators become even more outraged: why, these boxers – they are behaving in a violent and aggressive manner! In fact, Tyson's notoriety only helps generate more interest and put up his price. I don't know, maybe I'm being a bit cynical here, but it's almost as if somebody somewhere is more interested in the money than the sport. No, that's probably unfair, I take that back. If the boxing authorities had the long-term interests of boxing at heart, they would have nothing more to do with Mike Tyson. It would mean resisting the immediate prize of a huge multi-million-dollar fight, of course, so that's obviously going to happen.

But his continued presence only gives ammunition to those who would have the sport of boxing banned altogether. I can understand why some consider the sport to be barbaric, but these are often people who have had more career choices than those upon whom they would sit in judgement. When I was a young boy growing up in Maidenhead, boxing was the only way out of the Home Counties ghetto. It was either boxing or accountancy. Boxing, accountancy, law, medicine, the City, journalism, business consultancy or becoming a database developer for one of the emerging software companies springing up all along the M4 corridor. So for us, sportsmen like Frank Bruno were real heroes. We saved up to get a ticket to see him and those who were lucky enough to be there that night still talk about that incredible performance he gave as Widow Twankey at the Theatre Royal, Windsor.

Perhaps a career in pantomime could be the way forward for Mike Tyson; though it might be hard sticking to the original script with the former world champion on stage.

'Oh Buttons, my ugly sisters won't let me go to the ball.' Buttons spots the ugly sisters downstage, grabs Christopher Biggins and bites his ear off before punching Timmy Mallet into the orchestra pit.

'Okay, now you can go to the ball.'

'Oh, um, but you're not supposed to knock them unconscious . . .'

'Oh yes I am!'

'Oh no you're not!'

'Oh yes I fucking am!'

And the audience would shout back as one: 'All right, yes, you are! Whatever you say, Mike!'

It would be no more of a pantomime than what we have at the moment.

God Save the Queeeeen!

2 February 2002

On Wednesday the Queen will have been on the throne for exactly fifty years, but tragically this joyous anniversary seems to be regarded with widespread cynicism and apathy. Unemployed single parents lie around the house saying, 'Why should I care about some old woman who happens to be Queen?' 'Because I'm your mother!' she says to them. 'Now get off the couch and go and tour Canada or something.'

Social commentators are left wondering what has happened to this unpatriotic society when so little respect is shown to our head of state. How different from the happy innocence of Her Majesty's Silver Jubilee back in 1977, they say. Back then, in village greens across Merrie England, rosy-cheeked teenagers wearing black binliners and safety pins through their noses spat and pogo-ed to the sound of the Sex Pistols and the Clash. Yes, the whole nation came together in the unifying spirit of hate and anarchy, the poet laureate Sir John Rotten penned his jubilee poem 'God Save the Queen, the fascist regime that made you a moron', and thousands of young citizens with mohicans had 'No Future' tattooed across their foreheads. Ah, happy days.

In fact, the idea that Britain was always a nation of monarch-loving loyalists who spontaneously celebrated every anniversary is about as believable as today's royal wedding vows. Henry III, for example, ruled for fifty-six years but his Golden Jubilee was a complete flop.

'Henry the Third?' they said. 'Erm, now which one's that then? 'Cos Henry the Fifth is Agincourt, isn't he, and Henry the Eighth is six wives and all that, so Henry the Third – is he the one with the hump who killed the princes in the tower? No, that can't be right . . .' Charles I was just approaching his Silver Jubilee when the committee arranging the festivities decided it might be more fun to chop his head off. And then all the jubilee mugs had to be repainted with just the stump of his neck showing. Other royal celebrations were an even bigger washout: 'King Ethelred, have you made all the preparations for the street party?' 'Oh my god, is that today? I haven't even thought about it yet . . .'

And now, in the twenty-first century, we are all supposed to dash out into the street, introduce ourselves to the neighbours we've never met before and organize a spontaneous community knees-up. Street parties are a strange concept. You spend years telling your kids not to step out onto the road, nearly yanking their arms off if they so much as put one foot off the pavement. And then you plonk the kitchen table in the middle of the street and tell them to eat their lunch there.

'What are you crying for, darling?'

'I'm scared! It feels wrong!' stammers the terrified child.

'Don't be silly. Now come on, eat up before the table gets clamped!' (And then the following week her big brother wanders out of Burger King chomping on a Whopper and the parents say, 'How revolting! Eating your lunch in the middle of the street! Honestly, dear, can't you eat that *indoors*?')

Street parties, like the royal family, are just a bit out of fashion. Of course it is not so long since 'Palace' was the soap opera of the moment. In the 1980s we had royal weddings, even more royal babies and Diana and Fergie perfectly reflected the good taste and intellectual rigour of the age. But suddenly the fairy tale went into reverse and the princes turned into toads. Windsor Castle burned down after granny left her vests drying on the paraffin heater and Princess Anne got divorced, prompting a bitter court battle over custody of the horses.

So this year does present us with a wonderful anniversary. It is ten years since the *annus horribilis*, which is not some weird condition you develop from sitting on the throne for too long, but was the Queen's own phrase to describe the year when it all fell apart for the royal family. Nineteen ninety-two was the year the mask slipped and we saw the truth. So wave that flag and open that champagne. Because for a whole decade now nobody has cared about the monarchy. Hooray, we won't have to hold a street party and watch our neighbours waiting to race for that parking space right outside their house as soon as the cars are allowed back in the road. In one last-ditch attempt to appear relevant and with it, the monarchists are organizing a more modern type of party. Sir Paul McCartney, Mick Jagger and Sir Elton John are teaming up for a special Jubilee pop concert. 'Ah! Aren't they marvellous?' the old ladies will say. 'The way they just keep on going. They do so much for tourism and they work so hard and you shouldn't criticize them because they can't answer back.' Suddenly I agree with all the royalists saying things were better in 1977. It makes you nostalgic for punk. I don't blame the Queen personally, of course, she's just badly advised. No one's advised her to declare a republic.

As English as baseball itself

9 February 2002

Many years ago Norman Tebbit caused a political storm with his so-called 'cricket test'. An adapted version of this was later used by several Commonwealth countries – no one was allowed in unless they wanted to hit Norman Tebbit round the head with a cricket bat. Yesterday's White Paper on immigration and citizenship proposed that immigrants to this country swear an oath of allegiance to the Queen and demonstrate an ability to speak English that would have ruled out most of her ancestors. The full text of the pledge requires new arrivals to uphold British values and democratic traditions – so from now on they'll stop bothering to vote at elections and will just moan about everything instead.

Some immigrants to these shores do seem to have slightly naïve ideas about what life in Britain is like. Anyone who tries to get into the UK by clinging to the underneath of a train should have it politely explained to them that in this country the trains don't actually go any-where. But if there is going to be a test for British citizenship, it should at least reflect the reality of the British character. For a start, in the queue for applications, anyone seen twitching nervously, in case that man hovering near the front was thinking of pushing in, would get extra 'British-ness' points straight away. However, when someone does barge to the front of the queue, the ideal applicant should whisper to her husband, 'I'm going to say something,' to which he should reply, 'Shh, dear, best not make a fuss' and that couple will have then passed stage one with flying colours. Then comes the tough written test (and anyone who completes this without a single grammatical error or spelling mistake will be told to go straight back to Holland).

Question 1: Please list the following events in order of historical importance – (a) the French Revolution (b) the end of the Cold War (c) Brotherhood of Man's 1976 Eurovision triumph with 'Save Your Kisses For Me'. Question 2: What is the traditional accompaniment to spaghetti bolognese – (a) a light sprinkling of grated parmesan cheese, or (b) a large portion of chips and two slices of white bread? Question 3: A man trips on the pavement and bumps into you. Do you (a) cast him a slightly annoyed look and continue on your way, or (b) say 'Oh I'm terribly sorry, really – my fault entirely . . .'? Question 4: Which of the following would make you sufficiently angry to write to your MP – (a) Britain's involvement in a war with no foundation in international law (b) the sale of British armaments to repressive dictatorships, or (c) the shipping forecast on Radio 4 seems to have changed the name 'Finisterre' to 'Fitzroy'?

Immigration to Britain is nothing new, although in the old days the speed at which applications were processed often depended on how big your army was. Back in 1066, for example, the small immigration office at Hastings was completely overwhelmed.

'Right, sir, while your army is filling out form 7R(B) – *Application for Admission to Wessex by non-Saxon residents* – can I just ask you the purpose of your visit to the UK?'

'Well, to overthrow the incumbent Saxon monarchy, install a brutal regime based on fear and murder, and seize all wealth and property for myself and my fellow Normans.'

'Fine, just as long as you weren't planning to do any paid work while you were here . . .'

At which point one of the lancers had to go home because he'd been hoping to do a little bit of bar-work.

Today we hope to make assimilation a more peaceful process. But David Blunkett's White Paper (an unfortunate name in the circumstances) has now been upstaged by his comments about arranged marriages. He suggested that it would be better for people to choose their marriage partners from here in Britain rather than Asia, which greatly upset some fat old white men who were looking at a website based in Thailand. Of course, for most Britons it has not been customary for our parents to arrange our marriages. Instead we have both sets of in-laws come to stay at Christmas and there then follows an arranged divorce.

When politicians talk about race, and indeed religion, every single care must be taken, not just because it is so easy to give offence, but because there are racists in our society who need only the slightest mis-heard cue to justify racial violence. Which makes it all the more ironic that David Blunkett had to back down when he attempted to outlaw the incitement of religious hatred. Some people tried to claim this would make it illegal to impersonate a vicar, which was clearly ridiculous. What did they think the Prime Minister had been doing for the last five years?

Consignia Personnel Pat

16 February 2002

You'd think the woman from Scottish Widows would have got over it by now. She's been moping around in that black hooded cloak for years and, frankly, it's time she moved on. 'Och, come on, Morag,' her friends are all saying. 'You're still young. Put a nice bright dress on and come down the pub for singles nite.'

'Och no, it wouldnae be the best use of those wise investments made by my late husband Hamish . . .'

It won't be long till this particular actress is released from being typecast as a widow from the Highlands, because I expect Scottish Widows will be forced to change their name when the marketing men realize that the label actually gives a vague clue as to the sort of business the company does. The whole point of brand names these days is to disguise your purpose, not to clarify it. British Steel is now Corus, British Gas are Centrica, Tarmac Construction are Carillion, the Conservative Party are New Labour. Cheap gags aside, the stupidest rebranding of the lot has to be Consignia; another meaning-less word beginning with the letter 'c' which used to be something we knew as 'the Post Office'.

This week Consignia's chairman admitted that the expensive rebranding was a failure and that the new name and logo had attracted derision. Derision? Heaven forbid, I certainly wouldn't want to add to that. Well, maybe just a bit. So now that they have spent an absolute fortune changing their name from 'the Post Office', what name does the interim chairman of Consignia think they might try next? Apparently he thinks the name 'the Post Office' has a ring to it. Hmmm, yes, strangely it does sort of put you in mind of red pillar boxes, whistling postmen and queues of pensioners watching the video loop advertising Stannah stair lifts and moaning that there isn't a separate counter just for stamps. Clearly what is required now is some marketing consultants to spend a lot of time and money testing this new name out on carefully monitored focus groups, before finally unveiling the discovery that 'the Post Office' would indeed be the perfect moniker for that office where they handle all the post. In fact, 'Consignia' was not the original first choice of those clever guys from marketing. For a long time their preferred option was (and I kid you not) 'Mailtrack'. It says it all really.

Unfortunately, quite a lot of name-changing has been going on at the Post Office since it became a PLC. A 2 per cent pay offer is now known as a 'reasonable pay increase'. 'First-class mail' also has a different meaning, with over two million letters a day now being delivered late, and 'second delivery' now means some time later that week. The organization which in the financial year ending April 1999 made a profit of £493 million (its twenty-fourth consecutive annual surplus) is now losing £1 million a day. Some of the lowest postal charges in the world still saw 90 per cent of first-class letters being delivered the next day, but this was before it was made a public limited company. So much for private business acumen being superior to state-run public services. We are told that the Post Office has to change to survive in the globalized economy but there's nothing compulsory about this. The Tasty Plaice Fish Bar doesn't feel the need to diversify into international banking or insurance and rename itself 'Bolloxia'.

Of course modern global companies can't have names that really reflect their purpose, because the honesty would be too damaging: 'Rip U Off', 'Asset-strip PLC', 'Kwik-Profitz' and 'I Can't Believe We're Not Better'. And so they have quasi-Latin names that are deliberately bland and meaningless in the hope that nobody will take offence at what they actually do. The fashion is spreading fast; the

93

Al-Qaida terrorist network are soon to be renamed 'Convexia', Mossad are being relaunched as 'Creatia', and the LA street gang 'the Bloods' will henceforth be known as 'Cruxelsior PLC'.

When so much focus is put on image rather than delivery of service, it's no great surprise that things start to go as badly wrong as they have for what was once Britain's best known brand. And if the Post Office's customers are suffering, imagine what it is like for the ordinary employees. Things just aren't the same down in Greendale. Postman Pat is now 'Consignia Personnel Pat' with his black-and-white feline communications operative.

'Morning, Mrs Goggins,' says Pat.

'Any letters for me today, Pat?'

'No letters, sorry. But Consignia are expanding in a global market-place, offering financial services, home shopping, utilities and advertising and marketing sectors.'

'Oh, that's nice,' says Mrs Goggins. 'I would offer you a cup of tea but the rural Post Office is being closed down and converted into luxury second homes.'

'Oh well,' says Pat, 'at least Bob the Builder will still have a job. The bastard.'

Britain wins gold medal at Olympics!
(er, in the ladies' curling)

23 February 2002

What a day to have taken off work. For twenty years he had been BBC sport's only curling correspondent; two decades of trying to persuade *Grandstand* to cover the Strathclyde regional curling play-offs. And then on Thursday night he'd promised to be in the audience for his granddaughter's school recorder recital and the British women went and won the gold medal at the Winter Olympics. Oh well, there'll always be another time. No, on second thoughts, there won't be.

Britain's success in the women's curling is like the Polish cavalry winning the award for the best turned-out horses in the Second World War. You can't help feeling it's not the main event. But now we are supposed to look the world's athletes in the eye once more. 'Hey, we're not second rate at sport – we got a gold in the ladies' curling!' At Westminster, congratulations were given by the hastily appointed Minister for Curling. And how petty it was at this moment of national jubilation for cynics to suggest that this represented some sort of a demotion for John Prescott. To read the coverage in the newspapers you'd imagine that the whole world was focused on this one final. At the White House, President Bush cancelled all meetings and pretzels while he watched the thrilling climax to the ladies' final. In the Middle East, hostilities between Israelis and Palestinians ceased as both sides were gripped by the unfolding drama from Salt Lake City. In the BBC's *Question Time* studio, the programme was delayed by live coverage from the Winter Olympics, but the pundits put aside past differences as they too were consumed by the nail-biting climax. Nicholas Soames put a supportive arm around Harriet Harman as she nervously bit her lower lip. Ian Hislop and Mary Archer held hands under the desk, both secretly praying for the first British winter games gold since Torville and Dean broke both their hearts.

It's been a long time coming for the sport that now looks set to become as popular as synchronized swimming itself. As everyone knows, curling was invented at a Scottish public school during a game of association football. To the gasps of all around, one of the boys picked up the ball, filled it with cement, stuck a door-handle on top and slid it across a nearby frozen pond, madly brushing the ice in front with the school broom. 'What a splendid idea for a new sport!' said the headmaster of Curling School shortly before they were both led away by men in white coats.

Since then the sport has become almost popular in several cold countries, but despite this the British commentators were still struggling to explain what was going on. 'Um, and now we come to the bully-off, and the seeker has to get the puck past the quaffle, hang on, that's not right . . .' The women had looked unlikely gold medal winners at the beginning of the winter games. First, the bloke hiring out the boots couldn't find any their size and then when they finally walked out on to the ice, they slid about all over the place and refused to let go of the rail. But as the competition progressed, many of the favourites were knocked out. The American team, consisting mainly of US air force personnel, missed the ice completely as all their stones hit and destroyed a nearby hospital. The Lebanese team were disqualified for getting their curling stones past customs and then chopping them into little lumps and selling them on street corners. And so Great Britain suddenly found themselves in the final. Viewers who tuned in late may have been thrown by the sight of a manic-looking Scottish woman scrubbing the floor with a long broom – at any moment you expected her to look at the screen and say, 'Flash cleans floors without scratching!'

Then, with the scores at 3–3, the commentator said, 'How much more tense do you want it to be?' Well, quite a lot more tense, actually. Maybe Debbie Knox falling through the ice, where a killer whale is waiting to avenge mankind's ravaging of the planet, while Des Lynam, dagger in mouth, has to inch across the ice, spreadeagled on the cracking surface, holding out the broom for the brave Debbie as she cries out, 'Don't worry about me! Just make sure that last big stone gets inside the little circle!' Actually, even then I still think I'd rather have watched the repeat of Wimbledon's 1994 goalless draw with Leicester over on Sky Sports Sad. Apologizing for the cancellation of the advertised programme, the BBC's continuity announcer said, 'Due to the coverage of the curling final there's no time for Living Dangerously.' Well, quite. But at least this weekend the British can hold their heads up high, knowing that when it comes to sliding lumps of rock across the ice our ladies are the best in the world. Well done, Britain. It's as if in 1912 a survivor was pulled from the sea excitedly saying, 'Guess what happened on the *Titanic*? I won the deck quoits!'

Someone explain the Third Way to a fox

2 March 2002

'Government acts to stop hunting', say the headlines. Cue a hundred dismal cartoons of a fox with Stephen Byers'* face, running away from lots of dogs that seem to have 'Fleet Street' or 'MPs' written on their sides. In fact, there hasn't actually been a great deal of fox hunting over the past twelve months. All the foxes looked on confused as the humans apparently discovered a new rural hobby which involved piling up thousands of sheep and cow carcasses and then setting fire to them. 'That's even sicker than what they did to us!' said the foxes to each other.

But now the hounds are busy once more and the hunting enthusiasts are eager to make up for all those lost fixtures in their calendar. If 'country sports' really are a sport, how come the same side always wins? Does this always come as a surprise to the participants? Do the hunters look on excitedly with their fingers crossed to see whether the fox rips the dogs to pieces or vice versa? You don't get the fox being interviewed on *Sportsnight* beforehand saying, 'Well, Brian, I'm really confident about this one. I've had a couple of fights in the run-up; there was that easy win against Mr Rabbit, but this is the big one I've been training for.'

---

* Soon after this Transport Secretary Stephen Byers succumbed to pressure to resign from the cabinet. Byers had made the fatal political mistake of having a name that rhymed not only with 'liar' but also 'pants on fire'.

'So you're not worried that the bookies have you at a thousand to one against beating this pack of foxhounds?'

'What, you mean there's more than one of them? Er, excuse me – I've just got to call my agent.'

Last month the coalition in the Scottish Parliament managed to impose Labour's promise of a ban, which the House of Commons with its huge Labour majority still has not. And yet there are signs that the government are once more hoping to find some sort of compromise on this issue. This is where I have a problem with the philosophy of the Third Way. The fox either gets ripped to shreds by a pack of hounds, or it doesn't. You can't be a little bit barbaric. It wouldn't be much consolation to the fox that under New Labour's Third Way he at least gets to take part in a full consultation process beforehand and the hounds that kill him have to be fully licensed and registered.

But confronted with another historic set of seemingly implacable enemies, the Prime Minister cannot resist the chance to broker another historic peace deal. Under his latest proposals, foxes may have to withdraw from their new settlements in many urban areas and promise to stop tipping the KFC cartons out of wheelie bins. The hounds will be allowed to patrol the countryside but only in their new role as peacekeepers. Any dogs that mistakenly savage a fox will risk being told off when the inquiry is completed in twenty years' time.

In fact, the government is promoting a middle way which would involve fox hunting only being permitted under licence. This would be like solving the problem of burglary by issuing house-breaking permits and requiring the burglars to close the door behind them. Apparently there would be people whose job it was to ensure that fox hunting was not being excessively cruel or drawn out. How the neutral monitoring of fox hunting is going to work I cannot imagine. The supervisors would have to be like the parents of squabbling siblings. 'Stop fighting all of you – you're both as bad as each other.'

To which the fox says, 'No, we are not as bad as each other: there are dozens of them and one of me, and they are going to rip me to shreds.'

'Look, I don't want to hear any more! Why can't you just try and get on with one another?'

If fox hunting is to continue under new regulations, then we should campaign to make these new rules as obstructive as possible. For a start, foxhounds must be kept on leads at all times (thought not those extendable ones that get wrapped around everyone's legs). Harsh fines should be imposed for any hounds fouling the countryside, with the master of the hunt being made responsible for clearing up after his dogs. His little trumpet can be employed to alert everyone that another dog is doing his business – that familiar fanfare will now mean, 'Oh no, there's another one over here – pass us another little polythene bag.' Equal opportunities policy must be invoked to ensure that minority breeds of dogs are not discriminated against, forcing hunts to employ little shih-tzus and miniature chihuahuas, who may need to be helped over some of the larger clumps of grass.

But anyone who believes that a compromise is really possible should try explaining the Third Way to a fox. It is not a question of class warfare; hunting should be banned because it is a matter of principle and of democracy. The practice is barbaric, it's opposed by a huge majority of the British people and the people who do it are a bunch of snobby Tories with stupid posh accents. Oh damn, I didn't say that – damn, what a giveaway . . .

More power to those elbows with the leather patches

9 March 2002

At my kids' school a number of parents built a dinky little summer-house for the children to play in. And when it was finished a teacher squatted down inside it and said, 'Well, it's bigger than the flat I'm renting at the moment . . .' This week teachers in the capital voted in favour of strike action in a dispute about local allowances, or 'London weighting'; so called because teachers are still waiting for it. Like so many public sector workers, thousands of teachers simply cannot afford to buy homes in the South-east. So that's why we've been taking all those cereal boxes into the nursery. The teachers need them for building temporary dwellings behind the nature corner. 'Hello, mummy, look what I made today!' say the infants, skipping out into the playground with a brightly painted cardboard box, while their teacher comes running out behind them shouting, 'Oi, come back with my house!'

Perhaps the kids in Year One could go further towards solving the chronic accommodation problem. Many infant classes have a little teddy bear called Henry or whatever that they take turns to have on a sleepover. Well, instead of taking a soft toy home to stay with them, the five-year-olds could take turns to give their teacher a bed for the night. And as part of this exercise they could each write another page in teacher's sleepover diary: 'On Thursday I went back to Jessica's house, and we had Nutella sandwiches for tea and watched Pingu and I was very naughty because I didn't want to go to bed at seven o'clock and I kept saying I had to do my bloody lesson plan.'

The last time the teachers took industrial action on this issue was thirty years ago. The then Education Secretary soon regretted confronting the NUT, and was never heard of again. Oh, apart from becoming the Prime Minister for eleven and a half years and nearly destroying the entire trade union movement. But today's teachers have an advantage over their predecessors. Many of the present Labour government have kids in London state schools – the teachers have a direct line of communication to those in power. It would certainly liven up a parents' evening at the London Oratory School.

'Hello there, and whose parents are you?'

'We're Euan Blair's mum and dad – I'm Tony, this is my wife Cherie.'

'Well, I'll do my best to remember that – but I meet so many parents, you know . . . Now, young Euan, yes, well, I think he would do a lot better if his teachers were not burdened with so much administration and bloody bureaucracy.'

'Um, right . . . But what about his maths?'

'Hmmm, well, I gave him this basic sum this week: "If a teacher gets twenty-five thousand pounds a year and they have to spend twenty-five grand on their mortgage, pension and travel – HOW ON EARTH ARE THEY SUPPOSED TO BLOODY EAT!!!"'

'Oh, didn't he know that one?' says his disappointed dad. 'He should have said what a wonderful job the teachers did, adding that this government has raised education spending in real terms as share of GDP from four point six per cent in 1997 to five per cent in 2001.'

School reports for ministers' children might be another more direct route for teachers to get their point across. 'Kathryn continues to do well in all her studies and could normally expect to go to an excellent university. But unless you give us a big pay rise, I'm going to fail her in all subjects.'

Everyone keeps telling teachers how marvellous they are, but it doesn't pay the mortgage. The way forward is for teachers to attempt the same condescending tactic themselves. When the bank rings up asking about this month's payment, they should say, 'You do a marvellous job, collecting all that money, well done, you bank managers are marvellous; it's a vocation, it really is.' I'm sure Barclays would be happy to leave it at that.

Sadly, only 30 per cent of teachers actually took part in this week's strike vote, with the rest of them coming up with some very weak excuses for not bringing in the completed ballot papers. 'The dog ate it, sir.' 'I left it on the bus.' Or, 'My mum said I had to take my sister to Brownies so I didn't have time.' Several other teachers were seen copying off their friends in the playground before the bell went. The Department of Education suggested that the low turn-out in the ballot meant that the strike call lacked legitimacy; not the smartest argument to deploy from a government that was returned to office by only a quarter of the electorate. But Estelle Morris is right that strike action would be very bad news for London's schoolchildren – it would leave them with nowhere to play truant from.

Five thousand police march (police estimate much lower)

16 March 2002

People are always saying they'd like to see more bobbies on the beat. Well, this week there were 5000 policemen all walking down one road in London. Unfortunately, they still didn't notice that bloke smashing the car window and nicking the stereo.

In what must have been the most unusual demonstration in living memory, no banners were confiscated, no police helicopters drowned out the sound of the speakers, no activists were covertly filmed and the only unpleasant incident was when one officer became so confused that he dragged himself out of the crowd for being lippy and then beat himself up in the back of the van. Some of the marchers from outside the capital were not sure of the route to Westminster; they were hoping to ask a policeman, but you can never find one when you want one, can you? A few anarchists did turn up to act as impromptu stewards, but the police were not willing to do as instructed. For goodness sake, these anarchists are only trying to do their job, they are the thin multicoloured line who prevent our society from collapsing into, er, anarchy, no, hang on, that can't be right . . .

Of course, for every 5000 policemen going on a march to Whitehall, there are another 15,000 filling out the relevant paperwork back at the station. (This situation is repeated in every area of police work. For every police sniffer dog searching for drugs, there are another four Alsatians putting their paw marks on bits of paper.) The march's organizers claim that police morale is very low, although most policemen I encounter can never stop laughing. All I said was, 'So is there any chance of getting my bike back?' The trouble is that new recruits go into the police force with an unrealistic idea of what the job involves. They've watched *The Bill* and *Cops* and they imagined it would be all kicking down doors and finding villains in bed with forty-something peroxide blondes. Police dramas should be forced to be more honest about the mundane reality. Scene One: Inspector Hooper is sitting in the youth magistrate's court waiting to give evidence. Scene Two: He looks at his watch – it is an hour later. Scene Three: He is still sitting there. In fact, this new, no–holds–barred police drama continues in this vein for a whole hour until the final action sequence, when the clerk of the court wanders in to tell him that the case has been adjourned because the defendant couldn't be bothered to turn up. Roll credits as the continuity announcer says, 'And there'll be more real-life inaction next week, when Inspector Hooper escorts an extra wide load at ten miles an hour down the entire length of the M1.'

It is partly to free up the police to spend more time actually solving crimes that the idea of civilian community-support officers was conceived. But the police are also angry about other proposed reforms, including cuts to overtime pay. They don't blame David Blunkett for all this; apparently their chief suspect is a young asylum seeker who they say has just confessed to everything in a police cell in Stoke Newington.

There are currently no plans for another march, although personally I think it would be an excellent idea. Except next time they should march in uniform and spread out much more, so that there'd be a couple of them marching through every major crime spot of the inner cities. But it's hard to know where the police can take their protest next. They could try withdrawing goodwill, refusing to do some of the additional extras that so brighten up our lives. Imagine no more big yellow placards on the pavement saying 'Murder, Rape, Kidnap in your very road just the other day. Were you scared? Well, come on, you must be now.' Or in court they might resolve only to read out their evidence in a dull monotone, making it impossible for anyone actually to listen to what they're saying. But if none of this worked, then perhaps they'd be forced to break the law and down truncheons. A national police strike could be this Labour government's greatest test. Hundreds of ex-miners would have to be recruited to prevent the striking policemen from travelling around the country. Pitched battles would be fought as the police formed mass pickets around Wormwood Scrubs, trying to prevent the delivery of convicted felons.

'We are asking our comrades from the criminal fraternity to support our action by refusing to cross this picket line.'

'Oh, all right, I'll go home then.'

Conservative Party activists would set up strikers' support groups, providing hot meals of roasted pheasant and donating cast-off clothing such as old Barbour jackets and green wellingtons. At which point the public would decide the police had suffered enough. But of course we could never really have a police strike – if we did there might be lots of crimes and most of them wouldn't get cleared up. And a scenario like that – well, it's almost impossible to imagine.

Criminals in the community

23 March 2002

This week David Blunkett announced that thousands of non-violent offenders would be released from prison early. Panic spread around the country as everyone simultaneously had the same terrifying thought: 'Will this include Jeffrey Archer?' Prisoners will be released sixty days early but will have to wear an electronic tag which can only be removed by a designated police officer or by using that machine on the clothes counter at British Home Stores. Of course there is a danger that the tags will become something of a status symbol, and before long kids will be mugging each other for them. And some might argue that just wearing a little bracelet is not much of a punishment for somebody who was supposed to be in jail. But digital signals emanating from the tag mean the convicted criminal is prevented from having too much fun while he is out and about. For example, if the wearer goes to the cinema, the device keeps ringing like a mobile phone just to embarrass him. The gadget is also designed to block out all television signals except Channel Five and UK Living, a feature that has prompted widespread criticism from Human Rights organiz-ations. And at all other times, a built-in MP3 player plays 'Music Is My First Love' by John Miles over and over again. More serious offenders get a loop of 'Like To Get To Know You Well' by Howard Jones.

Electronic tags were originally piloted when New Labour was first elected to office. A specially selected group were forced to wear them at all times so that their every movement could be tracked and recorded. Back then the tags were called 'MPs' pagers'. The technology has now advanced to the stage where the movements of thousands of offenders wearing tags could be monitored, so if the satellite picture shows a particularly heavy build-up of criminals in one particular area then local radio stations could warn commuters. 'A lot of trafficking near the Hanger Lane gyratory system, where a lorry has just been turned over, so do expect further hold-ups at banks and post offices in the area.'

The idea of releasing criminals into the community was begun by Group 4 security a while back. The private firm who won the contract for transferring offenders from one prison to another were shocked to discover that their vehicles were not secure enough and that the convicts kept jumping off the back of the tandem. But now 'Criminals in the Community' has become official policy and the next stage will have to be finding suitable jobs for the people who are serving out their sentences in our midst. For some industries it is a great opportunity: 'Estate agent seeks experienced con-artist to lie convincingly and obtain large amounts of money for no work.' 'Electrical retailers require fraudsters to swindle gullible customers with extended warranty scam.' 'Experienced in daylight robbery? We need you to sell our designer greetings cards and wrapping paper!'

Tragically, one of the most obvious jobs for them would not be possible because their curfew would prevent them from turning up to sit in the House of Commons in the evening. Although, on second thoughts, that hasn't seemed to bother anyone else. The released offenders have to be inside their own homes by seven o'clock in the evening otherwise their tag bleeps and their carriage turns back into a pumpkin. So for twelve hours a day they are effectively swapping their old prison cells for their own houses. When offenders realized that this meant they had to pay for their own dinners they nearly rioted, but they'd just had the roof mended and didn't want to chuck any tiles into the begonias. 'I refuse to share a cell,' said the painted sheets hanging out of the windows. 'Conjugal Rights Now!' said another, and his wife shouted through the loud hailer, 'Well, make your bloody mind up!'

Apart from relieving prison overcrowding, the idea of the tag is to help reintroduce prisoners to normal society. They are prevented from going out after dark so that they end up just falling asleep in front of the telly and eventually struggling up to bed. So in that sense it works fantastically: they're behaving exactly like the rest of society almost immediately. The prison population now exceeds 70,000, which is about the population of Bedford. It's hard to imagine things getting much worse for prisoners, apart from having to live in Bedford. The chances for rehabilitation must be greater if former offenders are playing an active role in normal society, and now they can walk around our towns and cities once more and see how things have changed since they were first sent to jail. And then they can get mugged, have their car hijacked, be burgled and then be set upon by a gang of drunken yobs; at which point they'll go running back to Wormwood Scrubs, bang on the doors and shout, 'Let me in – let me back in – they're all bloody criminals out here!'

War! Hurr! What is it good for?

30 March 2002

Twenty years ago this week the news came through that Argentina had invaded the Falkland Islands. Details were sketchy in those first few hours, though some people thought they might be in the Indian Ocean maybe, or perhaps near Australia somewhere. While the Foreign Office were still leafing through their big dusty atlas with the British Empire bits coloured in pink, Margaret Thatcher had already decided to go to war. Almost overnight she went from being a vulnerable and deeply unpopular Prime Minister to being an unassailable politician who was then in a position to do to British industry what she'd just done to the *Belgrano*. A fascist dictatorship was toppled in Argentina, but apart from that, everything went the way she wanted it.

Now in the same way George W. Bush has been turned from discredited leader to popular national hero by embarking upon military action overseas. They are rewriting the lyrics to Edwin Starr's classic peace anthem. Now it goes: 'War! Hurr! What is it good for? Approval ratings for national leaders, yeah! War! Hurr! What is it good for? Deflecting attention from complex domestic problems! Say it again!'

Back in 1982 America supported Britain in the Falklands War on condition that the British government signed a special contract drawn up by the Pentagon which stated, 'In return for US backing, Britain hereby promises to support every armed intervention that America undertakes for ever and ever.' There can't be any other explanation for this country's consistent enthusiasm for every America bombing raid or new missile deployment. When the White House declared a war on drugs, British jets were scrambled ready to bomb a solitary dope-dealer in downtown Detroit. If the President's daughter reveals her battle with underage drinking, then the SAS are sent in to battle with the demon drink on her behalf.

But if we believe we can influence US foreign policy by sticking beside America, then we are deluding ourselves. Britain can no more affect the direction being taken than some teenage girl gripping onto the passenger seat as her joyriding boyfriend speeds out of control.

One day in the not too distant future, Tony Blair will appear in tears opposite George W. Bush on the *Jerry Springer Show*. 'On today's programme, "World leaders who promised special relationships".' The host will put a reassuring hand on the British PM's shoulder as a bitter Tony recounts how much he did for this guy; he went to war for him, he stuck up for him when no one else would, even though all his friends warned him not to get too close. Because George had promised Tony that they would always do everything together. But then Bang! Bang! and it was all over; George had got what he wanted and he wasn't bothered about Tony any more. And then the audience will boo George from Texas as he shrugs and sneers, 'Hey, I get into bed with whoever suits me – who knows what I promised Terry here.' Cue the shouting and the undignified scuffle as they cut to the ads and Jerry Springer says, 'Coming up after these messages: "My brother screwed Florida"!'

In the hysteria of the moment all wars can seem justifiable. During the War of Jenkins' Ear, all the woolly liberals were going around say-ing, 'Well, this Jenkins, chap did have his ear chopped off after all, so I think an all-out war against Spain is the only justifiable course of action.' But if the invasion of Iraq is such a great idea, why weren't we lobbying America to pursue this policy before they told us about it when they faxed through the infantry request form? We would all love to see Saddam Hussein being overthrown, but this has to be brought about by the people of Iraq. There are plenty of appalling regimes around the world and some we arm and some we bomb. In Saddam's case we have done both just to be on the safe side. If ever Arab support for peace in the Middle East needed to be courted it is now. So what does the American President think? 'I know! Why don't we invade Iraq? Because things are so quiet between Israel and the Palestinians at the moment that a US bombing of an Arab state would probably go down really well.' I had PE teachers more intelligent than George W. Bush. Tony Blair has to put some distance between himself and the Global Village Idiot. The Labour Party might be able to forgive its leader for behaving like a president, but they could never forgive him for behaving like *that* president.

And then our Prime Minister should explain to Bush that Britain can only go to war in extreme circumstances and when very precise criteria have been met. 'I'm sorry, George, but Britain can only bomb or invade a country where the leader has not been democratically elected and where the regime has recently executed British citizens. Oh no, hang on, that's America, isn't it? Um, look, I'll get back to you . . .'

Nationalized Grand National

6 April 2002

Today is the Grand National, the toughest challenge in the horse racing calendar and preparations are already under way. All leave at the glue factory is cancelled and the dog meat vans are reversing up to the side of the course. Perhaps it would be a fitting tribute to our recently departed Queen Mother's love of horse racing if the winners of this year's Grand National were used in Tuesday's funeral procession. It would certainly speed things up a bit to have the gun carriage pulled along by a couple of galloping racehorses, clearing the fence into St James's Park, leaping over the water and then speeding down the final straight of Whitehall as thousands of punters cheered them on from behind the crash barriers.

The Grand National used to be a special date in the British calendar because it was the one day a year when everyone would have a flutter; one harmless dabble in the world of gambling and that was it. Then suddenly the National Lottery had us throwing our money away fifty-two weeks a year, soon followed by a second mid-week draw just in case anyone had any income support still left by Wednesday. But still this wasn't enough. Now Britain's gambling laws are being relaxed after Robin Cook bet Tony Blair that they wouldn't be. The government has announced it is repealing those petty regulations that for some reason had banned one-armed bandits from nurseries, churches and operating theatres. Apparently the idea is to help tourism by turning Blackpool into a British Las Vegas. The gangsters of Nevada must be really worried – all those hardened American gamblers who now play poker and blackjack are suddenly going to be rushing over to Lancashire to try their hand at bingo. 'Guns on the table and clickety click, eyes down for a full house! Two lines of coke – eleven! A pair of Uzi pistols – seventy-seven!'

But where was the demand for all this? Where were the demonstrations from outraged citizens denied the right to give all their money away to dodgy casino owners? How often have you sat in a pub and thought, 'The trouble with this place is there just aren't enough fruit machines!' (It is no longer politically correct to call them 'one-armed bandits', following intensive lobbying by a number of people who are actually bandits by profession and have lost one of their upper limbs in robbery-related accidents.)

It's not a question of being a kill-joy, because there is very little joy in today's instant forms of gambling. Where's the fun or skill in scratch cards, fruit machines or the Lottery? You spend a quid, and in one split second suddenly realize you've just lost a quid. Wow, that was worth it! The reason that horse racing is such an infinitely superior way of throwing your money away is that it provides a narrative, an unfolding drama in which you discover that, despite all your expert analysis of the form and conditions, random factors have conspired against you, and so after a few minutes' thrilling or exasperating entertainment your money is finally lost. Or rather the money your partner put in that charity envelope by the front door is lost. And now you can even bet from home; online betting is replacing many bookmakers as computers are programmed to grunt at you and give you the wrong winnings.

The liberalization of gambling wouldn't be so bad if it was being used to raise more money for public services. But the tax charged at bookies was recently repealed so the Treasury no longer even gets 9 per cent of the child benefit back again. The National Lottery established the principle that gambling could benefit good causes, but this opportunity should have been taken to make all gambling give a similar percentage to charities. Or even better, nationalize all casinos, bookmakers and the Lottery and keep all the profit for our schools and hospitals. Imagine the scene in Park Lane at the glamorous setting of British Casinos, the new state-run gaming club:

'Place your bets, ladies and gentlemen!'

'Fifty pounds on thirteen black, please!'

'No, you can't really place your bet here – you have to go over to our other office in Peckham, fill out form CF/R7 – unless your stake is over a hundred pounds, in which case you need form CF/R12. Send it off to the sorting office at Didsbury and we should have that bet processed for you in three to four months' time.'

Today's big steeplechase would be a nationalized Grand National, though the tannoys might relay a slightly different commentary: 'We apologize for the late arrival of the runners and riders for today's three o'clock. This is due to jockey shortages. For those horses that wish to travel to Becher's Brook, a temporary bus service is in operation.'

But I still think it's a great idea. New Labour to nationalize all gambling? You'd be able to get pretty long odds on that one.

Does the working class exist?

13 April 2002

This week a writ was submitted to the High Court which stated, 'The words "working classes" are not now capable of any meaningful definition.' The judge looked up from his copy of the *Daily Star*, took a stubby pencil from behind his ear and said, 'Ooh dear, nah, mate, a court case like that's gonna cost yer innit? And we're booked up for ages – tell you what, I'll see if one of me mates can adjudicate for yer, I'll just get me mobile from the van.'

The assertion that the working classes no longer exist is being made by a property company who want to develop a site in central London for luxury housing despite a 1929 covenant which states that the land may only be used to provide housing for the working classes. The clause goes on to say that they must have stone cladding and a satellite dish on the front, a car stacked up on bricks in the front garden and a doorbell that plays an electric version of 'Maybe It's Because I'm A Londoner'.

The original 1929 clause was clearly intended to safeguard housing for ordinary people doing low-paid jobs, and today this need is greater than ever. Obviously the working classes are not the same as they were in the 1920s. They're not all wearing flat caps and saying to a wobbly black-and-white camera, 'Well, I'm just a simple working man and don't know nuffink about no gold standard but if that Mr Churchill says we's ought go back on it, well that's good enuff for the likes of me!'

To hear some of the commentators on this story over the past couple of days you would think they'd never met a working-class person in their lives. (Presumably their cleaners are from the Philippines so that doesn't count.) It's like we're talking about some near extinct species that could only be tracked down after days spent trekking through the urban jungle. You can almost imagine the next nature documentary from the BBC, featuring a memorable piece of footage in which David Attenborough encounters a surviving family group of the endangered species known as 'working-class people'. He whispers to camera that he is going to try to get closer. At first they are wary of him; the dominant male grunts and furrows his eyebrows before returning to feed on his natural diet of crisps and Tango. The mother seems anxious about her new offspring; he's still not back from the shop with her fags, but the older cubs are more playful, and before long are climbing all over David Attenborough and nicking his mobile phone.

In the old days you could tell what social class people belonged to by the way that they voted. The middle classes voted SDP and the working classes all voted for Maggie. If you go further back in history it was even more confusing: the rich people were fat and the poor people were all thin. Apparently the poor didn't eat much and had to walk everywhere; in direct contrast to today, of course, where the Royle family lie around all day in front of the telly eating bacon butties while the high earners are starving themselves on a lettuce leaf and spending an hour a day on a Stairmaster treadmill. But there are also all sorts of ways in which the classes overlap. I might decide to get myself a proletarian supper of fish and chips, but then I'll go and give myself away by asking if the vinegar is balsamic. (I hadn't had such a funny look since I asked if it was organic free-range chicken in the KFC bargain bucket.) Ultimately it still comes down to money. The working classes are embarrassed that they don't have more of it, and the middle classes are mortified that they have so much. All of these determining factors will be gone over in the High Court later this year. My prediction is that the court will rule in favour of the property company, thereby finally establishing in law that the British working class is indeed finally extinct. In other words, the law courts will have sided with the posh chaps from the property company in Surrey. And what more proof do you need that the English class system is alive and well and still screwing the working classes as much as ever? It makes my middle-class blood boil so much I want to tut and say, 'Honestly!', but best not make a fuss, I suppose.

Labour to increase taxes shock!

20 April 2002

The day before the budget the government heard some terrifying news. The Conservatives stated that they would not support increased health spending unless it was accompanied by reform. Panic spread through the cabinet. 'Oh no – the opposition have threatened to oppose us! What are we going to do? Without those crucial votes the budget will only be passed with a wafer-thin majority of a hundred and sixty-seven votes.'

By endlessly talking about the need to reform the NHS, political leaders are implying that the Health Service is somehow to blame for its own shortcomings. 'You can't solve these problems just by throwing money at them,' they say. What, problems like shortage of money? 'Exactly,' they continue. 'You might think that the solution to under-funding would be more funds, but nothing could be further from the truth.'

Maybe doctors should attempt this trick on the next politician to be rushed to casualty? 'Quick! He's lost four pints of blood; get him a transfusion quick!'

'Yes, but you see you can't just solve this shortage-of-blood problem by throwing blood at it,' says the doctor.

'But my blood pressure is dangerously low!' gasps the politician lying on the trolley.

'Not in real terms,' says the doctor. 'The rate of decrease is actually levelling out and it's still much higher than it was under the last government.'

'And my temperature is a hundred and five – that's critically high, isn't it?'

'Not when seasonally adjusted, and we remain firmly committed to a year-on-year reduction to bring it into line with the European average by two thousand and seven.'

It is of course wonderful news that this Labour government is committing £40 billion to the National Health Service so soon after ousting the Tories in, er, 1997. In the NHS the effects were immediate. There was a sudden drop in the number of Labour Party members being treated for severe depression. The budget was cheered by Labour back-benchers because, unlike previous budgets, they understood several words of it. The sentence 'more spending on the NHS' is actually five words in a row and constitutes a record for the longest any MP has concentrated on a budget speech without closing their eyes and dreaming that they are Martin Sheen in *The West Wing*.

The trouble is that most people on the left didn't get involved in politics because they felt passionate about a prudent stewardship of the national economy. Not many of us ever went on marches chanting, 'What do we want?' 'Abolition of the national insurance ceiling in order that NHS spending as a proportion of GDP can be brought into line with other Western democracies!' Our solution to the complex economic problems of this country was basically that there was this woman called Maggie, and we wanted her out.

Then the Labour Party rather threw us by actually coming to power and on day one they set about putting the economy straight. 'So, interest rates?' said Gordon. 'What do we think – up or down?' And the various junior Treasury ministers pretended to think really hard as a way of covering up the fact that they had no idea what was the expected answer. 'Um – I dunno, maybe just move them sideways a bit?' Ten minutes later it was agreed to hand this particular decision over to the Bank of England. Maybe that's why the Tories invented laissez-faire economics: it meant you didn't even have to pretend to comprehend any of it.

But this 2002 budget was different because everyone understood it. We're going to pay more National Insurance and get a better NHS. It is indeed great news, even if it shows how bad things had got that this should seem such a radical idea. 'Hooray, hooray! Labour government to raise money to pay for health service! You know that car we've had for all these years, well, they're going to let us put petrol in it too!'

While many Labour MPs cheered the news, some of the 1997 breed of New Labour clones were bitter about this betrayal of everything they stood for. 'Typical Labour Party sell-out!' they shouted angrily. 'Oh yeah, in opposition it's all "Down with the workers and up with big business" – but as soon as you get into power you change your tune!' Some of them are thinking of forming a faction called 'Old New Labour'. But most people in the country welcome last Wednesday's great news. This government is putting £40 billion pounds into the NHS because at last they finally understand what is most important to the people of this country. If that's how much it's going to cost to mend David Beckham's toe, then so be it.

Match abandoned (following inspection by accountants)

27 April 2002

There were ugly scenes in the Commons yesterday when rival supporters clashed over the collapse of ITV Digital and the future of the football league. Playing way out on the right wing, Blues forward Tim Yeo missed another open goal, prompting the usual groans from the dwindling band of long-suffering supporters behind him. Soon they turned their frustration on the yuppie supporters opposite, jeering at the hundreds of New Labour fans and chanting, 'Where were you when you were shit?' Afterwards new signing Tessa Jowell said she was 'sick as a parrot, but at the end of the day, we give it our best shot but it weren't to be and that's football innit?'

ITV Digital was born out of the presumption that there was no limit to the amount of football that the viewing public would watch. On BBC1 there was football, on Sky Sports there was football and on ITV, well, there were highlights of Leicester City versus Derby. Of course, there were still plenty of other things on telly. There was drama about footballers' wives or quiz shows featuring retired footballers. The clamour to get more football on television reached such a fever pitch I'm surprised that even infant school friendlies weren't televised. I'm sure Des Lynam and his guests would have done their best to provide expert half-time analysis:

'I'm worried about the shape of this under-eights team, Des. Instead of playing four-four-two, they've opted for the less conventional formation of eleven. If we just look at the replay here, watch the marking from seven–year-old Jamie. He should be tracking back to mark the centre forward, but no, he's waving to his mum and the striker goes straight past him and scores.'

'To be fair, Andy, the striker is from the same side and is scoring in the wrong goal there . . .'

'Well, that's another area of their game they're gonna have to work on, Des. At this level if you keep scoring in the wrong goal, you're going to lose games.'

ITV Digital paid hundreds of millions of pounds for the rights to the Nationwide League, but then to everyone's shock and amazement it turns out that no one was particularly interested in paying lots of money to watch Kidderminster Harriers v. Cheltenham Town. Who could possibly have foreseen such an outcome? That clubs that were only attracting a couple of thousand supporters in their home towns would not attract millions of viewers across the country! It's the greatest surprise since a stunned nation learned that Wales had failed to qualify for the World Cup.

Now dozens of minor clubs who had been promised large amounts of cash from the deal are faced with extinction. Century-old clubs that are part of this country's sporting heritage will be bulldozed to make way for garden centres and DIY superstores. But will anyone actually go to these garden centres? Will these supermarkets really make any money? All right, yes, they will, but that's not the point. There is more money in the game than ever before, and yet the smaller clubs are going bankrupt. When they said that football was a metaphor for life, now we know what they meant.

The Football League chairman is called Keith Harris, which was always a worry. How did we hand over our national sport to someone whose only experience is putting his hand up a duck's bottom? But the real soccer hooligans in this story are Carlton and Granada, the companies behind ITV Digital. They were very keen to make a quick buck out of the beautiful game (or 'the rather dreary game', when we realized which matches they'd bought), but despite their poor business judgement they're happy to walk away and leave the football clubs to perish. Those expensive set-top receivers will still have their uses, of course. Anyone in need of a sturdy paperweight or handy doorstop need look no further.

A major shake-up of the league structure now looks inevitable. At the beginning of next season the clubs will have to stand against a wall and then Nationwide Divisions One and Two will take turns to pick. 'Stoke City, we'll have you. Er, Coventry – over here!' Meanwhile Torquay and Lincoln will be standing there with their hands up saying, 'Pick me! Pick me!', knowing that no one wants them and they'll just have to play rounders instead.

Despite this fiasco, the onward march of digital technology continues. Because it's just better, apparently – if you had been reading this column online, for example, you'd be getting much funnier jokes than in the piece on the printed page. That's the brilliant scam about anything digital: it does exactly the same thing, it's just much more expensive.

'Excuse me, why is this cup of tea seven pounds eighty?'

'Well, it's digital – it's digital tea; everyone has got to switch over to digital tea soon, digital coffee, digital Ovaltine – they say the price will come down eventually . . .'

'Really?'

'Yeah, unless it all goes bankrupt, of course, and then no one will have any tea whatsoever. There's your digital sugar – that's another five pounds please.'

Talking ballots

4 May 2002

Lionel Jospin and his wife had a terrible row this morning. All she said was, 'I bet you never thought you'd be voting for Jacques Chirac tomorrow!' Honestly, some people can be so touchy sometimes. To understand the misery of French socialists this weekend, imagine yourself having to vote for Margaret Thatcher to keep out the BNP. Alone in the polling booth, your hand would shake and then recoil at such an unnatural act, and then your other hand would be needed to grip it and physically force it to put that supportive cross next to the words 'Thatcher, Margaret, the Conservative Party candidate'. Outside, Labour activists would be on hand to treat traumatized socialist voters, dispensing sympathetic counselling and vomit bags, while in the distance hard-left demonstrators chanted 'Maggie, Maggie, Maggie, In! In! In!'

In Britain's local elections this week, turn-out was up from appalling to just dismal, prompted in part by the French National Front's success and the spectre of gains for the BNP. The lazy excuse that 'they're all the same' now seems a little hollow.

'I mean, what's the point in voting? One lot say they're going to invest in education and the other lot say they are going to invade Poland – I can't see any difference between them frankly.'

'Exactly, one party promises more bobbies on the beat and the other promises to create lebensraum for the Nordic master race – there's nothing to choose between them any more.'

We won't always be able to rely on French fascists to push up our local election turn-out a meagre 5 per cent or so, and drastic action is still needed to tackle voter apathy. On Thursday all sorts of pilot schemes were attempted to encourage people to take part. In Hackney the entire election was done by postal voting and we are expecting the result as soon as last year's Christmas cards are finally sorted. Residents in other boroughs were able to vote using the remote control on their digital television. After pressing the wrong button residents in one ward have discovered that their local councillor is now Will Young from *Pop Idol*. Another experiment was internet voting, which was heralded as the greatest leap for democracy since the hanging chad. If only they'd had voting by computer in Florida, that would have made people less suspicious, wouldn't it? It's not just the idea of hacking that's so scary; it is the political opinions and interests of those anoraks who spend endless nights alone in front of their computers. 'And the winner of the Antrim North by-election, by over a million last-minute online votes, is Pre-Op Ladyboy Lola of the White Supremacist Bondage Party.' Other votes on Thursday were cast using text messaging. Imagine the arguments at the count while the returning officer tried to sort out all the messages that said 'IM VTNG 4 LB' between Labour, the Liberal Democrats and the zany Lord Dyslexia. Next they'll be suggesting voting by telepathy. Mystic Meg will be employed to sit in the polling station and say, 'I can sense that Mr Jones at twenty-three Station Road wishes to vote Lib Dem, but would mistakenly vote for only one council candidate instead of the permitted three.'

Next week a Private Member's Bill is to be tabled which proposes compulsory voting, but sadly no MPs will bother turning up to the chamber to vote for it: 'What's the point, you know, it never changes anything . . .' Maybe we should try thinking in terms of a carrot instead of a stick. Here is one possible idea to radically increase voter turn-out at a stroke. On the Saturday after the election there should be an additional Lottery draw for a £5 million jackpot. For this draw you wouldn't have to buy a Lottery ticket; all you'd have to do is to have gone and voted in that Thursday's general election. The prize money could come from within the system; every time there was no jackpot winner, half a million could be taken out of the amount rolling over to the following week. Over the year the fund would build up until there was a huge jackpot to be won on the Saturday after the election. But you are only in the draw if you voted. Turn-out would shoot up to 80 per cent – with just a handful of billionaires saying, 'I can't see the point, it wouldn't change anything . . .'

Obviously this 'Voter's Jackpot' idea would need to be piloted somewhere first, and I am happy to suggest my own ward as the ideal testing ground; in fact, just my road would probably be all you needed to try it out, maybe just odd numbers only. It might strike some people as a bit vulgar, but drastic action needs to be taken. In the first normal British election after the Second World War, the turn-out was 84 per cent. But it's not as if there's ever going to be another Nazi takeover of mainland Europe to make us sit up and realize the importance of taking part. Oh hang on, no, that's tomorrow, isn't it?*

*Jacques Chirac did of course go on to win the French Presidential election after the French answered the inspiring rallying call of 'Vote for the Crook, Not the Nazi!'

It's what one would have wanted

11 May 2002

It's the same in every family. First the shock and sadness at the death of an elderly relative, and then the mad scramble to get your hands on all their stuff. If you look back at the footage of the Queen Mother's funeral procession, you can see that it speeds up considerably towards the end, as members of the royal family compete to be first one back to the house to help themselves to the jewellery. No wonder Edward and Andrew stood guard over her coffin; they were there to stop all the other relatives nicking the crown off the top.

Like any pensioner, the Queen Mother had acquired a few bits and bobs over the years. Much of her fortune was tied up in a vast collection of coupons cut out of magazines, promising savings such as 10p off a tub of Asda own-brand margarine. A constitutional wrangle is developing over who gets the bundles of £5 notes that were discovered rolled up under the mattress. The old lady also had an impressive art collection, with such paintings as *Kitten Playing with Ball of Wool*, and on top of the telly were several porcelain figurines as advertised in the *Sunday Express* colour supplement (including the hand-crafted and individually numbered statuette *Man's Best Friend* – three monthly instalments still to be paid). There was one piece of abstract artwork that could not be explained: a small Haitian doll bearing a vague resemblance to Wallis Simpson with a lot of pins stuck in it.

But while most families squabble over who gets the carriage clock, the royal family have the additional matter of a number of palaces and castles that have to be divvied out as well.

'I think I should get Clarence House, the Royal Lodge at Windsor and her house at Balmoral, because, er – it's what she would have wanted.'

'Well, I think we should respect her last wishes, the ones expressed privately to me which were that, um . . . I should get the whole lot.'

Charles will now be moving into the granny flat known as Clarence House. It was about time he got his own pad; he was getting a bit old to be tiptoeing past his mother's bedroom at night, whispering to Camilla to skip the third step because it creaks a bit. The Queen Mother's Castle of Mey near John O'Groats has been suggested for Edward and Sophie.

'Ya, like a sort of holiday home thingy?' asked Edward.

'Well, kind of . . .' said the other royals. 'But don't feel under any pressure to hurry back.'

Meanwhile, second-tier royals such as Viscount Linley and Princess Michael of Kent are being asked to leave Kensington Palace. Two tattooed men in sheepskin coats with a couple of Rottweilers will be round with the sledgehammers first thing Monday, telling them to clear their stuff out pronto. Kensington Palace will then be let on the open market; Posh and Becks have already been round to measure up for curtains.

The Queen Mother's estate is reckoned to be worth around £50 million, a figure which could double once they take all the empties back to the off-licence. Normally the Treasury could expect to get about £20 million out of this, but apparently the royals won't be paying a penny in inheritance tax.

Presumably the Queen just has a very creative accountant who's somehow proved that the firm is operating at a loss. He's spent the last two weeks with Her Majesty trying to think up more and more elaborate expenses, while Philip sits in the corner scribbling random amounts on to a pad of blank taxi receipts.

'I know, Liz, how about we say you have to spend a grand a week on flowers? That's a business expense innit?'

'Um, well, one's public does tend to give one a lot of flowers for nothing . . .'

'Yeah, but the taxman ain't gonna know that, is he? Now how much shall I put down for crown polish?'

In fact, the Treasury will not be getting £20 million in death duties because of a so-called 'sovereign to sovereign' deal that was struck by John Major's government in 1993. Of course, it would be very easy for cynics to say that there was one rule for the rich and another for the poor. And the reason that it would be so easy is because it's true.

But the fact that Her Majesty isn't legally obliged to hand over the money means it would be a greater PR gesture if she did so voluntarily. Or why not donate the money to a specific social project which could bear her mother's name? The Queen Mother Crack Addicts Drop-In Centre? The Queen Mother Refuge for Bangladeshi Lesbians? It's what she wouldn't have wanted. But sadly the royal family will be too busy fighting amongst themselves over all those little incidental possessions, like Caithness, to think about giving any money away. The truth is that they have made millions out of her sad passing. No wonder they were always creeping up behind her and shouting 'Boo!'

Filthy lucre

18 May 2002

In last month's sizzling edition of *Big Ones* there was something familiar about one of the Readers' True-Life Confessions. Mr TB from Westminster wrote, 'It was my party and everyone kept giving me presents, but the biggest treat was more than I bargained for! I hadn't had an election for four years and suddenly this porn star with these big wads came up and offered to give me a good funding, just like that! Well, I was desperate for it, I can tell you. I've never had any cheques like it and I didn't feel guilty, even when everyone found out.'

On Thursday night *Newsnight* viewers were treated to the sight of Jeremy Paxman listing the titles of the pornographic magazines that were published by Richard Desmond, such as *Asian Babes*, *Spunk Loving Sluts* and *Big Ones*, and then asking the Prime Minister if he was familiar with these magazines. Just off camera, Alastair Campbell was waving at his boss mouthing 'No!' and shaking his head vigorously. Oh, that's cheating, thought Paxman. Just when Tony was about to tell us who were his favourite porn models and mime the most distinguishing features of the girls in *Big and Busty*: 'I tell you what, mate, that bird who was the centrefold last month – phwoar! Know what I mean, Jezza? Phwoar! Eh? I've got Busty Brenda pinned up in the cabinet office next to that list of New Labour's Aims and Values and no mistake!'

The PM pointedly refused to condemn the publications of the most embarrassing donor to give money to the Labour Party since Robert Kilroy-Silk resigned his membership. But the association with Richard Desmond finally caused the Prime Minister some grief at home when Cherie was sorting out Tony's old jumpers at the back of his wardrobe and discovered a grubby, well-thumbed copy of the *Daily Express*.

'Oh that!' blushed Tony. 'Well, um, there's actually some very good interviews . . .'

Meanwhile, round at Richard Desmond's house, the pornographer's wife was equally upset. 'What are you doing associating yourself with these people, Richard? Have you heard some of the titles that New Labour have published? *Towards a Public Private Partnership*! Ugh – it's appalling! *No Benefits without Responsibilities*! It sounds obscene!'

During an awkward discussion in cabinet, ministers admitted that Desmond's porn mags were not the sort of family publications with which the Labour Party ought to be associated. 'These magazines, they never show the love involved in sex,' said Robin Cook. 'And all the others that I researched – they didn't show any love either; very little sign of any love in over a hundred publications, which I thoroughly checked and rechecked.'

In the old days they used to say that the Labour Party tended towards financial improprieties while the Tory ministers would get caught out with sex scandals. Now New Labour have shown what is meant by the Third Way with a story that manages to combine both. The whole sordid episode raises many questions. Why did Desmond want to give this money? Why did the Labour Party accept it? And just who is that weirdo that goes into the woods and scatters pornographic magazines everywhere?

Clearly the decision to accept the cash was a political decision, not a financial one. To send the donation back would have stuck up two fingers to the owner of a major newspaper in the run-up to the General Election. It is quite possible that Desmond gave the money with exactly this test in mind. Perhaps he hoped that the association would make people see him as a respectable mainstream publisher. (Desmond does not like to be called a pornographer, according to people close to the pornographer.) Once upon a time Clare Short strode into W. H. Smith and took the pornographic magazines off the top shelf. Now the government has effectively marched back into the shop and put them back on the shelves lower down.

But if the Labour Party are going to take donations from a pornographer, why don't they cut out the middle man and just raise the money this way themselves? 'It's ladies' night at Spearmint Rhino. Live pole-dancing with Stephen Byers! You simply won't believe it!' Or 'Live on tour – The Full Monty, starring Jack Straw and John Prescott. Watch those dark suits come off to the tune of the Red Flag!' Soon the telephone boxes around Westminster will be full of little cards stuck up with Blu-tack, featuring pictures of eager young politicians with black bars across their eyes: 'Young politician – fresh in town – Lobby Me!' 'New Labour MP – I'll do whatever I'm told!' Or how about a live website: '"Tony-cam", featuring X-tremely X-citing X-certs of the PM's bedroom action, featuring Tony sitting up in bed reading "Whither the Euro"'? They might never need to have another Labour Party fundraising dinner ever again. Or is the depressing truth that more people are turned on by pictures of naked women than they are by our politicians? I suppose there will always be a fundamental difference between pornography and politics. With the magazines you only imagine you're getting screwed.

School's out

25 May 2002

Two major educational problems emerged this week: truancy and exclusions. It seems that if children are refusing to turn up for lessons, it makes it very difficult to expel them.

'Listen, lad, if you keep being absent from school like this, you won't be allowed into school, do you understand?'

'No.'

'No, neither do I.'

The DFES says that exclusions are only being used in extreme circumstances, such as when children are dealing in hard drugs or bringing weapons into the playground. Honestly, did these ministers never play swapsies when they were at school? 'I'll swap you my plastic snake for your Bobby Moore Esso Cup Coin,' or 'I'll swap you this kilo of heroin for your Kalashnikov semi-automatic.' Yet another innocent playground pastime banned by the do-gooders of the political correctness brigade!

Apparently some of these schools are so rough that the few kids having music lessons have to smuggle their violins into class hidden inside machine-gun cases. Last week an eleven-year-old girl was excluded for punching a teacher, which might be worth bearing in mind when they come to update *What Katy Did Next*. This week's figures represent the first increase in school exclusions since Labour came to power. And the number looks set to rise further, with whole classes expected to be sent home next month. The fact that this will happen to be on the days of England World Cup matches will be pure coincidence.

It is a bit hard to know what to do when teenagers have already strayed so far outside the system. Iain Duncan Smith has come up with a few tough suggestions of his own to punish Britain's errant schoolkids: officer cadets will be denied permission to wear their uniform on St George's Day and boarders won't be allowed to read the lesson in chapel. But it's possible that this may not be enough.

One mother was recently sent to prison because her daughters were consistently missing school. Except the prison governor suddenly spotted her with her daughters in the Arndale Centre. 'Hang on – you're supposed to be in jail – what are you doing coming out of Asda?' To which her daughters replied, 'Nah, she had to come shopping with us today. She might be in later in the week . . .'

Being teenage daughters, the girls were probably not too concerned that their actions had sent their mother to prison. 'Oh god, why's there no food in the fridge? Honestly, she's so selfish!' Suddenly teenagers have another means of bullying their parents. 'Right – either you let me get my eyebrow pierced or I'm skiving off school today and you'll be back inside. It's your choice, Mum.'

Obviously many of these problems start at home. My old English teacher told me that when he took a class on a school trip round the local police station his most disruptive pupil glanced into the cells and said a cheery 'Hello, Dad!' The way things are going, this might be the only way for truants to see their parents, but at least they'll be taking part in school trips.

However, the idea of taking child benefit away from the parents of consistent truants is not acceptable. You can take parents to court and the judge may choose to fine them. But child benefit is not a special treat for best-behaved parents, it is a hard-fought-for right for all. 'These parents are living in poverty and have lost control of their children.' 'Okay, well, the solution must be to make them poorer!'

Of course it's not always that easy to track down the kids who are playing truant. One effective method is for teachers to ring the phone numbers of their stolen mobiles and then when someone answers they say, 'Why aren't you in class today?' Some excuses are better than others:

'Why isn't your fourteen-year-old daughter in school this morning?'

'Because she's giving birth to twins.'

'Oh, I see. What about her little brother?'

'Well, someone had to drive her to the hospital.'

Most truancy actually takes place with the parent's permission. By 'truancy' we are obviously only referring to working-class children being off school – it is an entirely different matter if middle-class parents are taking their kids out during term time, because that was the only week the villa in Tuscany was available: 'Oh yes, I mean, think of the educational value little Henry will get from seeing the architecture in Florence and Pisa.'

'Quite, and last year he learnt several Italian words, like, erm, "pizza" . . .'

Local authorities are now employing truancy officers to question parents who are out and about with their kids during school hours. The next stage will be to patrol Legoland and Disneyland Paris, where they'll catch thousands at a time. They'll hide inside the Mickey Mouse costume and just when Mum and Dad think a giant cartoon character is hugging their kids, they'll suddenly realize Mickey is picking them up and slinging them in the back of a police van.

'What's this ride called?'

'Back to school-land. Now shut up.'

God bless the World Cup

1 June 2002

The Queen has been in a fantastic mood this week. Her Golden Jubilee appears to have prompted an enormous surge in patriotism, with pubs and cafés all decked out with the flag of St George.

'But why do all these people celebrating the Jubilee have "Come On England!" all over their white vans?' she asked her advisers.

'Er, well, Ma'am, they are urging the rest of England to "come on" and celebrate Your Majesty's Jubilee . . .'

'Oh, I see. But why does it say "Owen For Ever"? What's Owen?'

'Ah, that, well, yes, er, that's an acronym, Ma'am . . . It stands for, erm, "Onwards With Elizabeth's Nation" . . . yes, that works . . .'

'Well, I must say one hasn't seen such an outpouring of national pride since you pointed out that everyone was celebrating my fortieth birthday back in nineteen sixty-six!'

As a simple test of how the English people channel their patriotism, support for the national football team has totally eclipsed any interest in the Queen's Golden Jubilee. It's a complete walkover: England Flags 5, Union Jacks 1. (Of course all the flags were actually made in China, but that's another matter.) If the Queen had broken her lower metatarsal two months ago, it's hard to imagine the nation fretting quite so much as to whether she'd have been fit to do royal walkabouts in time for the Jubilee bank holiday. 'And the news from the Buck

House dressing room is that the Queen is looking fifty-fifty for the royal balcony waving on June the third. The physio laureate has said he doesn't want to push her too fast; some of those red carpets can be pretty treacherous.'

It seems logical that the only way for the royal family to increase its popularity would be to adopt some of the trappings of our national sport. Football has the advantage of constant television exposure, analysis from a panel of experts, post-match interviews – these are all things that Buckingham Palace needs to think about if they want to force themselves back to the centre of the nation's heart. So after a royal tree-planting is replayed for the third time in slow motion, we'll cut straight to the dressing room where John Motson is waiting to talk to a red-faced Prince Charles, as other exuberant royals run behind him, ruffling his sweat-soaked hair.

'So, Charles – a very successful tree-planting there . . . Congratulations!'

'Well, yeah, I didn't know much about it to be honest. The mayor picked up the shovel on my left, he passed it to me, inch perfect like, and I suddenly saw the base of the tree at my feet and I just buried it!'

The Duke of York, as President of the FA, is currently the only royal directly connected with the beautiful game and last week flew out for the opening ceremony. Apparently there was a terrible delay at the airport when Andrew's name came up on the computer as someone who had a history of travelling abroad with other English lads and getting involved in violence. 'Yes, that was the Falklands War, it doesn't count,' he said as he was chucked in the cells with all the tattooed Chelsea fans. Apparently the foul language and obscene sing-songs were quite shocking, but the fans soon got used to it.

Andrew's sister remains the only royal to have represented her country at the highest level on the sports field. In 1972 Princess Anne made the Olympic team for the sport of Poncing Around on a Horse. (The British selectors went on to get the gold medal for sycophantic toadying.) Her Royal Highness jumped all the fences as well as can be expected considering she had a police bodyguard sharing her saddle at all times. Anne's appearance was notable for the bizarre fact that she was the only competitor at the entire games who was not forced to undergo a sex test. The authorities carefully read through *Debrett's*

Etiquette and Modern Manners and there was absolutely no guidance whatsoever as to how one might tackle the tricky subject of whether a royal princess is a geezer or not. 'The thing is, Your Royal Highness, we do need to be one hundred per cent sure that you are not endowed with the old meat and two veg, as it were, so if you could just quickly lower the old jodhpurs for us, Ma'am, we'll be on our way.' A request like this could ruin your chances of being invited to a garden party at Buckingham Palace.

But not until one of the royals actually represents their country in Britain's favourite sport will they be able to claim some sort of stake in their subjects' football-inspired patriotism. Under FIFA rules the Queen could still qualify for this World Cup. Imagine the drama: England in the World Cup Final and Her Majesty in goal for the penalty shoot-out. It's just a shame she'd have to play for the Germans.

Snakes and property ladders

8 June 2002

When a great public building becomes vacant, the planning people must sit around for hours and hours thinking what on earth it could possibly be used for. 'I don't know, maybe this is a bit crazy, and shoot me down if I'm way off beam here, but how about – luxury flats?'

A stunned silence falls around the room at the incredible originality of this idea, the sheer audacity of such lateral thinking.

'What, you mean convert an old Victorian building originally intended for public use into small luxury domestic units to sell to young professionals? It couldn't be done, could it?'

'No, who in their right mind would pay two hundred and fifty K for a two-bedroom converted classroom?'

The price of property has got so ridiculous that you can't even get a rabbit hutch for under £100,000 these days. When rabbits have dinner parties, it's all they talk about.

'My owners looked at a two-bedroom hutch in Islington; it was a hundred and fifty K and that was without straw.'

'I know, it's ridiculous; we were hoping to start a family on Wednesday but we're going to have to wait until the weekend at least.'

Many central London pets are now having to rent one-room hutches way out in the Thames Estuary and then commute in every morning on the District Line. And once those hamsters start running the wrong way up the down escalator you just can't get them off it.

Figures released this week show the biggest leap in dinner-party conversations about house prices for five years. Discussions about the cost of a three-bedroom semi were up 5 per cent on last year, while smug anecdotes about how little couples paid for their own home a few years back are up a massive 17 per cent.

'My family only paid a pound for this place and now it's worth a hundred million.'

'Yes, but you are the Queen, Ma'am.'

In fact it had all started to go wrong way before that, right back when *Homo sapiens* started to shelter in caves. The supply of caverns was limited and prices started to rocket. Neanderthal estate agents would show prospective buyers around, trying to talk up the cave's best points.

'What about heating; what's that like?'

'I know it feels a little chilly at the moment but that's because we're in the middle of an ice age. But it's not a smoke-free zone or anything, so you'd be able to have a real fire just as soon as man discovers it.'

'Great! And the current occupier will definitely move out on completion, will he?'

'What, the sabre-toothed tiger? Um, definitely, yup, no problem there; just tell him you're the new cave-owner and he'll be only too happy to move on, I'm sure . . .'

Then primitive hunter-gatherers turned to agriculture and built the first farmhouses, soon adding a couple of spare rooms to let out for bed and breakfast. In those days you would work for a week or so and then you'd have your house. Obviously we've come a long way since then, except that now we have to work for twenty-five years before we own our homes outright. The reason that so many first-time buyers are struggling to get into the game of snakes and property ladders is not so much the price of property, but the exorbitant profits made by the mortgage companies. Imagine if a dodgy-looking bloke in a sheepskin coat with two hard men lurking behind him knocked on your door and offered you a loan.

'I'll lend you a hundred grand. You pay me back one hundred and seventy grand. But don't forget to pay, because we'd hate to see you lose your house, wouldn't we, boys?'

'Well, it's a big profit, but I suppose you have to cover your expenses.'

'Ah yes, the survey fee, that's another five hundred pounds you owe us.'

'Oh well, I suppose you've got all your paperwork . . .'

'Good point, that's another grand for our "arrangement fee".'

'Blimey, well, I suppose you have to think of the risks . . .'

'Which is why you'll also be taking out my insurance policy – tell him, Ron . . .'

You'd rightly think they were con men. But those are exactly the sort of mortgage figures you'd be quoted by the banks and building societies today. At least when Brazilian bandits drug you and steal one of your kidneys they don't charge you for the operation.

The spiralling property market is a symptom of the widening gap between rich and poor. With too many people earning more than they can possibly spend, they are buying flats to let out or little weekend cottages in Gloucestershire. Now when it's closing time on Friday night in the pubs of Kensington, the landlord shouts, 'Come on, haven't you got second homes to go to?' We have a property crisis because the rich are too rich. But you can't blame them for wanting to get out of the inner cities at the weekend. I mean, London can be so ghastly sometimes, what with all those homeless people on the streets and everything . . .

In-flight entertainment

14 June 2002

It's no wonder that ITV Digital couldn't get anyone to pay for their various satellite channels. Not when you can watch live footage from US spy planes for free. This week it was revealed that for the past six months it's been possible to watch transmissions from American spy planes with an ordinary satellite dish. What would normally require a secret video link was being broadcast unencrypted across the world via a commercial TV satellite, with a live connection to the internet just in case one or two terrorists had failed to catch the current US troop movements on their telly.

This bizarre lapse in security was discovered last year, but the broadcasts have still not been halted. If you failed to spot the wacky adventures of the American army listed in your copy of *TV Quick*, don't worry, you can still catch the omnibus edition that goes out on Sunday. If the US military wanted to keep the information top secret they could at least have switched transmission to Channel Five. If they'd stuck it between *Barney and Friends* and *Family Affairs* then maybe no one would have ever seen it.

You'd think suspicions would have been raised when the bloke from Dixons was called out to connect up a new satellite TV package for a Mr O. Bin Laden at a secret address in the Tora Bora cave complex in the Afghan mountains.

'So there's all your movie channels there – you've got Sky Sports, the complete Disney package and then on Channel seventy-one you've got all the latest movements of US peacekeeping forces in the Balkans.'

'Excellent! Now can you tell me when the Shopping Channel is selling anthrax warheads?'

For satellite customers bored of watching re-runs of *The Good Life*, the exciting new US spy plane package includes *The Terrorist Channel*, featuring all the latest movements of anti-US terror networks; *Terrorist Kids*, for younger viewers; and *USA Style*, which is a sort of homes and garden makeover channel. 'Okay, let's just remind ourselves how this Afghan village looked before the bombing, and watch the reaction of the red team when they get to see how the US air force have managed to completely change the layout of their home in just one hour!' Who wants to watch all that familiar footage from the Second World War on the Discovery Channel when you can watch all the preparations for the Third World War being broadcast live twenty-four hours a day? First the BBC do away with the globe and then everyone else has the same idea.*

The spy plane footage could also provide endless out-takes for other programmes. Between the home-video bloopers of bridesmaids fainting and toddlers getting stuck in their potties, there'll be other endearing human slip-ups, like NATO smart bombs accidentally blowing up the pharmaceuticals factory. Instead of watching CCTV footage of speeding joyriders on *Police, Camera, Action!* Alastair Stewart can tut about the dangerous driving of these irresponsible suicide bombers. 'Look at this idiot. If he carries on speeding that lorry load of explosives towards that building, someone could get really hurt!' Ever aware of the possibilities of advertising, it must only be a matter of time before the broadcasters find a suitable sponsor. 'And now back to part two of the War on Terrorism, sponsored by Taco Bell.'

Product placement will mean that, instead of chasing terrorists in helicopter gunships, US army personnel will be forced to cross

* The BBC had just done away with its famous globe logo. They were also considering replacing their historic motto, 'Nation Shall Speak Peace Unto Nation', with 'Charlie Dimmock Shall Speak Gardening Tips Unto Several Viewers.'

mountainous terrain in the latest five-door hatchback from General Motors. American military operations will be organized into eight-minute slots so that the broadcasters can cut to an ad break at just the right time. Each segment will end with a cliff-hanger in case the viewer is tempted to switch channels. 'Oh no! The Al-Qaida are about to escape over the border. And I forgot to ring my mom to say happy birthday!'

With the BBC, ITV and Sky now all pitching for the licence for ITV Digital, it would seem sensible to include these wonderful new American programmes in any new package on offer. The expertise demonstrated by their World Cup pundits could be employed at half-time in the latest global sport to hit the airwaves:

'Well, frankly, Gary, the Americans are going to have to work a lot harder to close down this Saudi star, Bin Laden.'

'I couldn't agree more, Terry; I've not been very impressed with accuracy of these American strikes so far. Here we see the action replay of this attack. Look: he completely misses and blows up the Chinese Embassy – and at this level you've really got to hit the target.'

With coverage like this it won't be long till we are all filling out our War on Terrorism wall-chart. And when all-out nuclear warfare does finally break out, at least we'll be able to say to our friends down the pub, 'Don't tell me who wins! I'm taping it and watching it later!'

PM-TV

22 June 2002

This government is fed up with being accused of an obsession with the media. So they're starting regular briefing sessions to be reported on the telly, on the radio and in the newspapers. 'No more spin!' said the press releases arriving in every newsroom in the country. 'Policy before Presentation!' said the hot-air balloons all over London.

We're used to seeing this sort of press conference from the White House, in which the President stands behind a lectern and answers really tough questions, such as, 'Just how evil are these Iraqis, Mr President?' Having British government policy announced in the same way as in the United States was the final adjustment required after it was decided we had to have all the same policies and opinions as them as well.

Tony Blair began his first televised session by announcing that the event was 'the first of what will become regular opportunities for question and answer sessions on anything you want to ask'. This was his first mistake. If you say 'anything' then there are all sorts of problems that people are going to want to know the answers to. Question number one – Andrew Marr, BBC: 'Prime Minister, I've got a new lambswool jumper but it's got chewing gum on it – what's the best way to get this off?' 'Put the jumper in the freezer and the gum will go rock hard; then carefully pick it off with a small kitchen knife.'

'Yeah, Jon Snow, Channel Four News. In the film *Toy Story*, if Buzz Lightyear thinks he's a real space ranger and not a toy, then how come he plays dead when the humans walk into the room?'

Although the PM is now answering questions directly instead of via his official press spokesman, it's a bit much to expect him to be up there completely on his own. That's why he now wears a secret radio earpiece, so that Alastair Campbell can dictate the correct facts and figures from a little radio booth in the room next door.

'Prime Minister, isn't it true that spending on health is actually falling compared to our European partners?'

'That's not true, Tony!' dictates Campbell.

'That's not true, Tony!' says the PM to a surprised-looking Elinor Goodman. And then, as is traditional, the radio signal starts to get interference from the mini-cab office up the road: 'This government has overseen the greatest hospital-building programme in our history,' says the PM resolutely, adding, 'and furthermore, we have always said Car Nine: pick up at Orlando Road, number ninety-seven, ring top bell.'

The idea of this initiative is to try to get past the cynical and negative press and talk direct to the British people, although it's hard to imagine bosses up and down the country allowing their workers to come in late so that they can watch the Prime Minister's live press broadcast first thing in the morning. If you want the great British public to tune in, then frankly it's no good holding boring old press briefings featuring politicians and journalists; you've got to put a bit more popular appeal in there to compete with all the other shows on TV. Basically, if it hasn't got Pauline Quirke in it, no one's going to be interested. If David Jason isn't playing a lovable maverick, you might as well forget it. What the government needs to do is to inject a bit of Sunday night drama into the proceedings. So the session will start with John Sergeant asking a tricky question about the Euro and then the PM begins explaining about the five economic tests. Suddenly Cherie bursts in and shouts in her strongest scouse accent, 'You said you'd be there for me and the kids, Tone, but since you've got this job it's just been work, work, work! It's not me you're married to – it's that little red box.'

'Not now, Cherie – I'm busy . . .'

'What, too busy for your own family?? I'm leaving you, Tony. I've met a holistic vet who lives on a canal barge. We're going to start a floating pet rescue centre with Robson Green and Amanda Burton – it's over, Tony!'

Ratings for the press briefings would soar. Every week the nation would tune in to watch the Prime Minister trying to cope with the pressures of life at the top as his private life crashes all around him.

'Prime Minister, what about this threat of all-out nuclear war?'

'You know, I think there may be another more important problem I need to deal with first. My family.' And then he'd push past the astonished hacks before running along the tow-path just in time to save the canal barge from going over the weir and taking Ross Kemp and all the injured animals with it. Rehearsals start on Monday . . .

No sex please, we're teenage boys

29 June 2002

During a recent secondary-school production of *The Sound of Music*, a teacher stood up in front of the audience and asked if all mothers with babies in the crèche could come and check if it was their baby that wouldn't stop crying. Half the cast walked off the stage. 'I am sixteen, going on seventeen,' continued Liesl, with a nine-month bump sticking out of her Mothercare maternity dress.

The problem of teenage pregnancies is in the news again, with the government announcing that it will be making free condoms available to schoolchildren. In practical terms, it is not very clear how these contraceptives will be handed out. Will each class have a condom monitor? Perhaps these boys will be sent down to the chemist to buy them, only to return shamefaced with thirty combs and a toothbrush. Or will the teachers just hand them out at morning registration? 'Right, take one and pass the rest back. No, don't open them now, Timothy, they are for after school, except for members of sex soc.' Or maybe they'll be sold in the school tuck shop (recently wittily renamed by the boys from 4B)? 'Er, yeah, can I have a sherbet dib-dab, 100 grams of lemon bonbons and a super-ribbed fetherlite Durex please.' Seeing who can blow the biggest bubbles will never be the same again. It is important that teenagers know what these things are for. Now that they're to be made more widely available, we can look forward to a dramatic increase in the numbers of condoms being filled up with water and chucked at passers-by from the top of the multi-storey car park.

Underage sex is not a new problem in this country. A report back in the 1970s showed that boys in their teens were having more sex than ever, although this figure would have dropped dramatically if they'd included me in the survey. Of course, these things can be quite difficult to measure. Approaching a class of sixteen-year-old boys and saying, 'Right, hands up who's still a virgin?' may not be the most reliable polling method available. In the developed world, only America manages an even higher teenage pregnancy rate than us, and there George W. Bush is funding an abstinence education programme, telling young people that they should not have sex, while every advert, TV show and movie is telling them the opposite.

It is fashionable on the left to laugh at the idea of abstinence education as misguided and reactionary, and if the only thing we were telling our teenagers about sex is 'don't do it' then we would obviously fail. But alongside better information, advice and access to contraception, I would venture that it is a good idea to just add that there is no compulsion for teenagers to lose their virginity quite so early on. Basically, what I'm saying is that if I didn't have constant sex as a teenager I don't see why they should. More education has to be the answer and Dutch caps off to the government for taking a brave stand on this. Obviously it's going to be a struggle to get fourteen-year-old boys to think about sex, but it has to be done. 'Oh but, miss, do we have to do sex again? Can't we do logarithms, please, miss, please?'

One way to reduce the pressure on kids to grow up so quickly might be to make sex education more brutally honest about the reality of the adult sexual experience. 'Sexual intercourse happens between a man and a woman on Sunday morning after *The Archers Omnibus*. Foreplay traditionally begins with the gentleman being more attentive to his wife than he has been all week, fetching her a second cup of tea and repeatedly sighing, "Well, there's nothing worth reading in the Sunday papers!" Three minutes after this the lady says, "Mmm, that was nice!" and remembers that she'd meant to get up early to dead-head the geraniums.' That should put them off the idea for a while. Or perhaps special books for children could be used to help educate kids on the subject. 'Oh dear, Mrs Goggins is very cross with Postman Pat.

He still hasn't guessed why she's been throwing up in the mornings.' You could have *Five Go Down to the Family Planning Clinic*, *Harry Potter and the Child Support Agency* and *Teletubbies Say Uh-oh!'* Or how about the pop-up *Joy of Sex*? Obviously after a few years it won't pop up like it used to, but hey – that's life.

Off with her head

6 July 2002

This government have finally lost touch. They have finally gone native. Somebody knocks the head off the statue of Lady Thatcher and they somehow try to suggest that this is a bad thing! Thousands of old lefties completely agree with them that Paul Kelleher should not have removed the head of Thatcher's statue. He should have, like, decapitated the original, man! It all could have been handled so differently. Tony Blair should have come out into Downing Street looking excited and proud: 'I would like to pass you over to our Minister for Culture as she has some news I think you might like to hear.'

The minister would then have stepped forward, trying not to look too smug as she read from the prepared statement: 'Be pleased to inform Her Majesty, that at approximately 12.00 hours GMT, a lone anti-capitalist protester entered the Guildhall in London and knocked Mrs Thatcher's block off! God Save the Queen!'

And above the cheers of the waiting crowds the excited journalists would have fired off dozens of questions, only to be chastised by the Prime Minister: 'Just rejoice at that news! And congratulate Paul Kelleher and Guildhall's security!'

Instead, the condemnation was universal. 'Politics is about persuading people through reason,' said Lady Thatcher to the sound of a million jaws dropping around the country. Of course whacking heads with cricket bats is not something that should be encouraged, even if it was a technique that Thatcher herself used to persuade stubborner members of her cabinet from time to time. Foreign commentators have asked why the assailant was not stopped by security when he entered the building carrying a cricket bat. They have to understand that, in England, if someone is in possession of a cricket bat it's just presumed that they'll never be able to hit their target. Perhaps this new feature should be incorporated into the English national game; it would certainly liven up *Test Match Special* a bit: 'And Atherton steps out, swings his bat high, misses the ball completely but it doesn't matter because he has knocked the head off the Thatcher statue! Marvellous – just listen to that applause! But oh dear, the wicketkeeper has managed to catch the head, and Atherton is out!'

Having failed to remove the head with a cricket bat, Kelleher employed one of the metal poles used to support the fancy bit of crimson rope that is supposed to prevent people from getting too close to the statue. You have to ask questions about the security system in operation here. Those dark red bits of rope have never been much of a deterrent to a really determined trespasser. In 1940, when Hitler was looking for the weak spot in France's famous Maginot Line, he identified the section near the Ardennes, which consisted of just a few poles linked together with twirly red rope, as offering the least resistance to the Wehrmacht's tank divisions. If I'd been the security guard on duty at the Guildhall, I would have just stuck the head back on with a bit of Araldite and hoped nobody would notice.

'Hang on a minute! What's that crack all around the neck with gluey stuff dripping out of it?'

'Honestly! It's supposed to be like that, you philistine. That is the artist's message, about the nature of, er – nothingness.'

'Oh right, yeah.'

It has to be said that as a work of art the original statue was a pretty vapid effort; if it had been eight inches high it would have been the sort of bland statuette that middle-class ladies place in back-lit corner units, on the little shelf above the crystal gondola. Exactly the sort of bland art that Mrs Thatcher herself might have gone for, in fact. But now, with the head removed and lying at her feet, it suddenly feels like a deeply symbolic and ironic statement. The leader who divided British society now lies in two pieces herself. For a woman who lost her marbles years ago, it all seems wonderfully appropriate.

Now the empty plinth in the House of Commons looks set to remain unoccupied for years to come. If they want they can borrow the old *Spitting Image* puppet of her that I have in my office and stick that in the empty space. It is a far better representation, and it might stop all the kids who come for sleepovers to our house having nightmares.

The artist is said to be deeply saddened by what has happened. So would you be if you had to meet up with her all over again for another half dozen sittings. But if a replacement is to be commissioned, shouldn't it be more in keeping with the more radical end of the BritArt scene? How about Lady Thatcher's unmade bed – with empty Glenfiddich bottles and chainmail knickers strewn across the sheets? Or how about a glass tank containing one of Mrs Thatcher's lungs pickled in formaldehyde? All right, so it might cause onlookers to recoil with disgust and nausea. But not as much as having an eight-foot-high realistic likeness staring down at you.

Talking rubbish

13 July 2002

This week the government took decisive action to help Britain's sketch writers and cartoonists. They published a great big document on the subject of rubbish. The humorists scratched their heads into the small hours.

'Hmmm, there's pages and pages of this thing, all about rubbish; there must be an angle in here somewhere?'

'Nope, beats me.'

The headline-grabbing idea was that households producing too much waste will have to start paying. It's a brilliant plan. At the moment we're saying, 'Please don't drop litter, please take your rubbish home with you.' And now we're simply adding, 'Oh, and it'll cost you a pound a bag every time you do so.' What greater incentive could there be to stop people dumping? We've seen what happens when people have to pay to get rid of their old cars or fridges; and all because those lazy dustmen somehow try to claim that they can't put a Nissan Sunny into the back of their cart. Even the Royal Navy has started simply dumping its battleships. (There's now a great big sticker on HMS *Nottingham* saying 'Police Aware'.)*

---

*Just as skiers go 'off piste' and owners of four-wheel drives go 'off road', this week the captain of HMS *Nottingham* went 'off sea'.

Fortunately, in this country all the appropriate spaces for fly tipping are very clearly marked; they have a big sign saying 'No Fly Tipping'. There's something about certain stretches of brick wall that compels people to think, 'You know what that spot really needs? A wet mattress and a broken kitchen unit – yup, that would really finish it off.'

'Super idea – and maybe some tins of hardened paint arranged around the edges?'

Something has to be done about all the rubbish produced in this country, other than putting it out on Sky One. Britain has one of the worst waste problems in Europe; we've all seen the ugly pictures of hundreds of tonnes of rubbish spread everywhere, bin liners split open as mangy looking seagulls pick over the stinking contents. Yes, that's what happens to the front garden when the dustmen don't get a Christmas tip. If the refuse does eventually get collected, it ends up in one of Britain's 1400 landfill sites (except for all the empty coke cans which go in my hedge). Britain has more landfill sites than most countries because of the number of mysterious holes in the ground located close to something once apparently known as 'the British Coal Industry'. So that's why Thatcher closed all the mines: she needed somewhere to put all of Denis's empties. It was a brilliant political scam: 'All right, Arthur Scargill, you can re-open all the coal mines if you want, but you'll have to get all the old disposable nappies out first.'

To cut down on the amount of rubbish that we bury, we're going to have to recycle more. It's suggested that people should recycle their vegetable waste by having a compost heap. Fine for some households, but if you're a single parent on the thirteenth floor of a high-rise block, you're unlikely to be worrying about whether the avocado skins would make good compost for the begonias. Paper is another obvious area where recycling should be encouraged. In Britain we throw away millions of tonnes of waste paper every day, and that's just the pizza leaflets. Where I live in Lambeth there is a scheme which involves putting all your newspapers outside your front gate for recycling. Countless hours are wasted every Monday night as couples anxiously argue over which publication would look best on top of the crate before it's put out for all to see.

'You can't just leave *Hello!* magazine on top. What will the neighbours think?'

'But I only put it there to cover up that Outsize Underwear catalogue we got through the post.'

'*What Computer?*'

'Too nerdy.'

'*Daily Mail?*'

'God forbid!'

'Look, hang on, the newsagent's still open. I'll pop down and get a copy of *Literary Review* – we can stick that on top.'

And then an hour later an old man in a grubby mac walks past and casually throws a copy of *Asian Babes* on top of the pile and the whole street has you marked down as a pervert for ever more. As well as publicly displaying your choice of reading material, you are also forced to advertise your weekly alcohol consumption when you put out the empty wine bottles. All I'm saying is that that Catholic priest in our road must do an awful lot of Holy Communions at home.

In future, anything that is not recycled will be weighed by the dustmen and a levy will be charged on particularly heavy wheelie bins. This will have people sneaking bags of rubbish into each other's bins under cover of darkness; at three in the morning the bedroom window will go up, followed by shouts of 'Oi, neighbour, that's *our* bloody wheelie bin you're loading up there!'

'Oh sorry, Cherie, it's so hard to see in the dark. Anyway it's not my fault – I've got tonnes and tonnes of useless scrap paper to get rid of. It's that huge report on rubbish from your husband.'

See, even jokes can be recycled.

Robo-squaddie

20 July 2002

The British army is going all hi-tech. Now when you phone them up you get a disjointed digital recording saying, 'Thank you for phoning the Ministry of Defence. If you wish to declare war on the United Kingdom, please press one. If you are the American President and require British forces to join your own to give the spurious impression of international co-operation, please press two. If you wish to register a complaint about the massacre of innocent civilians, press three or hold for an operator.' In which case you have to listen to Vivaldi for thirty years until someone's finally prepared to listen.

This week it was announced that British service personnel are to be armed with all the latest micro-chip technology to assist them in the war against terrorism. With so much of today's defence budget being spent on computerized equipment, they needed that extra £3.5 billion to pay for the printer cartridges. Modelling the 'soldier of the future' outfit for the BBC News was an embarrassed-looking squaddie weighed down by countless electrical gadgets strapped all over his body, while his face seemed to say, 'I haven't the faintest bloody idea how any of this stuff works.' There were satellite communicators, computerized weapons, an integrated monitor screen just above his eyeline; all in standard army camouflage colours, making the soldier impossible to pick out until the moment his mobile phone suddenly went off, playing *The Dam Busters* theme at full volume.

Of course, with the soldiers now carrying the latest in communications technology, terrorists will not be their only enemy. They're also going to have to watch their backs for teenage boys mugging them for their million-pound digital equipment which they could flog down the pub for a tenner. The computer packs are specially designed to be light and highly mobile; it's just a shame that carrying all those enormous manuals is going to slow them down so much. Hostilities will be delayed for months as combatants search through the weapons manual looking for the section on 'firing'. Yet the whole point of all this increased communications software is supposed to be speed. Soon NATO forces will be able to blow up their own armoured personnel carriers far more quickly than they have been able to do in the past. The ground forces will be in constant communication with reconnaissance aircraft, unmanned aerial vehicles and attack helicopters, right up until the moment the computer crashes and then all the aircraft crash as well.

But of course the test of all this technology will be the first time that this soldier is on the battlefield face to face with an enemy gunman. A split second can make the difference between life or death as he activates his computerized weaponry. But it doesn't take out the enemy; instead a little reminder wizard appears on screen: 'Click here to register your Microsoft Anti-terrorist software for great technical support, free upgrades and special offers on other Microsoft products.' The soldier frantically clicks the 'register later' icon as enemy bullets fly past his head. Grenades are now exploding on either side of him, as a smiling little animated Mr Bomb character bounces up and down on the screen saying, 'Are you sure you want to register later?'

That's if the technology works at all, of course. It's one thing to have your printer refusing to respond when you were hoping to catch the last post. But I'd say you'd get even more annoyed with modern technology when you are being surrounded by Taliban gunmen and the computerized missile launcher says, 'Error in weapon configuration – refer to helpline.' It's at times like this that you wish you'd sent that guarantee card back to Hewlett Packard.

With our armed forces increasingly dependent on computer

software, it won't be germ warfare we are worried about but virus warfare. 'Oh look, I've got an e-mail from someone called Osama – I'll just open that attachment and see what it is!' says the soldier brightly as the entire NATO communications goes down. Or maybe the enemy will be closer to home. I can't help worrying that the boys who left school to become squaddies tended not to be the same boys who were really brilliant with computers. The nervous brainy kids were forced to avoid all the tough boys by going along to computer soc. every lunchtime and will have spent the last fifteen years working their way up through the software industry, patiently planning their revenge. So when the tattooed meat-head of a squaddie is stuck in an Iraqi battle-field and has to rely on his computer equipment to save his life, he'll suddenly find his software freezing as a voice from the past pops up on the monitor: 'Hello Slugger. Timothy Johnson here, from Form 4B. You probably won't remember that every day for five years you broke my glasses and threw my violin case on top of the bus shelter. Well, now you are really going to wish you hadn't. Click here to leave a farewell message on Enemies Reunited.'

Look out! There's an accountant about . . .

27 July 2002

There was a major scandal in Wall Street this week when a rogue US corporation was found *not* to have been fiddling the books. 'We can't imagine how this has been allowed to happen,' said the shamefaced auditors. The chief financial officer immediate resigned in disgrace as it was revealed that the firm's profits were exactly what he'd claimed they were, with no trace of false accounting or the artificial inflation of share prices. However, it's thought the chance of this happening in other US corporations remains very slim.

The only thing that is surprising about the wave of financial scandals engulfing America is that everyone is so surprised. Well, who'd have thought it – the most aggressive capitalists making in-explicably huge profits turn out to have been cheating! You stop regulating big business and the directors take advantage to make them-selves huge illicit fortunes! And we'd all thought they'd made those extra billions by doing a paper round every morning before work.

The most common method of fraud has been to inflate share prices by artificially exaggerating company profits. Suspicions should have been raised when the revenue for the last financial year was given by an eight-year-old boy who excitedly announced the official figure to be a billion, trillion, gillion, quillion, zillion! Or when the figure at the end of the annual report had two zeros scrawled on the end in red felt-tip pen.

For a country obsessed by crime, the Americans are having to learn that criminals come in a variety of guises. Police officers are now making up for lost time as public opinion turns against the new hate figures in US society. America's isolated Accountant community, for many years shunned due to their strange stripy suits and incomprehensible language, are now being openly persecuted. 'We're not all fraudsters . . .' implored a spokesman for the accountants. 'In fact, only three point four per cent in the last fiscal quarter rising in line with projected forecasts . . .' he went on, but already he seemed to be losing the journalists' attention. Secret video footage has just been released showing traffic cops dragging an innocent auditor out of his car and beating him up. 'Thought you could offset projected profit shortfall by excluding capital outlay, huh, you four-eyed geek?' (punch!). 'Trying to overstate company revenues by hiding loan repayments eh? God, you pin-stripe punks make me sick . . .' (kick!).

In the nearby financial district, auditors reacted angrily, not rioting exactly, but the nearest equivalent for accountants. Desks were left untidy, computer keyboards were left uncovered by polythene dust sheets, calculators left switched on, caps left off fountain pens . . . Witnesses said they had not seen such untidy scenes since the great double-entry ledger protests of '68.

Now *Crimewatch* ratings look set to plummet. The only reconstruction so far showed a man sitting at his desk for a long time in front of a computer. 'Does this jog any memories?' said the presenter, as millions of viewers rang in to say they had a vague memory of witnessing a similar scene.

As the stock markets crashed, millions of ordinary citizens lost their pensions and savings and George W. Bush announced that he would take tough action to deal with whoever had done so much damage to American interests. US bombers were despatched to mete out the usual punishment, but then were swiftly called back when it was explained to the President that the perpetrators worked in Wall Street and bombing New York might not go down too well right now.

So then his advisers sat him down and very slowly explained the nature of modern corporate fraud from start to finish, finally declaring, 'So you see, Mr President, that's why billions of dollars have now disappeared.'

'I understand. So did anyone see the getaway car?'

'No, it wasn't stolen, sir. It was fraud.'

'So these are counterfeit dollars we're looking for. Do we have the numbers?'

'Sir, it's not real money; these are just figures in a computer.'

'Geez, they shouldn't have left the money in the computer – that's always the first thing these guys steal.'

The reason that this crisis is so damaging to the President is that this sort of unfettered capitalism is exactly what the current American administration is all about. Not only is he the champion of un-regulated business, but Enron and their like also paid for his election campaign. Maybe it was Enron's auditors who counted up the ballot papers which handed him victory after getting fewer votes than his opponent. Bush has promised to be tough on these super-rich fraudsters, so we can expect them to go to prison for the rest of their day. Because something tells me that America's billionaires will receive less punishment than an ordinary US citizen would. Of course, wiping out the pensions and savings for millions of ordinary people is a crime that deserves the sack. But once they're unemployed, let's just hope they don't make any false claims for minor social-security payments, because then they'd really be in trouble.

Rats!

3 August 2002

Yesterday cinemas around the country began showing a new horror film. In its final terrifying scene a pretty girl awakes in bed to find herself covered in a plague of filthy rats. Yes, it's the latest new release from those well-known purveyors of extreme horror action– the Keep Britain Tidy Campaign.

No one can accuse them of being at all sensationalist about this. All they are saying in this new advert is that if you drop litter you'll wake up with rats crawling all over your face – it's a very reasonable and moderate statement. 'We don't want to alarm you, but you drop one apple core and huge mutant rodents with razor-sharp teeth will swarm out of the sewers to gnaw through your skull and suck out your brains while you sleep.' And the cinema-goers all shrug and spill another kilo of popcorn all over the floor.

Apparently the making of this commercial was a rather tense affair for the casting agency concerned. 'So what's the part?' said the rats as they turned up for rehearsals. 'Are we the adorably furry pets that comfort the kiddies in the children's hospital? Or is it a *Stuart Little* type thing, cute rat with voice-over from Billy Crystal?'

'Er, no, no . . . it's pretty straightforward. We just wanted you looking a bit dirty, nibbling a discarded hot-dog.'

An awkward hush fell over the thespian rats. 'So we're playing vermin again, are we?' they said tersely.

'Well, that is sort of what the advert's about.'

'I see. It's just that as members of the rat community we do get a bit fed up of being typecast. I mean, we rats do do other things apart from breed in the sewers and scamper round spreading diseases, you know.' And the rats stormed off to their trailers to ring their agents, but then were distracted by some rotting burgers on the way.

This advert is required because so many people are discarding fast-food cartons that the rats are coming out of the sewers to feed on leftover McDonald's. So if the warfarin doesn't kill them then there's always heart disease. Apparently rats love the meat from fast-food outlets; now it seems they're cannibals as well. Rats are back as public enemy number one. Britain can no longer be a soft touch for rats. Politicians are suggesting that rats be confined to secure detention centres while their claims to be genuine rodents are processed. Others say our hostility is based on myth and ignorance.

There are now officially 60 million rats in the UK, and that's just the ones that bothered to return their census forms. Every year 200 of this number pass on Weil's disease to humans; so, as always, it's just a small minority who give all the others a bad name. In fact, British rats would have done well to fire their PR company years ago. When fleas gave everyone the bubonic plague, their spin doctor put out a story saying it was all the rats' fault and the brand 'rat' never really recovered. In any case the creatures involved were the Black Rat (*Rattus rattus* – it was late on Friday afternoon at the rodent naming office), which was later displaced by the Brown Rat (*Rattus norvegicus* – named after the first Stranglers album). But still all these years later it is presumed that the only good rat is a dead rat. Britain's domestic cat community has been censured for failing to do their bit to keep down the vermin population. At a press conference this week a spokesman for the cats seemed unmoved by the criticism. 'Yeah, what of it?' he shrugged before going back to sleep.

Meanwhile, increasingly cruel ways are being used to poison, trap and eradicate rats and nobody cares. Where are the fifty-something women who never had kids, weeping outside the Ministry? Where are the balaclava-clad hard men of the Animal Liberation Front, ready to burn down the warfarin factory? The British public have studied this issue very carefully and have concluded that any way you look at it, rats are just not as cute as dolphins and baby seals. Cruelty against fluffy doe-eyed animals is one thing – but smelly disgusting rats, well, sorry, you had it coming to you, I'm afraid.

But with fox hunting successfully banned, the solution to Britain's rat problem seems obvious. Could there be a more pleasing sight in the English countryside than dozens of huntsmen, resplendent in their bright red tunics, disappearing into the sewers and getting covered in crap? What could do more to gladden the heart of an Englishman than seeing the master of the hunt clambering out of a manhole, wiping the brown sludge from his jodhpurs? Soon we can look forward to our towns echoing with the sound of the huntsman's horn telling us that a traditional rat hunt has begun in earnest. It will be a signal announcing that the rural upper classes have just clambered into our sewers; a noise that says 'Right – everyone flush now!'

Football fans are revolting!

10 August 2002

Today is the first day of the English football season. Up and down the country will be heard that traditional cry of non-fans: 'Already? But it had only just finished!' In recent years the popularity of the sport has mushroomed beyond all expectations; violence is down, racist chanting is rare and the quality of the matches is significantly better. But still some commentators go all misty-eyed about times gone by: 'Oh it's not the same these days. I mean, when I were a lad, you'd be packed into the terraces behind a seven-foot chain-smoker, unable to see your team draw nil-nil after the defenders kept passing back to the keeper, and then on the way home you'd get beaten up for wearing the wrong scarf by that bloke who'd been shouting racist abuse. Ah, happy days . . .'

But a decade on from the formation of the Premier League, the majority of clubs that were left behind are now in trouble. The collapse of ITV Digital and the subsequent resignations have left the Football League in crisis. Supporters watching games this afternoon may already notice the lower-division clubs making one or two economies. Unable to afford proper kits, players will be wearing embarrassingly tight shirts and huge baggy shorts from the lost-property basket. The ball will be a plastic one from Woolworth's with Harry Potter on the side, and when it's kicked out of the ground, the rush goalie will be forced to go round and ask that grumpy old man next door, 'Excuse me, can we have our ball back please?' Final score two-nil.

'It wasn't two-nil, that second one was a post – it went straight over my jumper.'

'No, it would have gone *in-off*!'

Another worry for the Football League is that while arrests are down in the Premier League, according to tables published yesterday they actually increased in the first division. It's no wonder ITV Digital went bankrupt; the broadcasters boasted that their interactive coverage made it just like being at a real match. So when you leapt off the sofa to celebrate your team's goal they supplied a couple of opposing fans to beat you up. You have to question the wisdom of publishing league tables for football arrests. Did they imagine the perpetrators would weep with remorse at being brandished the worst trouble-makers in the land?

'I'm so dashed upset, Tarquin. We've really let down the vast majority of genuine peace-loving sports fans at our club.'

'Yes, Julian, the shame of it! I'll never be able to show my face down at my men's anger-management workshop again.'

Or is there perhaps an outside chance that the Neanderthals might take some sort of perverse pride in being top of the arrests league? Maybe the police could arrange a pitched battle between the fans that finished third and fourth to decide who gets a play-off place. They might at least have printed the tables the other way up, with the clubs with the most arrests at the bottom. It's the best chance I've got of seeing Fulham at the top of the Premiership. With Tony Blair helping to set up a new football league in Afghanistan, maybe other problems in the region could be solved with British football know-how by sending Stoke City and Millwall supporters to Iraq.

In fact, football violence roughly fits the Marxist analysis of war between capitalist economies. While working-class fans are beating each other up, the real enemy, football's ruling class, remains safe in their corporate boxes and chairmen's suites, becoming multi-millionaires as they bring poverty to the poorer clubs. Well, this season it's all going to change. Suddenly aware of their own strength, the supporters of the world will unite and throw off the chains of having to pay £45 for a replica shirt that cost 10p to produce in some sweat shop in China. Instead of pointlessly attacking each other, the newly politicized fans will storm the Manchester United Directors' Box, declaring the people's first socialist soccer soviet. The super-rich chairmen of the big clubs will be lined up and shot, but they'll survive because Andy Cole is doing the shooting. But no more will the big clubs grow ever richer off the players they have taken from the lower leagues; no more will the ordinary fan be priced out of the ground. At last it can be said, 'Chelsea fans are revolting!'

A supporters' revolution would slightly change the game, of course. 'Quick, pass!' 'Sorry, comrade, but such a move would have to be ratified by the people's executive committee!' But by bringing Marxist doctrine to the Premier League we'll prove that socialism is the only way forward for the rest of our society. 'The workers! United! Will never be defeated – because frankly a score draw is always the fairest result!' And imagine the thrilling climax to the season when you know every club will finish with exactly the same number of points and identical goal difference. Er, hang on – I think I'd better think this out again . . .

I'm a world leader, get me out of here!

30 August 2002

All week a conference centre in Johannesburg has been host to many of the most important people in the world. The security has been incredibly tight. One man who was thrown out is still hanging around outside the compound insisting that he is a bona fide delegate. 'I'm not making it up! There is such a country as Turkmenistan!' Meanwhle the girl on the reception desk has been having a terrible time trying to deal with all the complaints from the Western leaders who jumped at this chance to fly away in August. 'What do you mean it's winter in the southern hemisphere? It's just not good enough . . .'

In reality, this convention is not much different to any conference of middle managers taking place in the Jarvis Hotel on the A508 near Kettering. The reps all file in, collect their little name badges and then excitedly check their hotel rooms.

'Ooh, a trouser press!' says a thrilled Gerhard Schroeder.

'And look, miniature packets of cashew nuts in the mini-bar!' exclaims the Russian delegate, as he pops the free shower cap and little sewing kit into his suitcase.

During the first session all the world leaders sit there with anxious faces. Not because they are worrying about global ecology, but because they're all privately thinking, 'If I watch the adult channel tonight, will it come up on my bill as "Pay Movie" or "Pervy Porn Flick"?'

The first talk is done by a Scandinavian Environment Minister using Microsoft Power-point. 'So you see that within fifty years, Earth will be unable to sustain life and we will all be dead.' On the screen a little animated graphic shows the world expand and then go 'Pop!' and everyone gasps and turns to the delegate beside them.

'Ooh, that's clever, isn't it!'

'Yes, I can't do anything like that on my computer . . .'

After the coffee break there's a talk on teamwork and motivation from Will Carling and then in the afternoon they've arranged for some workshops.

'Right, if you chaps from the Balkans could get into small groups . . .'

'We already have done.'

'And if the South Americans can choose a team leader – no, don't use the army to install him.'

Soon they are all ready for the trust exercises. 'The Israeli minister here is going to fall backwards and these Arab leaders are going to catch him. You look a bit worried, Binyamin?'

By the end of the day they can't wait to get out of there and sit down to the evening meal, especially with the promise of a pro-fessional comedian as an after-dinner speaker. 'Oh no, who booked Jim Davidson?' say the African delegates, sitting there stony faced while Jim does his best West Indian accent for all his gags about 'my mate Chalky'. The whole dinner might have been more tactfully arranged. The Western leaders had a huge slap-up five-course feast, while over on the Third World table the waiters just dumped a sack of dried milk powder and left them to fight over it.

Back at home the ordinary voters remain cynical about their leaders' ability to change anything. People need to see their representatives getting stuck in, really making the best of a difficult situation, and so next time the gathering will take a completely different format. Coming soon on ITV1 is a brand-new docu-soap: *I'm A World Leader, Get Me Out of Here!* In order to understand the problems of the environment more fully, presidents and prime ministers will be forced to live in poverty in a hostile tropical setting, while Ant and Dec laugh at their efforts and dish out the next challenge. 'Oh no! The Canadian President has got dysentery from drinking that polluted water! And now he's got to go to the toilet in front of everyone!' they will chuckle. 'Whoops! Jacques Chirac has been bitten by a mosquito and now he's got malaria! I bet now he's wishing he hadn't cut back French medical aid to Africa!' they'll giggle.

Of course George Bush won't turn up again. Just like the original TV show, only D-list celebs will be available, and viewers will be left saying, 'Who on earth is that?' as the Prime Minister of Bhutan flirts with the President of Luxembourg. But that is the trouble with the whole Johannesburg conference: the people who really count aren't even there. Not just George W. Bush, whose country alone is responsible for a huge proportion of the world's greenhouse gases, but all the unaccountable people who run the global corporations and multinationals which are now more powerful and damaging than many nation states. So perhaps the only really effective way to help the environment and developing countries would be to get all the corporate billionaires to Johannesburg. If they saw the security they would be reassured of their own safety. 'That should keep people out,' they'd say, looking at all the razor wire, the lines of electrified fences and the heavily policed concrete barriers.

'What are you talking about?' would come the reply. 'That's to keep you in here.'

Atomkraft? Nein danke!

7 September 2002

Yesterday panicking crowds headed for the hills, holding up flimsy umbrellas and clutching handkerchiefs over their mouths. The newspapers had carelessly printed the terrifying headline: 'Britain's Nuclear Industry – Collapse Imminent'. It turns out that British Energy, which runs Britain's eight nuclear power stations, is on the brink of insolvency. Apparently the Sellafield Visitors' Centre Gift Shop is not selling quite as many Chernobyl shaky-snow fall-out scenes as they'd hoped. The sealed nuclear waste paperweights just aren't shifting and the kiddies' glow-in-the-dark plutonium bars are down to half price.

Although we are not about to be poisoned by a Chernobyl-style explosion, to listen to the shareholders in Britain's nuclear industry you'd think the reality was even worse. On yesterday's *Today* programme, British Energy shareholder Malcolm Stacey was incandescent that a government rule change had resulted in a 20 per cent drop in electricity prices for the consumer. Cheaper electricity for the masses or greater profits for shareholders, hmmm, that's one of those really tricky moral issues, isn't it? The sort of thing that would have kept Keir Hardie wrestling with his conscience for years.

Mr Stacey called on the government to bail out investors whose shares had fallen in value. On hearing this Gordon Brown must have leapt out of bed and straight into action. What greater priority can there be for a Labour government than compensating speculators who've lost money on British Energy shares? 'You know all that money we were going to give to schools and hospitals?' says the Chancellor. 'Forget all that; *this* is the reason I went into politics, to compensate nuclear shareholders!! These are the real heroes of our society. Sorry, nurses! Sorry, teachers! I need that money to hand out to City speculators who gambled and lost.'

British Energy was privatized the year before Labour came to power, but although the nuclear industry has been receiving massive subsidies for fifty years, it is still not profitable. Last year BE lost £518 million and remains heavily in debt. They tried to get a mortgage on Sellafield but the valuation had to be halted when the surveyors kept banging their little hammers on the side of the reactor. BE also own nuclear power stations overseas and are hoping to raise money by selling those. Apparently there's a man from Iraq who's very interested.

At last the nuclear lobby are no longer getting everything their own way. They knew they were in trouble when Tony Blair's ministerial Jaguar was replaced with a purple 2CV with a smiley sticker saying 'Atomkraft? Nein Danke!' It all started to go wrong for them when John Prescott was at Environment. They explained to him the complex nuclear physics that made atomic power possible and he just said, 'Right, but what if the pilot light blows out?'

Despite support from the Conservative Energy spokesman, British Energy have failed in their campaign for exemption from the £80 million climate-change levy. For some reason the government does not see nuclear power as especially environmentally friendly. Nuclear power *can* effect climate change; for example, it got much, much hotter around Chernobyl a while back. The chairman of British Energy, Robin Jeffrey, Britain's very own Mr Burns from *The Simpsons*, audaciously claims that nuclear is the greenest form of power because it doesn't emit any greenhouse gases. 'Doh!' as Homer would say. Yes, apart from the deadly toxic waste that remains radioactive for thousands of years, it really is a very green form of energy; apart from endlessly producing one of the most lethal substances known to man that has to be dumped underground to leak into the water supply and poison future generations, it's as green as an organic mung bean farm. But these bearded sandal-wearers always accentuate the negative when it comes to nuclear power, don't they? The environmentalists never talk about all those years when Chernobyl was supplying clean renewable energy as bunnies nibbled daisies in the surrounding fields. No, they always have to focus on that one particular day when Chernobyl exploded and contaminated hundreds of square miles with highly toxic radioactive fall-out.

Amazingly, British Nuclear Fuels Ltd have been lobbying to be allowed to construct a new generation of nuclear facilities. They might as well build power stations that burn £20 notes. But in the mind of the British public, the biggest worry will always be safety – no matter how many times we simple folk are told that British nuclear reactors are completely safe, that there is absolutely no possibility of an accident here. So what do we know? Maybe we should take their word for it that more nuclear power stations across Britain would be a good idea. Because it's not just the safety experts from the nuclear lobby who say this. The pilots at the Al-Qaida Flight School think so too.

United ~~Nations~~ States

14 September 2002

American officials are currently lobbying hard at the UN. It's the name they don't like: 'United Nations' – there's something not quite right about it.

'We're prepared to compromise,' they say. 'You can keep the first word.'

'United?'

'Yeah, but that second bit sounds wrong – what other words are there?'

'United Countries?'

'No . . .'

'United Places . . .'

'No, no, there must be another word for nation or country . . .'

'State?'

'Hmmm . . . United States, yes, that has a ring to it. So we'll call it the "United States", with its HQ in the United States . . . Now this UN flag. We're prepared to compromise: you can keep some of the blue, but it needs a bit of red and white in there as well.'

George W. Bush is trying to hijack the UN. Delegates thought it was just a routine peace-time trip; they were settling back in their seats for a snooze when suddenly a scary-looking American President broke through the flimsy doors into the United Nations cockpit, grabbed the controls and attempted to steer the UN into a catastrophe. Will anyone have the courage to overpower him or will they nervously sit it out, hoping that they might somehow survive?

Of course, he tried to appear conciliatory and courteous. But Bush's speech to the UN this week was like a headteacher pretending to respect the newly formed school council. It's not that he was patronizing to the UN, but at one point he stopped his monologue and shouted, 'Canada! Are you chewing? Get up here and spit it out!' His message was that the only way to ensure that UN policy was implemented around the world was to change it to American policy. Some of the more subversive translators were having great fun. Bush said, 'Will the United Nations serve the purpose of its founding or will it be irrelevant?' And into the headphones of one European minister came the translation, 'Listen, suckers, I'm going to bomb who the bloody hell I like, so sod the lot of you!'

'The world now faces a test and the UN a defining moment,' continued Dubya, as African leaders heard him apparently saying, 'I've never heard of half your countries! Why are you wearing those funny costumes? I might bomb you next! I've got B52s and sidewinders and everything, neeeeeoooow, boom! Bang! Ker-pow!'

Despite his efforts, Bush does not have the backing of the international community and so makes the most of his support from the British Foreign Secretary. Diplomatically he is a drowning man clutching at Jack Straws. Admittedly the United Nations is not the speediest means of deciding policy. At the beginning of the Afghan conflict a UN committee sat down to hammer out a resolution and this week they nearly agreed on whether it was 'Taliban' with an 'i' or 'Taleban' with an 'e'. But changing the world takes time. It is a laborious and painstaking process.

In North London an extended campaign by local residents recently managed to prevent a branch of Starbucks opening in their area. In my road another Starbucks has just opened and someone keeps smashing the windows. (It's amazing what you can get the Cubs to do in Bob-a-Job week.) Bombing Baghdad is the diplomatic equivalent of protestors who smash windows. It makes them feel tough and hard, it's quick and easy, but it doesn't actually make anything better for the people who really need help. It's instant espresso politics to go.

Meaningful change is brought about by long-term strategies, patience, painstaking persuasion and taking people with you. In this crisis we have to ensure that the United Nations is the ultimate authority; the UN has to agree a meaningful line and then eventually we might find a way to rid the world of the new Starbucks in my road.

Saddam might seem a little harder to shift, but quick wars don't bring long-term peace. American foreign policy is like their television. It has to keep jumping from one thing to another because the President has the remote control in his hand and his attention span is very limited. That thrilling adventure *Take Out the Taliban!* held his interest for a short while, but now the explosive opening action sequence is over and it's got bogged down in the complex story of rebuilding a war-torn country. Bush's finger is hovering over that button, itching to see if there's any more exciting stuff somewhere else.

'Don't you want to stick with this and see how Afghanistan turns out?' says Colin Powell.

'Nah, it's got boring now.'

'But we don't even know if they catch Bin Laden . . .'

'Ooh wow, look what's on CNN! *Bombers Over Baghdad!* Let's see if this baddie Saddam gets it instead . . .'

War on Iraq will not make the world a safer place. Perhaps the only way to make US policy successful is radically to change the aims. Then, as the troops are brought home and the flags are waved, the White House could declare that they'd definitely achieved all the objectives in 'Operation Kill All the Wrong People and Make the Problem Much Worse'.

The Quiet Man with a lot to be quiet about

12 October 2002

At school I was taught that the purpose of an opposition is to oppose, propose and depose. Frankly 'decompose' looks more likely at the moment. In fact, if you watched footage of this week's Conservative Party conference, a number of Tory members were forced to take their seats in the audience despite having died several weeks earlier. *Newsnight* interviewers did their best to get delegates' reactions to the various speeches, despite being unable to find any party members who were still actually alive.

'Were you concerned that Theresa May described the Tories as the Nasty Party?' *(Delegate stares open mouthed into the middle distance and then slumps forward on chair.)* 'Um, I see you're avoiding answering the question. Is this a make-or-break conference for Iain Duncan Smith?' *(Interviewee's head falls off and is hastily put back on by Tory Party activist.)*

Coming back from the dead was the challenge that faced the Tories this week and they told us loud and clear that they were on the way back. Actually it wasn't loud and clear; it was quiet and unclear. They were definitely looking to the future, but they'd be completing the unfinished business of the Thatcher revolution. I'm delighted to hear that they're going to carry on where Thatcher's ministers left off;

now we can look forward to seeing this lot banged up in prison as well.

When they took the register on Monday morning, there were a number of notable absences. Thatcher? Not here. Major? He just pulled out, sir. Currie – she's tucked up in bed as well, sir. Aitken? Absent. Hamilton? Absent. Archer – he might turn up later, sir, he said he'd see if he could get away. The remaining Tories unveiled twenty-five new policies or, put simply, one each. They tried to make it sound exciting but, strangely, the voters seemed to be less interested in opposition policy initiatives than they were in the sudden revelations about Edwina Currie shagging John Major.

Conference began with some tough talking from Theresa May, the new Tory Party 'chairman'. (The Tories couldn't possibly say they had a new 'chair'; it might make people think they couldn't afford a set of six.) She has obviously heard that it's a good idea to nick a few lines from your political enemies and so they spent the whole week saying 'Don't Vote Conservative! The Tories are dreadful!' Her job on Monday was to try to present the human face of the Tory Party. So she thought, 'Hmm – I think I'll get them to concentrate on the shoes.' Just in case the delegates did not believe that they were the Nasty Party, she then made way for a succession of unsavoury characters whose policy ideas were a combination of the unworkable and the dangerous. 'Localization' is just another word for privatization. The idea of tax breaks for using private health would leave the NHS as a skeleton service, pun intended. I'm not saying these ideas were written on the back of a fag packet, but when one shadow minister read out his new policy he shouted, 'We will let patients set up their own hospitals high tar, smoking causes heart disease!'

The conference ended not with a bang but with a whimper. Various newspapers reproduced Iain Duncan Smith's speech yesterday, but to really convey the sense of it they should have printed the text in an extremely small font. IDS needs to spend a few weeks at BBC1's *Fame Academy* learning how to project his voice and stop making strange hand gestures. But if I was IDS, I would whisper my achievements. If I was leading my party into third place, I wouldn't feel like shouting. If my policies were reducing the housing available to low earners or creating a two-tier health service or leaving the work of social services to charities, I'd mumble them as quietly as I could. This week we were presented with the new image of the leader of the opposition – Iain Duncan Smith is the Quiet Man. But then he has a great deal to be quiet about.

The Ballad of Lincoln Gaol

19 October 2002

For years now the left has been campaigning for a more humane penal system, protesting that British prisoners are forced to subsist in degrading and barbaric conditions, in desperate need of a more liberal and enlightened approach. And then they go and transfer Jeffrey Archer to an open prison. I mean these criminals, they might as well be at a bloody holiday camp. What sort of deterrent is that, playing table tennis and gardening and watching telly all day in their luxury penthouse suites while us law-abiding tax payers have to foot the bill? I reckon they should bring back the stocks and the birch, except those Tory public-school types would probably bloody enjoy it!

Campaigners for improved prison conditions have gained some unlikely new allies this month. The man who once roused Tory conferences by calling for young offenders to be locked up while awaiting trial has teamed up with that longstanding ally of Britain's convicts, the *Daily Mail*, to expose 'the shocking reality of the jail system'.

Of course Jeffrey Archer cannot be paid for having his prison diaries published in a national newspaper; indeed, he has had his prison pay docked as punishment for naming other prisoners. Twenty pounds it has cost him. That'll make him think twice next time. The estimated £300,000 payment for the diaries will be transferred later to the Worldwide Fund for the Assistance of the Former Prisoner, namely Jeffrey's bank account.

Not since the *Diary of Anne Frank* have readers been so moved by the private thoughts of an innocent free spirit locked away against his will. His transfer to the open prison this week was recounted in the usual truthful yet inspired literary manner: 'Suddenly the black Maria swerved off the mountain road and with a giant splashing noise we splashed into an icy river. I kicked open the back doors of the prison van and dived into the wet wet water. Swimming against the swirling current was not made easier by the iron ball and chain around my ankle, but my years as Olympic Backstroke Champion stood me in good stead and I dragged the panicking prison officers to safety, stopping only to rescue a frightened lamb that had slipped off the river bank. Overhead I noticed the famous Tamar Rail Bridge which I of course designed when I was at Harvard. As I handed the shivering lamb back to the grateful farmer, his hair turning grey from the ravages of Blair's countryside policy, he remarked, "Ooh-arrr! You be that novelist fellah, I've read all your books, ooh-arr! 'Tis not you who should be in prison – it be those Labour politicians and journalists what stitched ye up." Our simple country folk have such wisdom.'

So much of what Archer has said about himself in the past has been fabrication that it made me wonder if his prison diaries are a complete fiction as well. Perhaps Archer never really went to jail? Maybe the whole thing is another desperate bit of attention seeking by an experienced trickster used to pulling the wool over the media's eyes.

Now that he is safely installed in Hollesley Bay Open Prison, Archer will be able to give an honest account of a less austere regime. He will have access to a gym (or did they say access to 'Jim' – prison can do strange things to a man), there's a library and playing fields, all set in a 1400-acre estate overlooking the sea. The prison even has its own herd of cows, and one of the smarter prisoners has already begun work on a spoiler book entitled *Jeffrey Archer's Prison Dairy*. It is not clear whether Hollesley Bay allows conjugal rights but, on the off-chance, a number of prostitutes he's never met before have begun hanging around the gates in the hope that he might wander out and just hand over £2000. Archer will even be allowed home visits 'once he has satisfied the governor that he can be trusted'. So that shouldn't take long.

It is unlikely, however, that he will be permitted to do any more community work after the furore that surrounded his trips out from Lincoln Gaol. On one occasion he was taken from the prison to a cocktail party packed with Conservative MPs. One has to say – surely prison is punishment enough?

When you read Archer's harrowing accounts of life inside Belmarsh, the suffering goes beyond what any human being should be expected to endure. Time drags inexorably slowly as you read, you feel worthless and depressed with every passing paragraph, but the sentence seems to drag on and on with no prospect of its being rewritten, while you reflect upon the shame of having your friends and family know that you've been reading the *Daily Mail*.

But whatever the paper intended by publishing Jeffrey Archer's prison diaries, the accounts must have served as some sort of deterrent to Britain's would-be criminals. Make no mistake; commit a serious offence and there's a very real chance that you might find yourself sharing a cell with Jeffrey Archer.

Grate Britons

26 October 2002

There has never been an election like it. All the greatest people who have ever lived in these islands competing for the title of the greatest ever Briton. In the streets and council estates across the country, canvassers are knocking on doors trying to persuade the electorate to vote for their preferred candidate.

'Hello, I'm calling about the Great Britons election. I'm canvassing on behalf of Henry the Second – would you like a leaflet about his triumph over Geoffrey of Nantes?'

'Er, we normally vote for *Bohemian Rhapsody*, don't we, dear?'

'Well, you can't actually vote for a song, you see . . .'

'All right, put us down for *Emmerdale* then.'

Meanwhile on television, various commentators are urging us to vote for their Greatest Briton. Last night millions of viewers watched Andrew Marr nominate Charles Darwin. 'Hmmm,' he must have thought, 'should I choose Ernest Shackleton and spend two weeks filming in the frozen Antarctic or should I opt for Darwin and have the BBC fly me to a tropical paradise on the Equator just as the weather's turning a bit nippy? You know, when I think about it, Darwin just seems a greater figure compared to that bloke who went to the very, very cold place. But my mind is open – if you don't want Darwin I could always spend a couple of weeks discussing the inventor of the pedalo.'

It has to be said that some of the people in the current Top 100 have a fairly dubious claim to the epithet 'Great'. At number 89 is Donald Campbell (driving boats too fast and scaring all the ducks); number 17 is Michael Crawford (saying 'Oooh Betty, the cat's done a whoopsie in my beret'); and at number 51 King Arthur, whose only definite legacy is increased car-parking prices in Tintagel and inspiring the Guinevere Gift Shoppe. It makes you question why other 'great' figures have been left out. Where is Denis Howell, Minister for Sport in the Callaghan government? Where is Bunty James, co-presenter of the long-running kids' TV show *How?*

Predictably the radical vote is split among various factions. You would have thought that Thomas Paine, Nye Bevan and Tony Benn could have sat down and agreed which of them was going to represent the left, but no, they are all issuing poorly produced leaflets denouncing each other as splitters and declaring themselves to be the one true socialist candidate.

When it is all over, we will have an awards ceremony to end them all. When the Great Britons idea was pitched to the BBC, this was the star-studded show that finally clinched it. Cutaway shots of David Lloyd George goosing Jane Austen, slight embarrassment after Cromwell runs Sir Bob Geldof through with a sword, Lord Nelson struggling to hold his plate and champagne glass at the same time, Sir Winston Churchill being asked to put out his cigar, while Guy Fawkes is still stuck at the security desk. Generally speaking, most TV awards are dished out to the celebrity who is prepared to turn up on the night. Since many of the nominees have been dead for several hundred years, this could prove a bit of a problem. 'Sadly, Lord Horatio Nelson cannot be with us this evening as he was shot by a French sniper in 1805. But here to collect the award on his behalf is Carol Smillie.' In fact the very act of dying seems one of the best ways of getting yourself into the Top 100 – hence the presence of Princess Diana, Freddie Mercury and George Harrison, with Edwina Currie planning a strategically timed faked suicide in one last desperate bid to make the list.

These votes tell us more about current affairs than they do about British history. The only thing that this exercise measures is the type of people who take part. While there is room for Enoch Powell, there is not one black or Asian face in the whole Top 100. The fact that Owain Glyndwr is way ahead of Robert the Bruce simply tells us that more Welsh Nationalists are voting than Scots Nationalists. In fact, the whole undertaking is an elaborate way of finding answers to questions that the government didn't dare ask on last year's census forms. Every time an internet vote comes through another piece of information is added to the Home Office database.

'Mr N. Smith of Brighton just voted for Boy George, sir.'

'Okay, put him down as gay, then.'

'And we've had another vote for Boudicca.'

'Right, mark her as a militant feminist.'

'And another vote for Tony Blair, sir.'

'Tell Alastair to stop wasting our time.'

But despite all the tactics and lobbying, I for one will be treating the exercise with the serious historical consideration that it deserves. Irrespective of fashion or prejudice, I shall vote for whoever I sincerely believe has made the greatest contribution to the history of this country and its people. Oh, and most of all, for whoever's got the best chance of keeping Maggie out of the Top 10.

Je t'aime (moi non plus)

2 November 2002

Jacques Chirac lost his temper with Tony Blair this week, calling the Prime Minister 'rude' and cancelling the scheduled Anglo-French summit. All Tony had said was, 'So how did France get on in the World Cup?'* For a French president to call a British leader 'rude' is a bit like us accusing the French of having warm beer. One of the problems was that Tony Blair insisted that he got a B in his French O-level and said he was perfectly capable of conducting the summit without a translator. So the PM asked the French President in no uncertain terms 'Brother Jacques, Brother Jacques – Are you sleeping? Are you sleeping?' Things went from bad to worse when he added, 'Voulez-vous coucher avec moi, ce soir?' Now the diplomats and civil servants are working round the clock on the delicate rebuilding of trust and mutual respect between our two governments, which basically involves ringing their opposite numbers in France and slagging off politicians.

The row erupted over plans to reform the Common Agricultural Policy. The *Sun* editorial team wrestled for hours about the angle to take on this story. Which way should they go? Explain the complex

---

*The reigning world champions crashed out of the 2002 World Cup without even scoring a single goal. When I commiserated with the owner of my local French café, Monsieur Le Patron explained that it was because a lot of the French team played in the English Premiership. Of course! It was our fault!

subsidies of the CAP that have underwritten European food producers and undercut Third World farmers? Or just say that Chirac is a typical garlic-smelling frog with terrible personal hygiene who'd beg the plucky Brits to bail them out again as soon as there was another world war?

Anti-French sentiment has never been far below the surface in this country. Way back in the fourteenth century thousands of Englishmen were persuaded to join the English army fighting the French. 'Darling, I'm going off to fight in the Hundred Years' War . . .' 'When will you be back?' 'I dunno, it could be ages . . .' (The Hundred Years' War actually lasted 116 years, but the last sixteen years were spent arguing over which language the peace treaty should be in.) And to this day, in terms of domestic popularity it does not damage Tony Blair to fall out with Jacques Chirac. But this spat does not come at a good time for the European project as a whole. Negotiations are currently under way regarding the expansion of the EU to include countries such as Poland and Hungary, which is widely supported by British cabinet ministers because it would mean their *au pairs* could stay here legally. Meanwhile, one of Chirac's predecessors has just published a draft constitution for the EU, carefully worded to stir up the paranoia of the British Euro-sceptics. Among his suggestions for the future of Europe is the election of a European president. Whatever the merits of this idea, the prospect of lots of endless god-awful cartoons in the *Daily Telegraph* featuring badly drawn Adolf Hitlers and Napoleons might make it more than we can bear. These proposals represent something of a comeback for Valéry Giscard d'Estaing, who failed to retain the French presidency when it was realized that he had a girl's name. Other controversial suggestions were that the European Union consider adopting a new title (he thought the name 'France' had a certain ring to it) and that Terry Wogan be prevented from hosting the Eurovision Song Contest.

The British reaction to the falling out of Blair and Chirac underlines a deeper problem with the whole concept of European integration. There is no such thing as European patriotism. While people can be proud to be Scottish and British, or proud to be Californian and American, it's hard to imagine us sneering at the continent of Antarctica for being not as good as Europe. Each member of the Union is out for what's best for their country, which is why Chirac has put protecting the CAP above alleviating poverty in Africa.

The way to achieve greater understanding at the highest level is for our top politicians to do French exchanges. Tony should have to go and stay with Jacques' family for a couple of weeks and vice versa. Imagine what it would it do for Anglo-French relations to have the PM spending a fortnight in a Parisian suburb, taking up smoking and whizzing round on a little moped without a helmet. Then for the return visit Chirac could meet all Tony's friends. 'This is Jacques, everyone,' Tony will say and all the girls in the cabinet will gasp and swoon as the cool French boy raises an eyebrow and casually lights up a Gitane. Obviously there might be the risk of a diplomatic incident when on the last day of his trip Jacques is arrested for shoplifting in Carnaby Street. Stuffed into the pockets of his cagoule, the police will discover one stolen Big Ben cigarette lighter, a Beatles keyring and an ashtray from the Hard Rock Café. But by now Blair and Chirac will be lifelong friends. More importantly, Tony can say, 'Right, Jacques, either you agree to reform the CAP, or we're telling your parents.'

The butler didn't do it

9 November 2002

Let's just get this straight. Diana's former butler was just about to go into the dock to answer lots of awkward questions that would deeply embarrass the royal family when the Queen suddenly had a flash of memory. 'Oh yes, um, one definitely remembers now, he told me that he'd taken a load of Di's stuff for, er, safekeeping, read this out, Ma'am, so Paul Burrell gets let off. Whoops, I don't think one was supposed to say that last bit.' To slightly misquote *Measure for Measure*, 'There's something well bloody dodgy going on there and no mistake.'

Everyone will be trying this tack now; teenagers ripping car radios from the dashboard will claim they're just taking them 'for safe-keeping'. Next time Winona Ryder is done for shoplifting she'll say, 'Look, I told the Queen of England I was taking the stuff for safe-keeping . . .' and they'll call Buck House to check and she'll say, 'Look, one can't remember, she probably did . . .'

Frankly, if the Queen is going to interfere in court cases then I'm afraid she's going to have to take the stand in the witness box like everybody else. 'The Crown calls that old lady wearing the crown!' And then she'd walk past the jury, wondering why they weren't waving plastic union flags and handing her bunches of flowers.

'Would you tell the courtroom your name, please?'

'The Queen.'

'And your occupation?'

'The Queen.' That's if she could remember these pieces of information – her memory seems to have been a little dodgy of late. Before
long Her Majesty would be buckling under the aggressive cross-
examination of the prosecution counsel. 'One can't remember! You're
putting words into one's mouth . . .'

Eventually her suitability as a witness would come into question.
'Your Honour, I ask the jury to consider the background of this so-
called witness. She's been living off the state all her life, the police are
always round her house and her family's constantly in the papers.'

The tragedy for the Queen is that, although they managed to
prevent Paul Burrell revealing lots of embarrassing secrets in court, he
then went and revealed them in the *Daily Mirror* instead. The other
tabloids were appalled at this shameful betrayal that they failed to land
for themselves. Of course the *Sun* still ran the whole story with the
words 'World Exclusive' plastered across its front page. It's one thing
to copy everything from the *Mirror*, but you'd think they'd remember
to cross that bit out. Apparently when the Queen shed a tear at the
Cenotaph this week it was because the *Mirror* had got the rights to
the exposé and not the *Sun*.

Among Burrell's revelations, we learned that when Charles was in
hospital and needed a wee, he got his valet to hold the bottle. I suppose
it's better than Charles holding the bottle and the valet doing the other
bit. 'Shall I give it a little shake now, Your Highness?' We also learned
that Diana had a crush on Dr Hasnat Khan, and turned up at his
house wearing a sumptuous fur coat under which she was completely
naked. The great British public were appalled by this. They don't
mind their future queen having it off with all and sundry and
jeopardizing the future of the monarchy – but wearing fur, well, that's
just beyond the pale. Diana also had lovers smuggled into Kensington
Palace in the boot of her car – except on the nights when no one was
available, when she went to bed with a spare wheel and a load of newspapers that they'd been meaning to take for recycling.

No one seems to escape the wrath of Diana's former butler. The
Spencer family has come in for particularly severe criticism. Burrell
says that he would never have paraded Diana's life in a museum for

£10.50. Certainly not; he wanted £300,000 and not a penny less. He recounts how the Queen would ask him to keep her company when she was watching telly and that he had to stand to attention the entire time.

'I know, Burrell, let's watch the entire *Star Wars* trilogy!'

'Um, yes, Your Majesty, or we could just watch a couple of *Tom and Jerry*s and then call it a night.'

The trouble with our royal family is that this sort of deference and respect is hard to maintain when you start to find out a bit more about them. No wonder they desperately want total secrecy when each tiny revelation confirms how ludicrous they really are. Before she got him off all charges, the Queen told Paul Burrell, 'There are powerful forces in this country about whom we know very little.' That'll be your memory playing up again, Ma'am. They're called the royal family.

Dial 999. Ask for 'Fire'. And wait for strike to end . . .

16 November 2002

It has been twenty-five years since the last firefighters' strike, but those trusty old headlines and cumbersome puns that haven't seen active service since 1977 were dusted down and wheeled out once again. 'Blazing Row!' 'Burning Question!' 'Fanning the Flames' – they were all trundled out despite fears that they were no longer up to the job. Television news crews were eager to get some dramatic pictures of the first day of the strike, and they weren't disappointed when a spectacular blaze broke out at a fireworks factory in Manchester. One eager young TV crew seemed to be on the scene particularly quickly, getting all the best footage of rockets shooting out of the windows, pausing only to cover up the petrol can sticking out of their bag. The blaze spread rapidly; burning timbers crashed all around while the intense heat sparked hundreds of explosions as the inferno tore through the massive stockpile of fireworks. But still the bloody Roman Candle wouldn't light.

Military fire crews rushed to the scene, armed with mulled wine and parkin cake, and then stood back going 'Oooooh! Aaaaah!' as the multicoloured rockets lit up the sky. They did their best to stop the fire spreading to the jacket potato warehouse next door and one or two soldiers attempted to get closer to the blaze, if only to try to give a nudge to that Catherine wheel that wasn't spinning around properly. But it was striking firefighters that came off the picket line to rescue a man trapped inside who had made the mistake of returning to a fireworks factory once it was alight.

This is a peculiar strike in that the firemen are withholding their labour except when it is most needed. Despite a generally hostile press, the firefighters have managed to keep the moral high ground. They are not dealing with the smaller, less dangerous incidents; indeed in most news footage of picket lines, there have been small fires in oil drums right under their noses that no one has made the slightest effort to put out.

At this time we should, of course, all be taking extra care and I for one almost unplugged my television before going to bed. Nobody wants a house fire, but if it means having to re-set the clock on the video because you pulled out the wrong plug by mistake, then it's a risk most of us are going to take. Somebody ought to be using this opportunity to persuade more people to get smoke alarms fitted, because after all there is no surer way of finding out when somebody is making toast in the kitchen. (If these 'toast alarms' do go off accidentally, then it's a very simple operation to turn them off. You stand on a chair in the kitchen and yank out the battery, leaving a useless bit of plastic hanging from the ceiling until it is finally destroyed in the fire that burns down the entire house because you were too cheapskate to buy a decent one.) Other extra safety precautions taken this week brought severe disruption on the London Underground, which so delayed exasperated commuters that they almost made eye contact with one another and tutted. Meanwhile, Al-Qaida terrorists have been asked not to detonate any nuclear bombs in Britain until the strike is over.

But despite all the worry and inconvenience, public support for the firefighters remains high. Nobody believes that people who save lives for a living would suddenly become greedy or go on strike just for the sake of it. Forty per cent of a healthy wage would be asking too much, but that's not what firefighters have been paid in recent years. All they are asking for is £8.50 an hour, and if we think that's too expensive, then we deserve to see what life without them is like for forty-eight hours.

It's at times like this that Labour Party supporters would be so much more comfortable if the Tories were in power. The left can't really cope with being cast as management; we'd much rather be oppressed and victimized by a ruthless Tory government than find ourselves trying to be responsible and even-handed. The only way forward is to appoint an independent pay review body consisting of Norman Tebbit, Jim Davidson, Peter Hitchens and a Dalek. Then when the firefighters' wage demands are turned down, we can boo these tight-fisted Tories for their typically miserly response and reassure ourselves that things would be very different if it was Labour making the decisions.

The alternative is having to face up to the unsettling reality that Labour is not doing enough to reward public-sector workers once it's in government. And I thought the 'Flaming Idiots!' headlines were a cliché! John Prescott should remember his roots and announce a decent pay rise for Pugh, Pugh, Barney McGrew, Cuthbert, Dibble and Grubb. And while we are being nostalgic, he might want to ask Jim Callaghan about the last time Labour took on the public-sector unions. Because if we thought having no firefighters was scary, you should see what follows next . . .

Cut!

23 November 2002

This week a studio audience and various TV cameras looked on as the body of an old man was dissected and organs were removed and passed around. That'll teach that old bloke to stand up when the host asked for a volunteer from the audience. It was the first public autopsy in 170 years and apparently the viewing figures are way up on last time. The identity of the body in question has not been revealed, although there are so many desperate former celebrities who'd do any-thing to return to mainstream television that dying and being cut up would probably be considered a small price to pay to kick-start their comebacks.

Demand for this particular TV recording was high, and many dis-appointed members of the public were turned away and had to make do with watching a recording of *Kilroy* in the studio next door. Some were physically sick and had to be helped out, but that's Kilroy for you. The lucky few who got in to the autopsy prepared to witness the most blood and bone seen in a television programme since Roy Keane's last tackle to feature on *The Premiership*.

Professor Gunther von Hagens entered wearing a fedora and pro-ceeded to demonstrate how to cut up a human body, giving a Delia Smith-type running commentary as he sliced away. *His Home Autopsy Autumn Collection* book should be in your shops for Christmas. Some people have accused Von Hagens of perhaps erring on the side of showbiz spectacle rather than sombre deference, particularly when he put Punch and Judy puppets over each hand, pulled out the intestines and squealed, 'Here come the sausages!' Then he removed the sternum and a few ribs and these were handed around in a bowl. Most winced and passed them on, though there was a bit of a mix-up when a bunch of drunk lads who'd wandered in on their way back from the Chinese take-away were overheard asking for a fingerbowl.

Channel 4 have denied that the whole event was in poor taste and have just unveiled their winter schedules containing a batch of exciting new shows. *Whose Spleen Is It Anyway?*, *Colostomy Big Brother* and, more worryingly, *Heartbeat*. If there is any regret at Channel 4, it's that they only managed to get a single programme out of this. If they really wanted to make this idea run and run they should bring in the drama of elimination used so effectively in their most popular programme. 'Which organ is going to be removed next week? Will it be the pancreas? Or is the gall bladder Britain's least favourite internal organ? Remember – it's your votes that decide!'

Other channels will soon be hitting back with 'surgertainment' shows of their own, including a new TV makeover series where you are given a general anaesthetic and your next-door neighbour chooses whatever major cosmetic surgery they think is required. Not so much *Changing Rooms* as *Changing Sexes* – 'Just watch the expression on Philip, or rather Philippa's, face when he uncovers his eyes in front of the mirror to see what Handy Andy's done with a hacksaw!'

The trouble with TV surgery is that after a while we would become desensitized to it all.

'What a hideous sight!'

'I know – a green hat with that coat – what was Von Hagens thinking?'

There should be a plaque above the door of commissioning editors with the motto '*Use Shock Sparingly*'. Channel 4 have got lots of attention by cutting up a dead body live on telly. A while back Channel 5 managed some publicity by having Keith Chegwin in the nude, but it is all cheap and easy shock. In his fine film *Bowling for Columbine*, Michael Moore uses CCTV footage of the massacre at Columbine

High School to make a wider point about guns and a society gripped by fear. Shocking but cathartic.

In fact, the main objection to this week's TV autopsy has been about a lack of respect for the dead, which bizarrely seems to trump the novelty concept of 'respect for the living'. Yes, it is upsetting when an artist exhibits the body of a dead tramp in formaldehyde, but hey, not as disrespectful as it was to ignore that tramp when he was sleeping in the street. We now know from this week's showbiz autopsy that this particular man had drunk two bottles of whisky a day, and had not done a proper day's work for twenty years. Either he had been totally abandoned by society or he was a TV executive.

The tabloids were appalled at this dissection of a real human being and splashed their disgust over several pages. They would have said more about this unseemly intrusion, but their papers were full up with so much else – 'Inside: Was Diana pregnant? Pages 2–7', 'Barrymore groped Royal Butler!', 'Wills slams media overkill, pages 2–24!' And perhaps this is why carving up dead people will never really take off as entertainment. Because at the end of the day dissecting living people is so much more fun.

Weapons of mass distraction

30 November 2002

After four long years, the United Nations weapons inspectors this week resumed their search for those hidden Iraqi weapons of mass destruction. With their hands still over their eyes they breathlessly counted, '. . . nine million, nine hundred and ninety-nine thousand, nine hundred and ninety-nine . . . TEN MILLION! Com-ing!' How Saddam giggled as he watched them peeking in the cupboard under the stairs and behind the curtains. 'Cold . . . cold . . . ooh, getting warmer; no, cold again. Freezing!' But after a while it got a bit embarrassing for the Iraqi President, having them snoop all over the place.

'What's in this drawer?'

'Ooh no, don't look in there!' And they pulled it open only to find a pair of old pants from Millets with 'Sex Machine' emblazoned across the front.

'Look, they were a joke birthday present from my brother. I never wear them, honest.'

The work of the weapons inspectors is supposed to be top secret, giving the Iraqis absolutely no warning about which sites are to be visited. So there was a mild suspicion that they might possibly be being bugged when the first location they visited displayed a big banner saying 'Baghdad Fertilizer Plant Welcomes the UN Weapons

Inspectors!' and a choir of local schoolchildren sang a specially composed anthem as the delegates were directed towards the buffet lunch. Would that explain the wires trailing from the large bunch of flowers that was placed in the middle of their conference table? Is that why they were given a free mobile phone with their car rental?

First they had to decide where they were going to look. They tried driving around a bit, but despite all the helpful brown tourist signs on the motorway, not one said 'Nuclear Bomb Factory' next to a little picture of a mushroom cloud. They tried photocopying a picture of a missile and attaching it to a few lampposts with the caption 'Lost! Huge Chemical Warhead, Answers to the name of "Scud".' Of course, when you're looking for something you may never find it, but at least you come across a few other things that you thought you'd lost for good. So far the UN team have uncovered three Polly Pocket figures, a marble, the instructions to the tumble drier and a plastic clip which they think probably came with the micro-scooter. 'Oh look, a ten franc coin; is that still legal tender? Um, I don't think so, but put it back in the kitchen drawer just in case.'

But George W. Bush needs no further evidence. 'Imagine if these items fell into the hands of Iraq's elite Republican Guard! You could have someone's eye out with that!' said Colin Powell examining the sharp plastic edge of the charger from an old mobile phone. The reporting of the inspectors' discoveries leaves us in no doubt of Saddam's guilt. They have found paper cups of a type that would be used to refresh workers making weapons of mass destruction. Also uncovered was an atlas which included detailed maps of the United States and Britain and a keyboard which could be used to type the letters 'B.O.M.B.' Whatever they find, the verdict is already decided. Even if they unearth no glowing vats of kryptonite it will prove that Saddam has hidden them all away in his cousin's lock-up garage. The inspectors are there for appearances' sake, to give the impression of a legitimate process, like the 'review' of a pit closure or recounts in Florida.

Since the UN team are completely wasting their time, would it not be more worthwhile to get them searching for something a little more useful? 'After two weeks' hunting in British shopping centres, the United Nations weapons inspectors have finally located some

Beyblades at Toys 'R' Us, Merry Hill, Birmingham. Oh no – apparently they've just been sold.' Perhaps they could find us an unbreakable CD case, or the Marmite in Sainsbury's, or a programme on the History Channel that wasn't about the Nazis.

Or maybe they could find that international law that says that one nation has the right to decide there will be a 'regime change' in another country thousands of miles away. The whole world would like to see Saddam Hussein overthrown by his own people, but Bush needs this easy battle to help him win the really big fight the following year. Dubya's only interest in foreign policy is what it can do for him at home now they're over halfway through the presidential electoral cycle. So if I was a UN weapons inspector, I'd go back to the hotel, empty the mini-bar and hope there were enough miniature Johnny Walker bottles to drown the realization that I was a diplomatic patsy for the US Republican Party. Only I wouldn't stay there too long because there'll definitely be plenty of weapons of mass destruction all over Iraq pretty soon. They'll be dropping from US bombers to mark the start of the American presidential campaign, to make sure there's certainly no 'regime change' at the White House. And if the inspectors can't see that, then frankly they're never going to spot anything.

Miss World shows her age

7 December 2002

Tonight in London, around a hundred women will parade up and down in their swimming costumes until the judges finally select the most beautiful of them all. No, it's not advertising executives interviewing for their new receptionist, but the Miss World competition returning to Britain in the most controversial of circumstances. The original venue in Nigeria had to be abandoned after the event prompted rioting, arson and murder. Miss Wales commented, 'It is a shame that a small minority of people spoiled it for everyone else . . .' Well said that woman! It's always the way, isn't it? Just a small handful of troublemakers who have to go and murder over two hundred people and leave thousands injured or homeless. The Nigerian government had originally been very keen to stage the contest, as they hoped it would show their country in a good light. So that worked well then.

There were no prizes for guessing which nation would step in at the last minute to stage the naffest, most anachronistic event in the international calender. Sydney got the Olympics, Germany gets the World Cup, but Britain has Miss World and the Royal Variety Performance.

Obviously the logistics of getting over a hundred foreign contestants from Africa into Britain at short notice presented quite a few problems. The organizers were assured by that Turkish lorry driver that for just $200 and a big box of fags he could smuggle them all through the Channel Tunnel, no questions asked. But when it came to it he just turfed them out of the back of the truck outside Sangatte and told them to cling on to the Eurostar as it sped past. It's at times like this that one realizes that national costumes were not designed with practicality in mind.

Eventually the girls were rounded up by immigration officials at Dover who asked them a series of tough questions, every one of which was met with the answer, 'I'd like to travel and work with children . . .'

'Come on, tell us the truth, what are you hoping for?' snarled the officer.

'World peace,' beamed Miss Uruguay, glancing left and right and looking slightly puzzled that there was no applause.

Finally they were allowed to proceed to London, and as a hundred beauty queens boarded the train for Victoria, dozens of middle-aged businessmen were seen optimistically moving their briefcases from the empty train seats beside them. Some feared that the British girls might exploit their home advantage, but in fact they could not have gone further out of their way to assist their rivals. They helpfully advised contestants visiting our shores for the first time that the best way to get a really good agent is to stick your photo in telephone boxes with your mobile number clearly marked. Miss Croatia was given lodgings with a Hampstead family, but she's not being allowed to the contest this evening because she's got a huge pile of ironing to finish after she's picked up the kids from ballet.

This competition is now fifty-two years old, and frankly the lines started to show some time ago. Despite the botox and facelifts, there's no denying that poor Miss World has seen better days. This year the PR could not have been worse if Miss USA had insisted that Miss Iraq could only take part with a bucket over her head. But despite all the controversy, the promoters have been doing their best to try to whip up some excitement. One bookie's advert proclaimed, 'Place a bet and win a phwooarr-tune!' Ouch, my ribs are still aching from this joke. (Miss England is second favourite to win at 20–1, and you can get an each-way bet on the winner marrying Rod Stewart.) There have been some people who have suggested that, with so many deaths in Nigeria, the event should be abandoned altogether, but these are probably the very same kill-joys who for some reason wanted to cancel the Soweto

Black and White Minstrel Show. Muriel Gray said, 'The girls will be wearing swimwear dripping with blood.' That's the last time they get Damien Hirst to design the outfits.

In fact, a few of the more sensitive contestants withdrew some time ago. Some have returned now there's been a change in venue, which is a disappointing setback in the battle against sexism and patronizing attitudes towards women – but then you know what they say about a woman's prerogative to change her mind. The original boycott was to protest against the sentence passed on Amina Lawal, a Nigerian woman condemned to be stoned to death for having sex outside marriage. And now that hundreds have died in Nigeria as a result of this competition, there is something distasteful about the remaining contestants claiming that what they want most is 'world peace'. There's only one way for the organizers to salvage any dignity out of this farce – tonight, in her absence, they should crown Amina Lawal and see if the Nigerians would dare execute a reigning Miss World. But tell Rod not to propose to this one . . .

EU to include Narnia

14 December 2002

In 2004 the European Union will be joined by a further nine, or possibly ten, countries, depending on investigations currently under way to ascertain whether Slovakia and Slovenia are the same country or not. Most of the new EU members announced on Thursday come from behind what was the Iron Curtain, but after decades as part of the Soviet Bloc they finally broke free and now can't wait to sign up to the European super-state instead. And what better example of European co-operation could there have been this week as the Arianne space rocket was launched and then exploded into a thousand pieces, while the poor technician was still trying to thumb his way through an instruction manual printed in a dozen different languages?

Each new EU applicant has to meet a number of criteria before they can finally be admitted. They must have a functioning democracy, they should have a market economy and elderly widows will be expected to do something about their facial hair. No more smoking on the tram or letting dogs ride on mopeds. Rear seat belts must be fitted in all cars and then ignored as in the rest of the EU. No doubt the xenophobes will paint a picture of hordes invading from the Balkans. 'These Eastern European girls, I mean they come over here and do all our hoovering! But that's not enough for them, oh no, then they have to change the duvet covers, walk the Norfolk terriers and do six hours' babysitting as well! And what's going to happen to the good old British bar worker? They'll all have to go back to Australia!' English language schools will close in their hundreds as Slovakian *au pairs* no longer sign up just to get their student visa. New fast-food outlets will open. The traditional British kebab shop and Tandoori take-away will be replaced by Polish restaurants such as 'Beetroot U Like' and 'Yo Turnip!'

There was a great deal of intense negotiating over which countries actually qualified for the EU, and eyebrows have been raised at some of the new members, such as Estonia, Lithuania and most of all Narnia. Some objected that Narnia is not technically in Europe, but of course part of it is (well, the wardrobe bit anyway) and so Narnia scraped in. Naturally there have been concerns about their human rights record, not to mention the rights of fawns and beavers, but Jack Straw rightly pointed out that the Snow Queen's record on turning her subjects into stone statues has actually improved in recent years. 'The Snow Queen is gradually moving towards a more democratic and less wintry society and it is important that Western leaders are seen to be keeping the wardrobe door open,' he said. Further negotiations could take years, but it will seem like no time at all once the delegation is back home again.

The only other controversy was the application by the Turkish Prime Minister. He overheard Tony Blair saying, 'We're not having Turkey!' at which he immediately stormed out and attacked the racist elitism of the Western club. He should have hung around to hear the British PM continue '. . . No, we thought we'd have goose this year, but with all the traditional trimmings, you know . . .'

But at this seasonal time, the Christians did not vote for Turkey, despite a most helpful intervention by that popular European leader George W. Bush. This isn't the first time that Turkey have sought to be part of a united Europe – the last attempt was known as the Ottoman Empire. And for some years now Turkey have been knocking on the back door of the EU by getting themselves into the Eurovision Song Contest and the Champions League. What greater natural friendship could there be than that between English football fans and those of Galatasaray? And if Israel and Morocco are in Eurovision, then it's time the EU opened the door to Ecuador,

Madagascar and the Central African Republic as well.

I remember as a young activist I once stood up at a Labour Party meeting and said, 'Do the people of inner-city Battersea have the same interests as the fishermen of Greece or the sugar-beet farmers of Belgium?' and everyone rather threw me by replying 'Yes!' And while I was still standing there, various comrades mumbled, 'Better health care . . .' 'Good schools . . .' 'Decent housing . . .' 'Oh and, er, peace!' And so halfway through putting my argument, I completely changed my mind while still attempting to finish the original point I was trying to make. Turkish Muslims want the same things as European Christians: to get together in one happy internationalist family so we can all slag off the Americans. But try asking our leaders if we really want what was once a small common market to be expanded into a huge European super-state stretching from the Atlantic to Asia. Most politicians will say it is high time we had a full and frank debate about this whole issue. Which is their way of saying they haven't the faintest bloody idea . . .

Feeling travel-sick on the road to nowhere

18 December 2002

In December 2002, I sat in for the Guardian's *Parliamentary sketch writer, Simon Hoggart. The following piece is from that week.*

Like the distorted delays announced over tannoys in railway stations, the government statement on transport yesterday was completely incomprehensible. MPs glanced at one another, looking confused and irritated.

The monitors all over the Palace of Westminster had claimed this was a statement on the 'transport investment plan', although most MPs who get the train back to their constituencies every weekend were under the impression that there was no transport, no investment and no plan.

Members had bagged their places like passengers spreading themselves out on a double seat, though of course they would quickly move their order papers if Julie Kirkbride or Claire Ward looked like choosing the seat beside them.

The Transport Secretary, Alistair Darling, resisted the temptation to refer to honourable members as 'customers', but was received with all the incredulity of a driver proudly announcing that his train was delayed by four hours but this was much better than the five hours that was expected. 'We are committed to the long haul,' he said, clearly thinking of his next rail journey back to Edinburgh.

Increased road congestion was in fact a symptom of this government's economic success, he claimed, but amazingly no one opposite congratulated him. It's like spiralling drug consumption – it's only happening because more people have got the disposable cash to spend on cocaine, but nobody will give the government credit where it is due.

Alistair Darling once had a beard, but this meant people remembered which one he was, so he shaved it off again. Now he either dyes his grey eyebrows black or his black barnet grey, but either way he seems to have found a third way on hair colour.

Labour members leaned forward to congratulate him on his performance, but only because they were all competing to do the Blackadder joke and say, 'Excellent statement, Darling!'

The Tories' transport spokesman is the chinless puppy Tim Collins, who looks like central casting sent him in straight from filming 'The Upper Class Twit of the Year'. His website boasts that his mother is chairman of Epping Forest Conservative Association and that he got a better-than-national swing despite having an opponent with the same surname as him. This is the stuff of great statesmen! His swimming certificates and cycling proficiency badge are expected to be added shortly.

Collins's speech was more Thomas the Tank Engine than TGV. There was a lot of noise and puffing steam; he looked like he might hurtle out of control at any second. He talked louder than necessary, like a small businessman on his mobile phone trying to show off to other passengers.

Labour's Gordon Prentice said Richard Branson got a lot of stick in the House of Commons, but he was eager to report that he had recently travelled on a Virgin Voyager train and was staggered at how sophisticated it was. In a desperately sycophantic bid for free train tickets or a digitally remastered copy of *Tubular Bells*, he added that there had even been Braille in the toilets! No one told him that this wasn't in fact Braille, but the hardened deposits of passengers who had picked their noses and wiped it on the toilet wall. But the minister David Jamieson added that he too had travelled on a Virgin train and he confirmed that they are quite excellent. MPs now know it is possible to get travel sickness without actually going anywhere.

Throughout this hellish journey to nowhere, Tories looked as if they would rather have a first-class section separate from all the oiks on the standard-class Labour seats. It was all very entertaining for those present. It was a shame that most MPs were still stuck in a train outside Didcot Parkway and couldn't be there to hear it all.

New Labour, New Christmas

21 December 2002

It looks set to be a tense Christmas in the homes of New Labour ministers. When the families ask where their presents are, cabinet members will be forced to stand up in front of the telly and make a brief statement outlining revised targets for the purchase of Christmas gifts.

'What, you mean you haven't actually bought me anything?'

'Er, we remain fully committed to a full allocation of perfume and CDs, although revised targets mean that in some areas these may not come on-stream until June 2008.'

'What about Granny? She was hoping for a teasmaid.'

'We hope that by returning to employment many of our elderly will have the opportunity to provide themselves with teasmaids which otherwise might not be affordable within the projected savings gap.'

'Well, happy holidays to you too!'

'Ah yes, about the holidays . . . with the emphasis now on wealth creation we are seeking to discourage people from taking more holiday than is needed, so it will no longer be compulsory for people to take December twenty-fifth off work. Quite the opposite, in fact.'

And then a full-blown row ensues, with the minister's wife saying she has lost patience with this government and tearing up that nice

Christmas card from the PM with the message 'Peace to all Mankind except those concealing weapons of mass destruction'.

Which will make it all the more tense when the neighbours pop round to 10 Downing Street on Christmas morning. William Straw and Euan Blair will skulk in a corner saying how fascist Christmas is, while Cherie goes around offering drinks.

'Bitter, Gordon?'

'I am not!'

'Or Scotch on the rocks?'

'How dare you!'

Tony will be wearing his wife's present of a bright red-and-green jumper (chosen by Carole Caplin) while the younger kids will be arguing over who gets to board up the last window on the advent calendar.

Then it's into the drawing room where the little ones perform a moving recreation of the Christmas story. Despite having travelled many miles, Jesus and Mary find themselves detained at Sangatte Detention Centre. In the humble stable a cow looks on, but then staggers sideways and falls over before being quickly whisked off to the abattoir. 'Though I am a single mother,' says Mary, 'I am determined to get back to work and create wealth!'

'Good idea!' says Joseph. 'Then maybe the Child Support Agency will get off my back!' The shepherds get their lines all wrong and start waving Countryside Alliance banners and then come the three Wise Men who had been following a bright star across the Middle East. 'No, you idiots!' says the innkeeper. 'That's not a star – it's a rocket from the US Missile Defence system, on its way to Baghdad.'

The younger children at the party will at least have had the consolation of all the presents that were left in their stockings, but even that looks set to change. This will be the last year in which children get free presents from Santa. As from next December, the government is planning to introduce a system of loans whereby children will eventually have to pay back all the money spent on toys and games that generations of kids have always taken for granted. It is estimated that by the time the average British child goes to secondary school he or she will owe Father Christmas approximately £10,000. The government has defended these so called 'Santa Loans', pointing out that they will be at a low rate of interest and there will be exemptions for children from poorer families. Children in the capital will be particularly badly hit following a ruling that Santa's sleigh will not be exempt from the congestion charge, which transport groups say will inevitably be passed on to the kids, or 'customers' as they are now known. Last year a misguided attempt to get Santa off his sleigh and onto public transport backfired when he spent the whole of Christmas Eve stuck in a tunnel on the London Underground with a load of drunken office workers in nylon Santa hats. Many of them were later sued for having unofficial Santa merchandise.

Labour left-wingers do not know where to turn, particularly since Naomi Klein's recent exposé on the appalling working conditions endured by the elves in Santa's sweatshop. A press spokesman for the Father Christmas Corporation denied that any elves were being paid three cents an hour to work fourteen hours a day in dangerous conditions, but this is probably because he no longer employs any elves – production was recently shifted from the North Pole to sub-contractors in Indonesia.

The traditions of Christmas have always changed to reflect the spirit of the age, but suddenly it seems that so much that we took for granted has gone out of the window. So this will in fact be the last year that there will be any Santa, any presents, any days off work or indeed any peace for all mankind. But hey, Happy Christmas anyway.

Election battle

28 December 2002

In the United States it is the custom to include in your Christmas card an annual update on all the things that your family have been up to during the previous twelve months. Needless to say, this practice has become the excuse for highly selective reporting, thinly veiled boasting and general one-upmanship between friends and relations.

Colleagues of ex-President Bush were particularly irked by the round robin they received from George Snr and Barbara this Christmas: 'Young George W. is getting on just fine in his new job of President of the United States (thanks for the help, Jeb!). He is looking forward to starting World War Three in the new year and Dad has been helping him find Iraq on the old family atlas. Coincidentally, this is also the time that he'll be beginning his campaign for re-election, and as Dubya says: "I will not be impedemented!"'

Yes, believe it or not, we are now more than halfway through the American electoral cycle, which is of course a far more important factor in the timing of any war than Iraqi winters or UN resolutions. You can understand why George W. Bush wants a military victory a year before his presidential election, but why do British troops need to be involved in his crude bid for electoral popularity? Apart from all the death and suffering that British squaddies would inflict upon the already oppressed Iraqi people, the troops themselves would be at great risk of being killed, injured, or entertained by Jim Davidson. So wouldn't it be safer and far more honest if our boys were simply deployed in key marginal states across the pond to go canvassing for the US Republican Party?

Instead of helping George W. Bush get re-elected by joining a war in the Gulf, Her Majesty's armed forces would be parachuted into New Hampshire, where they could give out glossy leaflets saying 'Re-elect Bush and Cheney 2004!' Dubya would still be grateful to Tony Blair, but no horrific war crimes would be committed and British servicemen would all come back safe and sound, except for the unfortunate few who got lost in downtown Detroit.

Obviously, getting the SAS to do a little light political canvassing on a Saturday morning might involve a small amount of retraining. On their first attempt, the elite forces would probably try to make contact with the voters by abseiling down from the roof and smashing through the upstairs windows, before detonating stun grenades and smoke canisters. The residents, lying quivering on the floor with a British army boot pressed down on their head and an SA80 assault rifle pointing at their temple, would then be asked a couple of politely worded questions about their current voting intentions. And when they stammered that they would probably be voting for Ralph Nader, they'd be shot through the back 127 times. So the SAS's usual approach is probably going to need toning down a bit, though in its favour no one would accuse these particular Republican canvassers of being soft on gun control.

Other British servicemen could be brought in as well. Instead of blowing up Baghdad, the RAF could just blow up thousands of red, white and blue balloons. Chieftain tanks could be converted to fire tickertape and streamers, and the band of the Royal Marines could learn to trumpet their way through such US election classics as 'Simply The Best' and 'You Ain't Seen Nothing Yet'.

Of course we would all prefer it if the delivery of US Republican Party leaflets could be done by the whole of the United Nations working together. But if the UN fails to take this historic opportunity to make itself relevant to the post-9/11 global scenario and it falls to US and British forces to get George Bush re-elected on our own, then we will not shirk from our moral duty to mobilize our troops to give out little lapel buttons with pictures of George W. to key voters in swing states.

Between you and me, there is another reason why this is by far the best solution. During the last Gulf War, there were so many military cock-ups and disasters that you can be sure that the same thing would happen if the US and British armies were in charge of Bush's re-election campaign. The 1991 conflict saw allied troops killed by friendly fire, Patriot missiles repeatedly failing to knock out Scuds, and SAS troops being dropped in the wrong place with the wrong equipment. Bringing all this inexpertise to bear on Bush's election campaign is the only chance that the Democrats have.

So call up the reservists, send our boys over the Atlantic with their jamming rifles and their crashing Royal Navy destroyers and, God speed, with our help Dubya will be cast out of the White House in 2004. Some have said that it is not the job of the British army to bring about 'regime change' in a sovereign country. But in Bush's case I'm sure we can make an exception.

Intelligent hominids (due any century now)

11 January 2003

Anthropologists are hailing a major new breakthrough that occurred this week in Spain. Sadly, it was not a British holidaymaker attempting a few words of Spanish; that may yet be hundreds of generations away. This was a discovery concerning another primitive human sub-species known as *Homo heidelbergensis* who died out after several million years of evolution having only just learned how to pronounce their own name. The unearthing of an axe head in a primitive burial chamber has proved the existence of intelligence and abstract thinking 300,000 years earlier than was previously thought. An organized burial chamber with tools for an imagined after-life suggests that these early cave-dwellers had some sort of religion. Many of them may have been awoken early on a Saturday morning by smiley Neanderthals calling round to the cave to ask them if they'd heard the good news about the Sun God. 'Molten rocks will fall from the sky and the seas will freeze over,' preached the zealots, and the cavemen sighed, 'No change there then . . .'

While the excavation of the site in Spain continues, archaeologists can only guess as to how the prehistoric funeral service might have been conducted. 'What can I say about Ug?' says the priest. 'He liked the simple things in life. Which is probably just as well. And he certainly didn't suffer fools gladly!' he adds, and there's a brave, affection nod from Ug's brother whose arm was ripped off and eaten during a particularly lean bit of the last ice age. Cremation may have been an option, although this would have involved a slight delay while they waited around for someone to invent fire. But however primitive this society, we now know that some sort of social order and culture did at least exist – setting the earliest hominids apart from the rest of the animal kingdom. (Although intelligent social behaviour has been observed in other primates such as chimpanzees, many scientists now believe that the chimps were put up to behaving like this by PG Tips.)

Of course the evolution of *Homo erectus* was a slow and painful process. Indeed, we still haven't reached the stage at which we are sophisticated enough not to want to giggle when we hear the name *Homo erectus*. Neither did it progress in a straight line – it was greatly affected by external factors such as the coming of the ice age, when all the cavemen went outside during their lunch hour to throw snowballs at one another.* But no other species has developed religion, art, abstract thought, science or little tear-off strips to prevent static in the tumble drier. This journey now has its first milestone in central Spain, where thousands of sub-humans migrated because of its warmer climate and lack of any extradition agreement.

Primates had begun using the first tools several hundred thousand years earlier – a crucial moment of human history, memorably re-created at the beginning of Stanley Kubrick's *2001: A Space Odyssey*. What did that apeman do with his new club? Did he use it to break open fruit for his family or was his first instinct to smash in the skull of his fellow man? Perhaps another apeman bowled a pine cone at him and that's how cricket got started. A million years later and we are no closer to knowing the answers to these questions or indeed to under-standing what the hell is going on in *2001: A Space Odyssey*. Thanks to an earlier film, *One Million Years B.C.*, starring Raquel Welch, many people are still under the misapprehension that primitive man inhabited the Earth at the same as the dinosaurs. In fact, the film is

*This week had seen the first heavy snowfall in London for over a decade and hundreds of grown adults spontaneously ran out of their workplaces and started throwing snowballs at each other, with only a minority of the cabinet hiding lumps of brick inside theirs.

full of wild anachronisms: dinosaurs occurred much earlier and fur Wonderbras came much, much later.

What is also not generally understood is that there were various branches of hominids in competition with each other. Neanderthals were not our direct ancestors but another branch of the genus that were in all probability wiped out by us, *Homo sapiens*. Ugly battles must have taken place between grunting troglodytes with thick necks and protruding foreheads – a bit like when Millwall fans turn up at Chelsea. The remains discovered this week in Spain are also of a sub-species that was killed off and now we are presented with the depressing conclusion that our particular branch of mankind may not have triumphed because we were the only highly intelligent branch of the family, as we'd arrogantly presumed, but because we were the most vicious and brutal. We know that early *Homo sapiens* looked like a chimp and was dangerous and aggressive. And when you look at President Bush, you can see how far we have come. On the same day that this prehistoric discovery was announced, the respected World Watch Institute in Washington declared that we only have one generation to save the planet. A million years getting to this point and we are going to blow it all away in less than a century. This week the anthropologists were excitedly debating when the first intelligent humans appeared. But somehow when you look around you can't help thinking that we're still waiting.

Grounds for concern

18 January 2003

Football teams are under all sorts of pressure these days. Peterborough United were recently told they could no longer use the nickname 'Posh' because that now belongs to Posh Spice. Next thing you know George Michael will object to Fulham calling themselves 'the Cottagers'.

The origin of Fulham's nickname comes of course from Craven Cottage, by far the most charming football ground in the country. But this week it has been reported that the club's owner, Mohamed Al Fayed, has already received a £15 million down-payment from a property company seeking to build luxury homes on this prime riverside location. It wasn't clear whether the cash was handed over in plain brown envelopes.

Chairman Mo insists that this is just a precautionary option that he is taking alongside his primary objective of redeveloping Fulham's historic ground. Clearly there is no contradiction here; property developers and football players will work alongside each other. The team will play a normal ninety minutes except there will be cement mixers and piles of rubble all over the pitch. It'll certainly liven up the match commentary on *The Premiership*: 'Oh and a fantastic piece of improvisation there from Steve Finnan! The Irish international jumped into the JCB, picked up the ball in midfield, steered it round the visitors' defence and delivered it right into the box. But oh dear, Marlet's still missed it!'

Craven Cottage has been the home of Fulham FC since 1896 and if ancient rights of way are still used by ramblers through the estates of country houses, then this development should proceed only if the historic right to play footy there is maintained. The new residents will only be able to park their Porsches after Malbranque and Van De Sar have finished playing 'three-and-in' against the garage door. In the lobby, the game of keepy-uppy may have to be abandoned due to chandelier failure. Will the jacuzzi still be as inviting after eleven foot-ballers have jumped into it wearing muddy boots and sweaty football kits?

Former season-ticket holders must also have some sort of rights as sitting tenants that would mean the incoming millionaires having to share their living rooms with the previous occupant of that particular space. Any purchaser who imagines herself curled up on the sofa watching a period costume drama on BBC2 should realize that the charmer who sits behind me at Fulham every week will now be sitting directly behind her settee, swearing and shouting at her television: 'Oi, Darcy, you stuck-up twat, tell Mrs Bennet to go fuck herself!' Dinner parties just won't be the same with the squatters sitting there chomping on hot-dogs and burgers, with mustard and red sauce dripping out all over the place mats.

But of course none of this will have to happen if the local Labour council have the courage to refuse planning permission for this development. Until now Fulham FC has been a great example of what can happen under Labour. When Tony Blair became PM, Fulham were in the bottom division. By the end of his first term, Fulham had been promoted to the Premiership – what clearer evidence do people want of Labour's competence in power? Of course, Al Fayed's millions may have also have had something to do with it. But the club's chairman is in his seventies – in ten years' time he may no longer be funding the club, Fulham will probably slip out of the Premiership and the memory of a few seasons in the sun will not be adequate com-pensation for being permanently homeless or having to travel out to the edge of some god-awful industrial estate twenty miles away to watch the team.

Obviously, as a season-ticket holder at Fulham I cannot pretend to be neutral on this issue, but I would not wish the loss of their ground on any club. Well, except Chelsea, of course. Every site in the capital is worth more as luxury flats, whether it's a hospital, a school or an old football ground. But there's a difference between price and value. What is it that gives our cities character and charm: quirky places open to all and full of memories for thousands, or gated private housing with CCTV cameras? Football fans from any club will agree that Craven Cottage is special. I have watched hundreds of games there, often followed by a reflective pint overlooking the river as the sun went down on the Thames. The idea that this might be gone for ever fills me with such sadness that it makes me want to top myself – or worse, start supporting Manchester United. There is something wrong with our society when we are prepared to surrender our sporting heritage for luxury apartments. And the only people who'll be able to afford those sort of prices will be Premiership footballers. It's a shame they won't actually have anywhere to play any more.

London Olympics (indoors if wet)

1 February 2003

This week the cabinet postponed a decision on another British bid for the Olympics while they focused on the more pressing problem of Saddam Hussein. The thinking is that bombing Iraq will make Baghdad's chances of hosting the 2012 Olympics even slimmer and suddenly London might be in with an outside chance.

Our recent record on landing major sporting events has not been too impressive. For the 2006 World Cup we lost to Germany without so much as a penalty shoot-out. And strangely, Olympic delegates were more attracted by the prospect of a few weeks in Sydney than they were by sunny Manchester. Now it's even looking touch and go whether London will get to host the London Marathon. Despite all this, it seems that the government will eventually back a British bid for the 2012 Games. Having had such a wonderful experience with the Millennium Dome, they are keen to multiply that PR triumph by a thousand. Why limit ourselves to being humiliated inside the sporting arena when we can be humiliated outside it as well?

As part of the bidding process, each city has to spend a week hosting the IOC Committee, showing them the very best of what their home town has to offer. The suggestion that this occasion might provide opportunities for a certain amount of corruption is grossly exaggerated. While other countries will be laying on high-class prostitutes, cocaine and suitcases crammed with $50 notes, in London the delegates will be surreptitiously slipped two free tickets to see David Essex at the Labatt's Apollo. There will be a chance to see all the sites, of course; a coach will set off from Tower Bridge en route for Trafalgar Square – so that should take up the first three days. What greater treat could there be than being stuck in a traffic jam with Sebastian Coe? And while the international committee search through their pockets to cough up for the congestion charge, they'll be given a running commentary on London's sporting heritage: 'The British people love sport and find many ways to get involved; notice that chap on the corner holding up a sign saying "Massive Golf Sale". And as you can see, our young men are already in practice for the relay race, grabbing mobile phones and running off at great speed!' Then it's a traditional London tourist's slap-up lunch – wandering down Oxford Street eating a warmed-up slice of pizza saying, 'Pleeze, where is Penny Lane and Ze Cavern?' as office workers hurry past presuming they're being accosted by a drug addict.

This initial bidding stage will cost £13 million – or twice that if they buy them lunch at Prêt à Manger. But should we be successful and beat off bids from Harare and the Lost City of Atlantis, then the money gets really serious. The current estimate is that it would cost the UK taxpayer £2 billion to stage the Olympics in London. Now I'm going to really stick my neck out here and make an outlandish prediction. *The actual cost will end up being more than the estimate.* There, I've said it, and in 2012 historians will dig out this column and say, 'How could he possibly have known such a thing? Was he a time traveller, some sort of mystic visionary, a second Nostradamus? For he actually foresaw that the cost of this major construction project would exceed the original estimate! And he also predicted that there would be delays in construction. Yea, a true prophet did come among us!'

The question is whether the benefits of hosting the Olympic Games would be worth three or four billion quid. Is London the part of Britain that needs this sort of investment, or did someone decide that the 'Warrington–Runcorn Olympics' didn't have the right ring to it? Imagine if that sort of money was invested in sport at a grass–roots level all across the country. This was the policy pursued by François

Mitterrand in the 1980s and great national sporting achievement duly followed, with a French World Cup victory and an impressive crop of Olympic golds, far exceeding Britain's usual handful in the small-bore rifle shooting and synchronized queuing.

Do we really want the whole world watching an opening ceremony where the lighting of the Olympic torch is delayed because the man from the gas board never turned up even though the sports minister waited in all day for him? Do we trust our police to watch Carl Lewis's successor breaking the 100 metres world record without pulling him over to ask him why he's in such a hurry? And if the Olympic village was like any other village in the south of England, all the foreign athletes would have to live there for five years before anyone said 'Good morning' to them. No, instead Britain should limit itself to bidding for the Winter Olympics. Now that would be really impressive: 'We apologize that the skiing, skating and bobsled events have all been cancelled. Apparently there's been a bit of snow, so nobody can get anywhere.'

Off the wall

8 February 2003

Why is everybody so quick to label Michael Jackson? Who among us can honestly say we haven't gone shopping and bought things we didn't really need? Who hasn't wished they could change their appearance a little? Who hasn't built their own private funfair, zoo and fantasy park and got twelve-year-old kids to come over and stay the night in their bedroom? Okay, so just Michael then.

Martin Bashir's documentary was certainly compelling entertainment, especially now those guided tours through Bedlam have been stopped. We learned that Michael wants his kids to have a happier childhood than he had. So he calls his son 'Blanket'. Yup, that sounds fine to me; I can't see any school bullies or sadistic teachers finding anything strange or laughable in that. In any case, when they're older, kids with unusual names always have the option of switching to their more conventional middle name, which in this case happens to be 'Duvet'. Michael Jackson's attempt to bottle feed the baby did not fill one with confidence. There was an incredible amount of shaking going on, probably coming from the baby who at that moment looked up to realize that this complete weirdo was his dad. But young Blanket is rapidly growing up to be a normal toddler and should be moonwalking any day now.

Another great moment was the sight of Michael going shopping.

He dashed around a boutique crammed with ornate gold vases and giant jewel-encrusted urns, each costing tens of thousands of dollars, buying everything in sight while the store-owner rubbed his hands like Uriah Heep behind him. I wish this scene had been filmed in Britain.

'Ooh, no, sorry, that's a display model, I'm afraid, and we won't have any more of those for another six to eight weeks.'

'But look, here's a million in cash – just let me have whatever you've got.'

'Nah, sorry, you have to order those in advance.'

Of course the element which has grabbed all the media attention has been Jackson's relationship with a twelve-year-old boy. The parents of young 'Gavin' are apparently perfectly happy for their son to go and sleep in Michael Jackson's bed. It's marvellous that such trust still survives in this world, that they can confidently send little Gavin off with his overnight bag, his toothbrush and half a dozen hidden microphones while a crack team of private detectives and lawyers are parked in a mobile listening command centre at the bottom of the lane praying that this will be the night they can hit Jacko with a billion-dollar lawsuit.

'Did you have a nice time at your friend's, dear?'

'Yes, Mommy.'

'Damn! You mean you didn't get trampled by one of his pet elephants or anything?'

I wonder if Michael ever goes back for a sleepover at Gavin's house? 'Hello, Michael, we've put up the camp bed for you in Gavin's room, and got the oxygen tent down from the loft, and put up sun screens and hired a few aardvarks and camels to wander about the place to make you feel at home. Now, would you like some ice cream, dear – it's five million dollars a scoop?'

Of course it is not normal or healthy for a forty-four-year-old man to have twelve-year-old boys over to stay, but what is it about our society that makes us so eager to scream 'paedophile' before we're sure what is really going on? It seems more likely that Jacko, as part of his rather tragic childlike behaviour, is having 'other' kids over to stay. Yet since the film was broadcast there has been an almost tangible hunger to brand Jackson as a pederast because in the modern Salem witch hunts it's been a few weeks since the last public show trial and the mob are screaming for more. We've had paediatricians attacked because people got that confused with paedophile. Who's next? I've got relations in Ireland called 'Paddy O'Farrell'; that sounds a bit like 'paedophile' – maybe the mob should storm their houses as well. And as for Iraqi paedophiles posing as asylum seekers, well, they're the worst of the lot.

The eagerness to tar Jacko with the worst possible brush is like one of the cheap thrills in his empty funfair. Yes, he is creepy and self-deluding but that doesn't automatically mean he must be evil. Nothing is black and white – especially in Michael Jackson's case. Apparently he was horrified by Bashir's documentary, saying, 'I am surprised that a professional journalist would compromise his integrity by deceiving me.' Blimey, he's even more detached from reality than we thought. Jacko's PR adviser should have warned him that doing this film was a bad idea, that it might be edited in such a way as to make the singer seem a trifle eccentric. Sadly, Michael's PR adviser is a llama and so was unable to do this. And so now Bashir's really put the star's nose out of joint. That should keep the plastic surgeons busy for a while.

Genetically modified asparagus (an end to strange-smelling urine)

22 February 2003

This is the year that the government is supposed to make a decision on whether to allow commercial growing of genetically modified crops. The farm trials began three years ago and they had hoped that they'd get away without having to decide one way or the other because there wouldn't be any farms left by now. The immediate problem is remembering exactly which fields the farmers planted the GM crops in. 'Was it that one?' 'Er, might have been, or it could have been that one . . . I dunno, us farmers have had a lot on our minds you know.'

This month's conference on GM crops did not cause quite the stir that had been hoped. One appalled environmentalist spoke from the platform about the terrible threat to one of our best-known native species. 'Unless action is taken soon,' she implored, 'we will see the deliberate extinction of the stinging nettle!!' There was an awkward silence as delegates contemplated such a scenario. 'Imagine the stinging nettle completely disappearing from our gardens and footpaths!'

'Erm, yeah, well, I think I could probably live with that,' said someone at the back.

'Me too,' echoed a couple in the row in front and a positive murmur went round the whole hall as delegates imagined their kids falling into a bed of the GM 'tickling nettle'.

The geneticists promise us that GM plants offer a brave new world in which you could park your car underneath a sycamore tree without the windscreen getting all sticky. One day it will be possible to eat a three-bean salad and then lay a carpet with confidence. All sorts of adjustments can be made to everyday plants: there'll be a mould that is the same colour as the non-slip bath mat, an end to the trauma of that one unopenable pistachio nut and a new minty-fresh garlic redesigned so the skin doesn't get all stuck in the garlic crusher. One inspired scientist has even managed to put a cannabis gene into a cocoa plant so that you can get stoned and cure the munchies all at the same time.

But many opponents of GM food are wary of the Hitlerian concept of genetic super-species, even if this time round we are talking about broccoli. Can the Americans really be trusted to meddle in the incredibly complex genetic make-up of plants without adding tomato ketchup to everything? The balance of the natural world is very fragile, with many animals and plants depending upon one another for their propagation and survival. For example, the lily has evolved so that its pollen can be dispersed only by people with clean white shirts brushing against it at drinks parties. History has shown us that every change we make to the ecosystem will have a knock-on effect that we did not foresee. For example, we are rapidly losing the natural habitat of that special moss that grows only on the bumpers of Triumph Heralds. Of course, mankind has been interfering in nature since prehistoric farmers first learnt to apply for subsidies. Without selective breeding and the development of new species the world would be a very different place. There'd only be one sort of lettuce and husbands would no longer come back from the supermarket in fear that they'd got the wrong one. David Blunkett would have a 'Guide Wolf for the Blind'. And the guide wolf would sit patiently at his feet during Home Office questions while the opposition took great care to agree with every single point the minister made.

But interfering directly with the genetic make-up of crops is very different indeed because of the scientific process involved. What the geneticists do is, well, it's hard to explain exactly, but um, there's this DNA stuff and then, er, chromosomes and well, I think they take out all the genes and then they mix up the GM with the DNA or something – well, anyway, I don't like the sound of it. However, one thing that we can all understand is that increased food production won't automatically feed the starving millions. The promise that GM crops will bring an end to malnutrition is a bogus one. We already have enough food to feed everyone in the world. Increasing food production with GM crops might boost profits and surpluses but it won't make any difference to the way that food and, more importantly, power is distributed in this world. Meanwhile we are being hurriedly led down a rather treacherous path through a field of GM triffids, and this time I'm not sure I trust the bloke with the Ordnance Survey map who claims he knows where he's going. Two things are certain with GM crops: firstly, there are bound to be disastrous ecological side-effects that no one ever foresaw; and secondly, they'll never modify Brussels sprouts enough for kids to try one on Christmas Day. And in the meantime the food companies will keep assuring us that eating GM vegetables has no dangerous side-effects. Yeah, right, so how come the Jolly Green Giant ended up looking like that then?

Tories in turmoil (Part 7)

1 March 2003

It is a dilemma that has split Europe, that consumes Washington, NATO and the corridors of Westminster. Should UN troops be used to bring about regime change at the top of the Conservative Party? Is it really morally acceptable for us to stand by and watch the terrible suffering that IDS is causing Conservative supporters? Would it not be more humane in the long term for the UN to step in and topple his extremist military leadership and install a regime that offers some hope to desperate Tory Party members?

From his bunker in Central Office come reports of increasing paranoia and panic as Duncan Smith ruthlessly 'disposes' of any former ally that he imagines might threaten his position. His deputies walk in terror that they may be next to be 'disappeared' or, worse, may be forced to endure the terrible torture of listening to IDS explaining his position on the Euro.

The latest crisis in the Tory Party was triggered when prominent Conservatives Mark MacGregor and Rick Nye were dramatically sacked. Newspaper offices were thrown into a frenzy when this news came down the wire.

'So, um, who's going to cover this one then?'

'Er, sports desk, maybe? I've got a feeling one of them might be manager of Farnborough Town.'

'No, it must be an entertainment story – they're actors in *Emmerdale*, I'm sure of it . . .'

But for the more liberal Conservative MPs who understood that these sackings represented another lurch to the right, their fury could not have been greater if someone had passed the cannabis round the wrong way.

Michael Portillo promptly launched an attack on IDS's leadership, accusing him of surrounding himself with pygmies. As it happens, there are indeed a number of four-foot-high Equatorial Africans working in IDS's private office who were rather offended by this remark. The leader duly hit back and the political row reached such a pitch over the weekend that *Breakfast with Frost* was actually watched by someone who wasn't a politician or living in an old people's home. Thank goodness Norman Tebbit was on hand to add some measured sanity to the debate on modernization. 'I could count on the fingers of the right hand of a Finsbury Park Muslim cleric the number of voters who have asked me to support the legalization of sex in public lavatories or instruction in oral sex in schools.' But surely all three parties are agreed that these are key planks in British domestic policy! I suppose we should just be grateful that there were no veiled personal attacks on Michael Portillo.

With the threat of war damaging the government's standing in the polls, the Conservatives ought to be brimming with confidence. In fact, many Conservatives are suggesting to him that the Gulf crisis might be the one issue on which Duncan Smith could really make an impact.

'What you should do, Iain, is go to Iraq for a bit.'

'What, to negotiate with Saddam Hussein, you mean?'

'Er, if you want, but just get a feel for the place. We've rented you a little flat next door to the Baghdad armaments factory – it's a six-month lease.'

But of course we don't have to wait for the Conservatives to remove him as leader of the opposition. It is theoretically in the gift of the Parliamentary Labour Party to make the Liberals the official opposition. A hundred or so Labour backbenchers could decide to cross the floor of the house to join the Liberals, so that the Lib Dems then became the second largest party. Admittedly Labour would not be in such a commanding position in the Commons, but it wouldn't matter because these former Labour MPs would have a curious tendency to defy the Liberal whip and consistently vote with the Labour government. Iain Duncan Smith would then be the leader of a minor party which would finally tear itself apart in a mire of back-stabbing and recriminations.

But of course the government actually want IDS in place for as long as possible, so for once the crisis in the Tory Party is bad news for Labour. It's a chilling thought that it's not Portillo who is the covert ally of New Labour, but Norman Tebbit and the other far-right supporters of the current leadership. Meanwhile the Tories remain fundamentally divided on the major issues of the day, such as 'Which one's Ant and which one's Dec?' More importantly, there is growing panic in the Parliamentary Party that Iain Duncan Smith consistently fails to make any impact. Their leader strenuously denied this, although no one can quite remember what he actually said. Journalists have reduced his name to three letters, but even typing 'IDS' feels like more effort than he really justifies. Tory MPs had been hoping that their leader would grow into the job, but it turns out that there is less to him than meets the eye. Unless the Tories make major gains in May's local elections, then IDS may well be in his job for even less time than Saddam Hussein's anger therapist.

Who wants to be a military Blair?

7 March 2003

Accusations of fraud in TV game shows are nothing new. Police are currently looking into a claim that a number of the participants in *I'm a Celebrity, Get Me Out Of Here!* were not in fact celebrities at all, but rather tragic rejects from the provincial panto circuit. On another occasion an imposter on *Mastermind* was prevented from entering the studio when police noticed he was wearing vaguely fashionable clothes. And there was also outrage recently on *University Challenge*, when the captain of some Oxbridge team actually allowed the token female to give her correct response herself, rather than confidently repeating her whispered answer as if he'd known it all along.

But the allegations currently occupying Southwark Crown Court are far more serious because of the prize involved. I'm not saying that the commemorative glass bowl that the BBC dished out to the winner of *Mastermind* was a worthless piece of tat, not at all; it's just that given the choice I suspect many of the winners might have preferred a million quid.

But now the third person to win the ultimate prize on *Who Wants To Be A Millionaire?* stands accused of cheating. This week the defendant took the witness box and the prosecution's cross-examination began. 'Are you Major Charles Ingram from Easterton, Wiltshire?' The courtroom lights dimmed, and the electronic heartbeat of the *Millionaire* theme tune pulsated underneath as all eyes fell on the Major. But they always start off with a really easy question and Ingram came straight back with the correct answer as the jury breathed a sigh of relief and burst into applause. 'Question number two: Are you guilty or not guilty of the charges brought against you?' At this point he considered going fifty/fifty but opted instead to phone a friend, in this case his lawyer, who reckoned he ought to plump for 'Not Guilty'. Final answer? asked the judge. 'Final answer,' he confirmed.

Of course, the key difference with this particular quiz show is that the longer the lawyers can string out the questions, the closer they get to earning themselves another million. On Wednesday the video of the entire show in question was played in court. When Chris Tarrant said, 'What is butterscotch?' the judge was jumping up and down saying, 'Ooh, I know this one – it's D: brittle toffee. It's definitely D!' and the lawyers felt obliged to applaud His Honour's impressive display of general knowledge. Then came the next question: 'For two thousand pounds: In *Coronation Street*, who is Audrey's daughter?' and with all the jury nodding to each other about the correct answer, the judge lost patience and said, 'Look, do we really have to watch this all the way through . . .'

The allegation is that this contestant won his million with the assistance of someone in the audience coughing at key moments to signal which choice was the correct answer. More worryingly, it appears that this covert method of prompting the right response is spreading beyond mere entertainment shows. Over recent weeks our own Prime Minister has repeatedly been in the hot seat and forced to answer some very difficult questions on the subject of the impending war with Iraq. Allegations have now been made that at each stage the PM was being assisted by a man called George W. Bush who was sitting in the audience coughing emphatically at crucial moments. Now the transcript of *Who Wants To Be A Military Blair?* is published here for the first time.

'Prime Minister, would you support a war against Iraq that did not have the backing of the United Nations?'

'Hmmm . . . I'm tempted to say that we must have UN support.' Silence. Blair then appears unsure about this answer. 'But then again, maybe we have a duty to support the Americans with or without the UN . . .' A distinctive cough is heard from Mr Bush sitting in the third row. 'Yes, yes, I think that's the right answer . . .' Another loud cough. 'Definitely, I'm sure of it now. I'm going to plump for support the Americans whatever.'

As is traditional, the questioning gets harder. 'Okay, now remember this question is worth billions of pounds in defence and re-construction contracts for British companies. So, for ten billion pounds: Would you begin the bombing of Iraq before there has even been a second UN resolution or a vote in the House of Commons?'

'Hmmm . . . not sure,' says Blair, seeming deliberately to consider his choices out loud. 'Should we start bombing Iraq now?' Suddenly Mr Bush can be clearly heard coughing like a heavy smoker with bronchitis. One or two of the splutters even sound like a thinly dis-guised 'Yes!' 'Actually, I think I do know this one,' says the British PM. (There's no point in Tony asking the audience because he did that right at the beginning; they all voted against the war and he chose to disregard them.) 'Yes, definitely! In fact, the bombing has already started.' It's confirmed that this is true and Tony leaps up and punches the air.

'Congratulations! And here's your prize – an enormous blank cheque made out from you to the Americans . . . Oh, but before you leave, there are some gentlemen in the wings. They want to talk to you about breaking international law . . .'

That's slaughtertainment!

28 March 2003

The auditions to be Saddam Hussein's lookalike must be rather nervous affairs. All of Iraq's finest impressionists are summoned to the Imperial Palace, along with make-up artists, prosthetics experts and the proprietor of Moustaches 'R' Us. And then the Iraqi equivalents of Rory Bremner or Robin Williams have to stand before the brutal, vain and famously short-tempered dictator and do their very best parody of him.

'Why are you twitching like that? I don't twitch!' barks Saddam as the Republican Guards try to suppress their laughter at the brilliance of the caricature.

'We will defeat the American criminals . . .' continues the impressionist, twitching satirically as the soldiers collapse into uncontrollable laughter which they have to pretend are tears of love for their glorious leader.

'And you are nowhere near handsome enough – why have you got a great big bulbous nose, I don't have a bulbous nose. We should get Richard Gere to be my lookalike.'

With an atmosphere like this, it's no wonder that Saddam's broadcasts end up being such dull and unwatchable affairs. The format is wooden and old fashioned, with none of the intimacy or clever camera tricks that Western broadcasters have learned. For example, Saddam would surely benefit from having a co-presenter; someone like Judy Finnegan with whom he could flirt on the *Breakfast Time* sofa before they glanced through next week's newspaper headlines.

'So, Judy, what is next Wednesday's *Baghdad Times* saying?' he could ask with a little wink.

'Well, Saddam, they've got you leading the victory parade over the vanquished Americans – and very handsome you look too!' and they'd share an affectionate giggle as they cut to their resident zany weatherman predicting a light south-easterly breeze giving way to huge clouds of oily smoke all over the country.

So apart from losing the military battle, Saddam is also currently losing the propaganda war. These days military spending is wasted if you don't have the media back-up to show the war from your viewpoint. Alfred Hitchcock maintained that in a thriller the audience's sympathies had more to do with where you placed the camera than they did with accepted notions of morality. Take an everyday burglary, for example. Film it from the victim's point of view, following him as he walks nervously down the stairs because he's heard an intruder, and you are obviously on the homeowner's side. But if the camera had followed that burglar through the window and then suddenly he'd heard someone coming down the stairs, you'd think, 'Oh no, quick, get out!' And in this war it's the intruders who have got the most cameras. The Americans understand the Hitchcock Principle all too well, which is why they built an enormous media centre in the middle of the desert almost before they did anything else.

More problematic Hollywood rules also apply, of course. The attention span of the modern audience is nowhere near as long as it used to be. In centuries gone by not only were the plays and epic poems much longer, but the wars were too. But there's no way that a modern scheduler could tolerate a six-year war today, not with all the competition from the movie channels and reality TV shows. That's why these days we only go to war against really easy opponents, to make sure it's all over before we start reaching for the remote control. Otherwise they'd have to come up with new ways to keep us all interested – introducing *Fame Academy*-style phone votes to let the viewers decide who wins the mother of all battles. 'If you want George Bush to win the war, phone or text the number on your screen now! If you want Saddam Hussein to win, phone this second number and hold for a visit from the CIA . . .'

As it is, the new concept of twenty-four-hour slaughtertainment that's hit the airwaves is still compulsive television. The Oscars have had their lowest audience for years, because viewers want to catch the ending of the action adventure movie happening over on CNN. Perhaps this branch of showbiz should have its own awards ceremony. Best Supporting Actor: Tony Blair. Best Special Effects: the American Air Force. Best Editing: award to be shared between all the American news channels. George W. Bush would go up to the podium to collect his special award: 'I would like to thank my dad, without whom this war would not have been possible.' And then there would be a little bit of controversy and the microphone would disappear into the lectern because one or two speakers used the occasion to criticize Hollywood films they'd seen that didn't quite work for them.

Except that they probably know it was Hollywood that taught them all the rules. America's point of view is dictated by the 'p.o.v.' in the movie director's meaning of the phrase. More westerners would have cried at the close-up human fiction in *Saving Private Ryan* than shed tears to see real-life explosions lighting up a distant Baghdad. No wonder the US military were so keen to destroy Baghdad's main television station this week. Mao said that power grows out of the barrel of a gun. Now it comes out of the end of whichever gun has the cameras right behind it.

Free market forces

4 April 2003

The following article is reprinted from the journal of the Washington Freedom Association, which has been hugely influential in shaping George W. Bush's foreign policy due to its uncompromising far-right Republican outlook in easy-to-read large print.

The war is now two weeks old and it seems incredible to many of us on Capitol Hill that Saddam Hussein has not yet surrendered. Has his translator not explained to him exactly what George Bush said: that 'Baghdad will endure bombardmentalization'? That 'the Iraqi people must be freed from this tyrannosaurus regime'? What bit of 'non-conditional capitulization' does Saddam not understand?

The Washington Freedom Association is of the opinion that American foreign policy and the principles of free enterprise must go hand in hand. Yet we are permitting this war to be pursued by Federal Government instead of outsourcing the operation to American private companies. War pursued by central government necessitates higher levels of federal taxation and is thus incompatible with the very freedom for which American service personnel are risking their lives. 'Free enterprise warfare' would not only result in an army unfettered by federal bureaucracy, but by fielding an army employed by a limited company rather than a nation state, troops would not be impeded by excessive petty international regulations such as the Geneva Convention. In addition, the boost to share prices of the companies conducting the conflict would have a regenerative effect on the US economy as a whole. Already a number of private companies have put in tenders to the State Department to take over the running of the Iraq war. Our finest supermarkets already have large supplies of guns and ammunition on their shelves; Exxon have extensive experience in laying waste to large areas of countryside; Enron is looking for new spheres of influence; and there are many more companies that so enthusiastically share the President's vision of freedom that they contributed to his election campaign.

The idea is already a reality. To pilot the idea of 'free market forces' a small squadron of privatized vehicle immobilizers from the Bronx was recently despatched to secure strategic bases in Iraq. Admittedly, early reports of this covert operation have been disappointing. Although a number of key bridges, power stations, etc., were success-fully neutralized, it seems that despite their extensive know-how the clampers destroyed major sections of infrastructure in the wrong country. Reports from Iran indicate significant levels of hostility were provoked by these private contractors blowing up the wrong nation. However, the former traffic officers were then able to bring all their experience to bear, refusing to enter into any dialogue or even make eye-contact with the so-called 'victims', and instead impassively filled out their paperwork before handing them a pro-forma letter explain-ing how to appeal against an allegedly erroneous carpet bombing.

Teething problems are to be expected, of course, but by out-sourcing military operations the Secretary of Defense will be freed up to concentrate on the more appropriate diplomatic work of central government, extending full spectrum dominance across the globe. It is not sufficient that the United Nations has been sidelined while there remain countless international organizations operating independently of American interests and security. It has come to our attention, for example, that every four years there takes place an event known as the Soccer World Cup, in which America has repeatedly been denied the freedom to field a team reflecting superior US economic and military strength. Instead FIFA has unilaterally decided that the US may only field just eleven players, the same number permitted to

Third World countries such as Brazil and France. Like the UN, FIFA cannot be permitted to dictate the rules of engagement where American participants are involved and English President Toby Blare has promised he will back a rule change permitting a quarter of a million US soccer players on the field at any one time. Similarly, the organizers of the Miss World competition will no longer be permitted to allow winners from non-compliant nation states. France will only be allowed to enter a man.

This will be a world in which opponents of liberty will be rendered inoperable. Enemies of free speech will be silenced. Iraq will be just the first country to benefit from the opportunity of reconstruction by US companies after the bombing has been completed. Saddam knows that our democratic ideals will not permit us to see his son installed as Iraqi leader. George Bush is against this and so was George Bush Snr when he was President. He cannot be permitted to cling to power without the democratic backing of his people. Saddam Hussein, that is, not George Bush.

Gary T. Bush is the nephew of the President and owns an emergent enterprise opportunity taking over the executions of prisoners in private penitentiaries in Texas and Florida.

garytbush@executions_r_us.com

McDonald's to go, please

11 April 2003

This was truly a historic week as a much hated regime finally seemed to lose its grip amid scenes of jubilation across the world. The McDonald's Information Minister, dressed in the official stripy uniform and proudly wearing the three stars that he received for managing to work in one of their restaurants for more than a month, appeared before the world's press angrily denying that the fast-food giant had finally lost the burger war. 'Our heroic leader Ronald McDonald has scored another momentous victory,' he declared as the famous Golden Arches came crashing to the ground behind him. 'Our glorious Egg McMuffins have never been more popular!' he shouted as the share price tumbled and outlets were being closed around the world.

Meanwhile, the whereabouts of Ronald McDonald himself remain a mystery. Some reports claim he may have died of heart failure after a lifetime of eating saturated burgers. Though the figurehead's iconic pictures are still displayed all across the crumbling McDonald's empire, many believe that it was a lookalike clown used in the recent propaganda film shown on Western television featuring him giving out balloons to young children. There is, of course, still much anxiety for the future. Huge reserves of oil can be found in their hamburgers and who knows what dangerous chemicals may yet be found when the inspectors go back into the restaurants. Ordinary McDonald's employees seemed dazed and confused in the midst of the crisis. Asked by a journalist if she could have evidence of the brutality of the regime, a pale and poorly fed looking young worker just stared blankly and said, 'Do you want fries with that?'

There is a rather satisfying symmetry that the most symbolic American corporate brand should be plunged into crisis just as the US army are reasserting the military dominance of the world's only superpower. You might say that it was a delicious irony, but that adjective doesn't really feel appropriate here. The more aggressively the old 'military-industrial complex' asserts the rights of US companies to trade around the world, the less the global consumer wants to hand them their cash. Hostility to the brand is such that earlier this week a bomb went off in a McDonald's in Beirut. It could have been really dangerous, but fortunately no one bought any Big Macs because a bomb went off. A few years ago there was an extended battle as the citizens of London NW3 attempted to prevent a branch of McDonald's opening in their neighbourhood. The Hampstead residents wanted something more useful in their High Street, like an antique clock restorer's.

The brand that says 'America' has lost its appeal. The world has taken a big bite of the American dream and is now feeling a bit queasy. In response to the first ever loss in its fifty-five-year history, the American fast-food giant has announced that it is going upmarket. So soon you'll be able to see teenagers hanging around in bus shelters eating McChateaubriand and McCaviar with their bare hands. Obviously, when the corporation say 'upmarket' they won't be going as far as indulging in unnecessary ostentatious extras such as cutlery. But in future you will get a better class of worm in your fillet of fish.

Despite the attempt at rebranding, the McDonald's share price has failed to recover. Maybe they should make the shares a bit more attractive by giving away little free gifts with them. Then embarrassed middle-class parents would say, 'Well, we wouldn't normally buy a stake in the McDonald's Corporation but little Timmy had been desperate for the wind-up plastic dinosaur . . .'

McDonald's remains the most potent symbol of the freedoms for which the American troops have been fighting these past few weeks.

The freedom of choice to have the same food served by the same corporation in every high street in the world. The only minor rules are that any employees attempting to form a union will be instantly sacked; any workers attempting to speak out against the corporation will be hit with massive lawsuits; and if you haven't got chronic acne, well, don't even think about applying for a job. Their fast-food mentality has spread to everything: US foreign policy is quick and easy and don't think about the consequences; 'Big Mac to go . . . fries to go . . . United Nations to go'. And despite closing hundreds of outlets in the West, McDonald's are still seeking to expand in the Third World and soon there will be very few cities in the world without a discarded vanilla shake splattered across the pavement. The West has got wise, so let's force the stuff down the throats of the rest of the world. So that's what this war was all about. Opening soon, McDonald's Restaurant, Al-Takhrir Square, Baghdad. Surely the Iraqis have suffered enough?

The thief of Baghdad

18 April 2003

The Baghdad branch of Neighbourhood Watch has been completely overwhelmed this week. 'If you notice anyone behaving in a vaguely suspicious manner, please contact the police immediately,' say their little signs on the lampposts, but these were all brazenly nicked along with everything else in the city that wasn't nailed down.

As the war stumbled to a confusing and chaotic end, lawlessness swept across the country as thousands of people helped themselves to computers, stereos and other electrical goods. Such is the state of anarchy in the country that many of them haven't even sent off the little guarantee postcards yet. Western leaders have been reluctant to condemn the looters, perhaps because the clamour for material goods is partly what this war was all about: bringing Western-style consumerism to a former Islamic 'socialist' republic. With sufficiently aggressive advertising, within a few weeks the rioters will become vaguely dissatisfied with that Sony Playstation they seized and will feel the urge to go out and loot the new Playstation 2 with integral DVD player.

Meanwhile, in Iraq's own version of *Supermarket Sweep*, the population have been fighting their way out of the stores with as much as they could carry (though there was a separate aisle for those looting eight items or less). Particularly popular were all the goods with special promotional stickers on: 'All this week – two for the price of none!' or 'Nick one – get another one free!' And then isn't it always the way – you load up the car with looted goods, check the wads of bank notes you grabbed when they said 'Do you want any cash back?', and then you realize you forgot to get your parking money back from the girl on the till.

In the traditional Arab markets, traders attempted to haggle with the mob as they eyed the various trinkets and souvenirs on display.

'That is a beautiful hand-carved statue, sir. That is one hundred dinar.'

'Hmmm . . . tell you what – I'll give you zero dinar for it.'

'All right, eighty dinar – I can't go lower than that, sir, look at the craftsmanship . . .'

'No, I think I'm going to stick with zero dinar actually,' said the looter as he brandished an old Russian machine gun.

'Um, well, you drive a hard bargain. Zero dinar is my final price – take it or take it.'

The former palaces of the Ba'ath leadership were also stripped, and the gold taps and erotic paintings are expected to fetch a fortune if anyone can transport them to Romford market. In wartime the media have a duty to convey a certain number of disturbing images, but showing us Saddam Hussein's taste in art is probably going too far. Snakes wrapping themselves around missiles being ridden by naked women – surely the artist will have to stand trial for crimes against humanity. I suppose he was just grateful for the work after he lost that job designing all those 1970s heavy-metal album covers.

Some commentators attempted to argue that this was the dispossessed taking back what was rightfully theirs – but the looting of the palaces probably had more to do with the mob knowing where all the best stuff would be. Once they'd symbolically pulled down one statue, they forgot about the politics and got on with helping themselves to as much gear as possible. Which is why their former dictator managed to hide so easily; in the midst of all the chaos, Saddam simply painted himself in metallic paint and is standing very, very still in a busy town square somewhere.

Gradually, it seems, some sort of order is being restored in the cities, with some stolen goods even being returned (although the

Baghdad branch of Marks and Spencer's are now refusing to exchange looted clothes for a different size). But just when we thought the lawlessness was over, even more blatant incidents of looting have begun out of sight of the television cameras. With handkerchiefs masking half their faces, two rioters roughly the height of George W. Bush and Donald Rumsfeld kicked in the gates of Iraq's largest oilfield and started to grab all the keys of the oil tankers. International onlookers were powerless to prevent the illegal behaviour of these heavily armed looters, and billions of dollars' worth of crude oil, gas and petroleum were seized, not to mention all the free glasses.

'Yee-haw! It's all ours!' laughed the bandits.

'Millions of barrels of the stuff! We can just help ourselves and no one can stop us!' shrieked the grey-haired one as he filled up the first tanker and headed for home.

'Yup, and this mask guarantees my anonymousinity!' said his leader.

So after all these years there really is such a person as the Thief of Baghdad. Except, strangely, his accent sounded vaguely Texan.

An American in Paris (in a Sherman tank)

25 April 2003

This week another dangerous dictatorship has been added to the 'Axis of Evil'. Forget Syria, North Korea and Iran; the next rogue state on the United States hit-list appears to be France. Colin Powell declared on Wednesday that France will have to 'face the consequences' of failing to back the United States on the UN Security Council and all-out war can now be only a matter of time.

A few weeks back, French fries were renamed 'freedom fries' – which is clearly a far more sensible choice than our awkward word 'chips'. Since then, American makers of French polish and French horns have gone bankrupt and teenage boys have been walking into pharmacies and plucking up courage to ask for 'freedom letters'. As Gallic food products are boycotted, exports of British cheeses to the US are up, with the finest Roqueforts and Camemberts being replaced by Asda's own-brand Microwavable Cheese Strings. No one can now say that the Americans haven't suffered as well.

'May I order the Châteauneuf-du-Pape?'

'I'm afraid not, sir, but we can offer you this British gooseberry Riesling as an alternative.'

Now an extensive UN dossier has been published giving detailed accounts of French abuses of human rights. There are disturbing reports of nonchalant shrugging by French waiters. CNN has broadcast astonishing footage of French bureaucrats actually being rude and obstructive to foreigners, though surely this must have been faked. American mothers have been appalled by photographs of French women having a glass of wine when pregnant, though there is also a certain amount of pity for a population forced to watch all those intellectual French films that won the *oeuf d'or* at the Bruges film festival. But what's really annoyed the Americans is the provocative way they eat all this fancy rich food and just don't seem to get fat. The French must fall into line with Western levels of obesity or face the consequences. George W. Bush is now drawing up a list of the most wanted Frenchmen, which so far names only Gerard Depardieu and Babar the Elephant.

Hostility between the United States and France goes back quite a few years. A lot of bad feeling was created by the Louisiana Purchase when Napoleon's estate agent managed to get the price up by claiming that there was another couple who were also very interested.

'They're bluffing,' said the American President, but Mrs Jefferson had fallen in love with the big garden with that pretty 2000-mile river frontage onto the Mississippi. 'I'm going to tell them that there's a few other properties that we're going to look at. I'll say we might decide to buy Florida off the Spanish instead . . .'

'But, darling, we could lose it altogether – and look at the estate agent's details: "A rare opportunity to purchase this eight hundred and twenty-eight thousand square mile estate with its own mountain range, plains, lakes and several outbuildings." Oh darling, can we, please, please, please . . .' she begged, staring at the picture in *Country Life*. But, of course, when they moved in it was nothing like the description: half of it was swamps and deserts, and the neighbours were unfriendly and kept threatening to scalp everyone. America sulked for a century and refused to forward all the mail. Then in 1966 President de Gaulle took France out of NATO and said all American troops should leave French soil. ('Does that include the dead ones?' quipped an American cynic at the time.) The US then had to find another way to install American service personnel there, and this was the origin of Disneyland Paris. It was very hard to argue with Ronald Reagan at the best of times, but when he had this idea that thousands of US marines should be stationed in Northern France hidden inside

Mickey Mouse and Goofy costumes, they thought he'd finally flipped. Battle-weary soldiers were kitted out in their new uniforms as Sneezy or Baloo the Bear. B52 pilots were retrained to man Space Mountain and the flying Dumbo ride, and amazingly the plan worked. The soldiers were delighted that the locals seemed to wave and cheer them every day as they rode past on the way to Sleeping Beauty's castle. Never before had US troops been hugged and photographed with their arms round the native population.

But all this is now set to change when these agents suddenly reveal themselves at the outset of America's cunning plan to bring about regime change in Paris. The bombing of French cities begins next month, although no doubt those obstinate French politicians will find some reason to object to this as well. All the White House seeks is a French President who'll back the United States, a leader who'll support America whatever its policies. No wonder Tony Blair's been having those extra French lessons.

Responsible owner sought for sawn-off shotguns

2 May 2003

The desk sergeant at Hackney police station is having a few days off. He has just had the most stressful month of his life – every day during the month-long gun amnesty he would look up from his paperwork to see hardened criminals striding through the front door brandishing automatic sub-machine guns.

'Excuse me?' they would shout, waving their Kalashnikov around at an apparently empty desk. 'Oi, mate, I can see you; it's no good crouching down there with a computer cover on your head . . .'

And the quivering sergeant would then stand up slowly with his hands in the air, having passed across his wallet and the keys to all the cells.

'No, I've come to hand my gun in – to put it in safe hands.'

And then various bystanders would say, 'So why are you giving it to the police then?'

The Home Office's gun amnesty ended this week with over 20,000 weapons handed in at police stations around the country. There were old shotguns, antique duelling pistols and a 1970s Johnny Seven with all the original plastic white bullets recovered from under the piano. However, much to the government's disappointment, at no time did an Iraqi man with a moustache wander in and hand over a few weapons of mass destruction that he'd forgotten were still lying around in his attic.

It seems a bit unfair that the criminals have been called to put their weapons permanently beyond use with no concessions whatsoever from the other side. Shouldn't the police be made to change their name or something? What about a truncheon amnesty? Or a promise to attempt to recruit more officers from the criminal community (no, on second thoughts there are quite enough already). The reality is, of course, that the weapons handed in were not from gangland killers but from law-abiding citizens who were getting increasingly uneasy about having Granddad's old Second World War revolver rattling around in that kitchen drawer with the garden twine and old Allen keys from Ikea. The idea that Interpol's most wanted villains were going to voluntarily walk into a police station was perhaps a little naïve.

'Excuse me, I was the mystery second gunman in the Kennedy assassination and I've been meaning to get rid of this vital clue for ages, so I thought "Where better than Scotland Yard?" '

'Right, many thanks, sir, just pop it there next to Abu Nidal's rocket launcher.'

'Um, that CCTV camera is definitely switched off, is it?'

'Oh yes, we're not at all interested in the fact that you happen to be a professional hit-man in the pay of organized crime. As long as we've got this old gun. Mind how you go now . . .'

Apparently drug dealers and gangsters were struggling to imagine such a scenario.

That's not to say that the gun amnesty was not worth doing. Every gun taken out of circulation makes this country a safer place. Of all the bills passed by this government, the ban on handguns was surely one of the most sensible and right. Having to choose between the risk of another Dunblane and a few sportsmen losing their pastime – there is simply no argument. And yet former handgun owners are still moaning that their human rights have been infringed. Why don't they just get another hobby? Take up macramé or making amusing novelty paperweights by sticking swivelly eyes on shiny pebbles or something? Gun ownership is simply not worth the risk. Fatal shootings committed by Americans are now higher than ever (particularly when unarmed Iraqi demonstrators happen to be in the vicinity).

The gun amnesty has been such a success that they are now thinking of repeating the exercise with other dangerous objects. Hospital casualty departments are pressing hard for a 'power tools amnesty'. Middle-class husbands who were given electric saws, high-speed drills and nail guns as Christmas presents and are too scared even to get them out of the packaging will soon be able to hand them in anonymously without risk of embarrassment.

In the meantime, the government is now left with the problem of what to do with thousands of knackered old revolvers and shotguns, so look out for a Junior Minister of Trade explaining that we only export such arms to Third World dictatorships who intend to use the weapons for peaceful purposes. Perhaps the firearms should be melted down to make a symbolic statue for the 'Lefty-Council Peace Garden'. When it was discussed in cabinet it transpired that many of the guns are rusted up or jammed.

'Perfect,' said the Minister of Defence. 'Then why don't we just issue them to Britain's front-line soldiers?'

Testing, testing . . .

9 May 2003

This week a headteacher was reprimanded for cheating during his pupils' SATS exams. He was made to wait outside the office of the General Teaching Council and when he was finally told to enter, he knew he was in really big trouble because his mum and dad had been called in too.

'We're not angry with you, David, just disappointed . . .' said the officials. 'You know, you're only cheating yourself, aren't you?'

And the disgraced headteacher mumbled 'Yes, miss' while staring open-mouthed at the floor.

This month hundreds of thousands of pupils will be sitting SATS tests, and teachers will have to find more sophisticated ways of improving their school's performance. As their pens hover over the multiple-choice questions, pupils will suddenly hear some carefully timed coughing from the headteacher looking over their shoulder. Despite the fact that the vast majority of teachers are against the national testing of seven-, eleven- and fourteen-year-olds, the government refuses to abolish Standardized Assessment Tests. Because let's face it, without SATS we would have no way of discovering which schools are concentrating on the SATS. Without these tables we'd never know that those middle-class kids at the village school in Surrey were doing much better than children who had English as a second language in that run-down estate in Tower Hamlets.

This is surely the whole point of academic league tables. Parents of the posh kids got fed up with their kids losing football matches 13–0 to the tough boys from the school on the estate, so another sort of league table was devised where they wouldn't always come last. Of course, more progressive newspapers like the *Guardian* print the schools in alphabetical order so as not to imply any sort of order of merit, although Aardvark Primary in Abbas Coombe still boasts about being top. (Arsenal have just contacted the sports desk to see if they might adopt the same policy for the Premiership.)

Apart from the undoubted stress placed on staff and pupils, the tables are misleading because there are so many variables that generally do not get taken into account. For example, in one–class–entry schools each child represents over 3 per cent, so a few low-achieving pupils in a particular year group can make it seem as if the school has slipped back drastically in twelve months. Say just four children in a class of thirty had numeracy problems, then that's four times 3.3 recurring, which makes, um, twelve, no, thirteen point something – er, well, anyway, these numeracy skills are overrated.

Many liberal middle classes are instinctively against testing children at such a young age: 'Oh, I mean, it's ridiculous, putting children under that much pressure,' they say, as they drive their children round to the private tutors. 'I mean, there's enough pressure on children already. Jennifer's got her grade four cello test, her gymkhana, ballet, Brownies and bridge lessons – frankly, school ought to be the one chance they have to relax a bit.' You see these over-keen parents running behind their children in places like the Science Museum. As their kids are maniacally pressing buttons and pulling levers, Mummy and Daddy are standing behind them desperately attempting to précis the explanatory notes: 'You see, darling, that's called "refraction" and there, you see the light breaking into different colours, that's because um . . .' But it's too late, because little Timothy has already dashed off and is barging his little sister off the plasma lamp. At least if the government introduced tests for neurosis we could guarantee those scores would get higher every year.

Maybe it would be fairer if children were able to choose the subjects on which they were tested. Ofsted reports would be far more positive: 'Students were stimulated and focused with a majority of them attaining Level Seven or higher in Mortal Kombat on their Nintendo GameBoys. There was also genuine progress amongst the boys in the standard DFES test for seeing who could wee the highest.'

It seems that the only way to make things fair would be to introduce testing and league tables for government ministers. Critics of this idea might argue that it would only increase stress for our front-benchers, and that ministers' mums and dads might have them tutored in advance. 'It takes no account of the intake,' they'll say. 'How can a working–class kid like John Prescott be expected to do as well at verbal reasoning as a privately educated pupil like Tony Blair?' And what would it do for the morale of ministers, to see themselves near the bottom of the cabinet league table just because they failed a minor numeracy test such as balancing their departmental budget?

'Okay, we'll have to publish the cabinet league tables in alphabetical order,' says Tony Blair. 'Oh, and tell Hilary Armstrong she's sacked . . .'

Halal Dolly

16 May 2002

It's always the same in every group: there's always one bloody leftie stirring things up and spoiling the atmosphere for everyone else. Take Britain's farms, for example – apparently there's one cow going around claiming that the humans keep animals so they can sell them for slaughter.

'It's true, I tell you, the farmer gets paid to let other humans murder us all,' she says, failing to sell a single copy of her radical newspaper as all the other animals wink at each other because the nutter with the conspiracy theories is off again.

'Don't be ridiculous, Daisy, humans like animals; why would they want to murder us?'

'Well, um, look, I know it sounds outlandish, but they kill us because, well, they like to eat our flesh . . .'

At which point the other cows and sheep fall about laughing and shake their heads in pity at this demented individual who has to bring politics into everything. 'Yeah, sure thing, Trotsky. And I suppose they like to rip off our skins and wear them on their own bodies as well?'

But of course the reality gets worse than that. The biggest growth area in the British meat market is for halal meat; that is, meat from sheep and chickens that have been ritually slaughtered by having their throats cut until they bleed to death. This is not a pleasant sight and a visit to the halal abattoir is not recommended for the infants school trip. But now a government-funded committee is expected to conclude that traditional Islamic methods of slaughter are inhumane. The timing of this judgement could not be better, because clearly Britain's Muslims are nowhere near alienated enough at the moment.

'Okay, so the UK has supported Israel, bombed Iraq, elected BNP councillors – how about outlawing halal meat as well?'

'Hmm, yes, that'll go down well at the mosque.'

This moral conundrum goes right to the heart of what it means to live in a multicultural society. There are many things that British WASPs do not understand about other religious traditions. Like where in the Koran does it state that Muslims must have ornate gold tissue-box holders in the back of the Datsun? Or, when the Jewish scriptures sensibly forbade the eating of pork or prawns, why didn't God add the codicil 'until you invent the fridge'? But this impending report from the Farm Animals Welfare Council looks set to cause well-meaning *Guardian* readers to implode with liberal angst.

'So you are against the traditions of Islam, are you?'

'No, of course not, the kids learn all about Eid at school . . .'

'Oh, so you're in favour of cruelty to animals then?'

'Er no, we're against fox hunting . . .'

'But it's okay if it's done by Muslims?'

'Um, yes, I mean no, look I must dash, I promised the kids chicken curry for tea. Free range, obviously . . .'

Until now I've always wondered who those wet people were that always answered 'Don't know' to every survey. 'Are you part of the twenty per cent of the population that always answers "Don't know" to everything?' 'Er, dunno.' 'Do you think some people are perhaps too lacking in confidence to offer any opinions on current affairs?' 'Er, dunno . . .' Suddenly this seems like rather an attractive camp to be in. Whoever has to make the final decision on this one will cause enormous offence to one group or other. Of all the topics guaranteed to get the British public writing angry letters, the most potent are religion and cruelty to animals; so maybe this is all an elaborate scam designed to save the Post Office.

There are examples where opposing moralities clash when I would not be so hesitant. If a child was likely to die because its parents were

Jehovah's Witnesses and were refusing a blood transfusion on religious grounds, I'd argue, as sensitively as possible, that the state should step in and overrule that particular religious doctrine (oh, and tell the parents to get back to the Planet Quargon). But halal meat is more blurred, partly because however the creature is slaughtered we're still talking about the moment of death, when surely it is the farm animal's quality of life up to that point which is the bigger issue. We cannot call ourselves a multi-faith society and then only tolerate the aspects of other religions that match our Western liberal values. Halal slaughter sounds horrible and cruel, and when you think about it almost enough to make you have the vegetable biriyani. But many animals are in fact stunned before the blood is drained away to produce what Muslims maintain is the most hygienic meat available. If we are to be genuinely tolerant and inclusive, we have to be extremely certain before we go dictating our mix-and-match morality to other cultures about what they eat or how they prepare their food. I believe we should let sleeping dogs lie. Even in Korean restaurants.

Sunday Dads

20 May 2003

The problem of fathers who don't spend enough time with their families is an issue throughout the animal kingdom. The worker bee, for example, spends all his time out with his mates supping pollen, while the poor queen bee is stuck inside producing around 100,000 eggs a week. No doubt when she was younger she had all these plans about travelling and starting a career, but then one day she had an egg, and then three seconds later she had another one, and suddenly she found herself trapped in the hive, feeling fat and fed up and stuffing her face with royal jelly all day.

After billions of years of evolution, however, *Homo sapiens* has finally reached the stage where the male is occasionally prepared to get more involved in the care of the little ones. Some of the more advanced men relish this opportunity, but for most it is something they do reluctantly and as infrequently as possible. This sub-species is known as the Sunday Dad. He spends time with his kids once a week and, according to my wife, even then he has an ulterior motive. 'Typical male!' she says. 'He's only looking after them to get out of clearing up after lunch.'

You see these Sunday Dads looking lost in public parks, pushing the baby's buggy with only one hand to give the impression that it's not actually theirs, that they're simply looking after it for someone. Just as less socially aware dog owners pretend not to notice when the Great Dane on the end of their lead leaves a pile of dog mess that can be seen by passing aircraft, the Sunday Dad will try to make out that those noisy children clutching his leg and shouting 'Daddy!' are nothing to do with him. Sometimes his determination to ignore his kids reaches heroic proportions. He may be sitting in a ball pit, with his offspring screaming and throwing brightly coloured plastic balls at his head, but he will still give the impression that this is a perfectly normal place for an adult to go and read the Sunday papers. Wherever he is with his children, his mind is somewhere else.

Of course what he's really afraid of is embarrassment. His affected detachment is his way of appearing cool. For if he was to throw himself fully into playing with his kids, the rest of the world might see that he's not actually very good at it. When it came to learning how to deal with the children his wife somehow seemed to have a head start on him. This made it easier to take a back seat, and so the gap in their childcare skills grew even wider. At a dinner table he always sat wherever it would be impossible for him to get out when the children needed seeing to. During the night he pretended to be asleep when his wife went to the crying baby for the fourth time. And now he might try to justify all this to himself by imagining that he works very hard; but deep down he knows that it's easier to be rushing about looking important than sitting in a freezing cold playground being bored out of your head pushing a swing for the four thousandth time.

It is often the case that the more successful a man is at work, the less use he is in the home. He gets so wrapped up in his job, he forgets to give a second thought to what his wife and children are up to. When Neil Armstrong touched down on the moon, he said to Mission Control, 'The Eagle has landed! Oh and Houston, will you call my wife and tell her I won't be home for dinner tonight.' The career high-flier who works long hours is also used to getting his own way and having everyone do as he says. But this cuts no ice with his two-year-old and so the Sunday Dad gets a bit of a shock when his toddler lies down on the floor, kicking and screaming and shouting 'No!' to every suggestion or demand. Maybe his secretary should try that sometimes.

As they get older the kids soon learn that Dad doesn't really have the faintest idea what they're not allowed, and so he'll find himself coming back from the shops and then getting all defensive with his wife: 'Well, how was I to know that the kids aren't allowed flame-throwers?' The only other shopping that the Sunday Dad has to do with the kids is choosing a present for Mummy's birthday. Every year he will suddenly realize that he has left it too late and that the only place still open is the petrol station. That's when he can be spotted dragging the kids around the Texaco mini-mart trying to decide if Mummy would prefer a packet of barbecue briquettes, some Castrol GTX or a polythene-wrapped copy of *Penthouse*.

Sunday Dads are physically absent six days of the week and mentally absent for all seven. But rather than try to change their worker bee husbands, perhaps their wives ought to look at the example of another insect – the praying mantis. The female of this species has learned to tackle the problem of the absent male head on. She chooses the father of her children, mates with him just the once and then eats him. Apparently this approach goes quite a long way in tempering the resentment than can build up in a marriage. My wife, however, still feels it does not go far enough. 'Typical male,' she said. 'He's not there when it's time to clear up after dinner either.'

I don't want spam!

22 May 2003

Millions of men in Britain are getting private e-mail messages suggesting they might want to have their penises enlarged. 'How did they know?' they are thinking. 'Who told them? Was it Janice in accounts after last year's Christmas party? That's not fair, I was drunk and it was cold on that fire escape . . .' Of course part of them suspects this is just another bit of 'spam', the unsolicited junk e-mail that is swamping the net, but they're not going to shout about it just in case. Perpetrators of these scams must depend on this sort of embarrassment. If the operation went horribly wrong, you're not going to go on BBC's *Watchdog* and say, 'Okay, it used to be small but at least it worked. But now, Kate, just look at what a botch job they made of it . . .' And so unscrupulous businesses have continued to bombard our electronic in-boxes with offers of Viagra, free passwords to internet porn sites and the offer of tickets for the new Cliff Richard musical.

Spam is the small-ads section of the global village newspaper. And yesterday Yahoo predicted that soon it will overtake the number of normal e-mails flying around cyberspace. Just as the small ads of a local rag reveal what its readership is really thinking about (Answer: Sex and Money), so the most common junk e-mail messages offer hard-core pornography and confidential money transfers out of

Nigeria. It's hard to know which is more depressing, the baseness of human nature that this reveals or the stupidity of all the greedy people who fall for these scams. 'Wow, what a fantastic offer! I transfer $200 to this overseas bank account and they pay off all my credit card debts! I can't see how this could possibly go wrong!' If I want to spend hundreds of pounds for absolutely nothing in return, I'll stick to holistic healing, thank you very much.

Of course the problem of unsolicited mail is nothing new. When the Penny Post started in 1840, masked highwaymen would hold up the mail coach and go through all the letters to see what goodies they might steal. 'Ha-harrr! What do we have here, Black Bess? Hmm, offers to apply for a new type of credit card and forty-seven Boden catalogues. Damn!' And now, in the twenty-first century, electronic mail involves so many hours' sorting through all the junk that frankly you'd be better off popping that letter into a pillar box. Computer programmes have been designed to randomly mix letters and numbers which are then combined with Internet Service Providers. For example, there's bound to be a billgates1@hotmail.com; in fact, I think this was the very first e-mail account ever set up. And then Bill just sat at his computer for a few weeks feeling vaguely disappointed every time he checked his e-mails.

It's estimated that spam currently costs businesses £9 billion a year, although I can never quite understand how they work these figures out. The presumption is that if people weren't wasting their time deleting e-mails, they'd be hard at work increasing company profits. In fact, they'd only be wasting their time with some other mindless computer diversion, like playing Minesweeper or entering their own name on Google and then being slightly indignant that there are lots of other David Smiths around the world.

However, not content with being at war with drugs and terrorism, America has now declared war on spam as well. Last month the state of Virginia (home of AOL) outlawed the sending of unsolicited e-mails, making it a Class 6 felony carrying a five-year prison term (or ten years for anyone who on hearing the word 'spam' starts to recite the Monty Python sketch). The new law also gives the state the right to seize the assets of these companies, which is how the Governor explained all those boxes of Viagra that his secretary found in the filing cabinet. There remains the slight problem that the internet is no respecter of national borders or regional laws, but if those Russian gangsters did ever decide to move to Virginia and go public about their business practices they could be in serious trouble. Opponents claim that this law is in breach of America's sacred First Amendment, 'Congress shall make no law abridging the freedom of speech, or of the press; or the right of the people to send out thousands of e-mails an hour offering live web-cams of group sex featuring pre-op transsexuals.' But other US states and EU governments look set to follow and then they will tell all the computer users of the world about their new legal rights and these new protections. And we'll see this historic message in our in-box and think, 'Well, that looks dodgy, I'm deleting that one for starters . . .'

Life on Mars?

6 June 2003

'Cinque . . . vier . . . tres . . . two . . . un! Nous avons eine lift-off!'
Agreeing the language for the countdown of the European Mars
Express was always going to require a degree of compromise. During
the research period they realized that the rocket would actually be too
heavy to get off the ground unless they got rid of that manual printed
in all thirty-seven European dialects. But in the end this week's launch
was a magnificent example of European co-operation and every
country agreed on one thing: that it was their own scientists who had
made the greatest contribution to this success. What's more, this milestone shows that Europe now rivals the United States when it comes
to space exploration. 'The idea that European rocket technology is not
as advanced as the Americans' is a patronizing slur,' said the chief
scientist as he stood the rocket up in the giant milk bottle before lighting the blue touchpaper with his little glowing joss stick. Then as
Beagle 2 roared away into the night sky, TV science correspondents
ended their reports by wondering if we would finally discover the
answer to that age-old question, 'Is there life on Mars?' And back in
the studio the editor shouted, 'Okay – and cue track 3, side one of
Hunky Dory by David Bowie!'

For centuries mankind has been fascinated by the possibility that
life might exist on our neighbouring planet. 'Earth and Mars

exchanged material in the early days when life was forming on Earth,' said Mark Adler of the US space agency this week. 'Was Mars part of our past? Maybe we are the Martians!' he added, at which point people edged away from him nervously, trying not to make eye-contact. There was a surge of speculation about life on the red planet in the 1950s, mostly involving low-budget black-and-white films with wobbly sets, papier mâché masks and thinly veiled allegories of the threat of communism. Then the first unmanned craft landed on Mars in the 1970s, an era which set the standard for the technology and the scientists' fashion sense. But when Beagle 2 touches down in six months' time the search for evidence of life will begin in earnest. A special robot has been programmed to roam around the planet turning over rocks and then going all squeamish when lots of little creepy-crawlies scurry away. If the European space probe does in fact discover some form of life on the planet, then Mars is expected to join the European Union in 2006. 'Take me to your leader!' the Martians will say and we'll have to explain that there is no overall leader as such, nor any formal constitution as yet, but greater economic and legal harmonization has been achieved outside a federal framework. Of course, any life forms that may be discovered are not expected to be very intelligent, but to have the IQ of an amoeba or someone who sends off money for a genuine piece of Martian space rock as advertised on the internet.

This ought to be a mission to inspire our imaginations, but there are plenty of us on the left who are instinctively cynical about any sort of technological breakthrough. And this because, underneath it all, there's a vague suspicion that all science is somehow a bit right wing. That everything from double Physics on Thursday afternoons to man landing on the moon is the sort of nerdy boys' stuff that ought to be automatically sneered at by any self-respecting old leftie. Never mind that science has brought us the cure to countless diseases and clean water and warm homes and laser-jet printers that work almost 50 per cent of the time; the bottom line is that the kids who wanted chemistry sets for Christmas were not the ones wearing 'Rock Against Racism' badges or going on the CND marches; indeed they could probably only see nuclear explosions as a fascinating cosmic phenomenon. So for generations on the British left there has been a lazy hostility to any major scientific achievement, whether it was cloning a sheep or keeping Margaret Thatcher's hair fixed in place.

'What are they going to Mars for? They should give that money to the health service!' we say.

'But this project is being paid for by business sponsorship . . .'

'Oh, typical! They're even privatizing space now!'

But we should fight our cynicism about the motives for this mission; we should not use space exploration as another stick with which to beat our governments. I for one look forward to the day the probe begins to burrow beneath the surface of our neighbouring planet, seeing what lies beneath those far-off Martian rocks and craters. In any case, they've looked everywhere else for Iraq's weapons of mass destruction and this is the last place left.

United Nations Closing Down Sale

13 June 2003

Hans Blix had never planned to be a United Nations weapons inspector. But when he filled out one of those multiple-choice questionnaires at school, ticking off all his interests and qualifications, that's just what came out of the computer. His sister got 'nurse', his brother got 'engine driver' and Hans got 'United Nations weapons inspector'. That'll teach him just to tick all the boxes at random as a joke.

Hans Blix is stepping down from his controversial post at the UN, but just before he packs away his souvenir Baghdad shaky snow scene he has broken with the usual niceties of diplomatic language to attack the current US administration. Claiming that he was smeared by 'bastards' within the Pentagon, he added that there are hawks within the Bush regime who would like to see the United Nations 'sink into the East River'. 'I believe that there were consistent efforts to undermine me,' he told reporters, as Donald Rumsfeld stood behind him tapping his forehead and miming that Hans had gone completely gaga.

Hans's leaving card is already being passed around the Pentagon and one or two of the comments certainly reveal a slight hostility towards the retiring diplomat. 'Sorry you are leaving the United Nations, Hans. THAT'S IF YOU CAN FIND THE GODDAM DOOR TO YOUR OFFICE!!' or 'Hope you like your present, Hans, though I expect you'll get a bigger one from your buddy Saddam.'

Since he first went out to Iraq with his *Observer's Book of Weapons of Mass Destruction* Hans Blix found himself to be a target for both sides in the dispute. Republican hawks felt that Blix was not doing his job properly because he failed to exaggerate the threat posed by Saddam Hussein. If they'd had their way he would have gone into the Baghdad marketplace urging reporters to wear helmets and protective clothing before they approached the fruit and vegetable stall. 'Look at this – a weapon of mass destruction cunningly disguised as a grapefruit. Plus anthrax cluster bombs in the shape of bananas. And look at these blackcurrants; if thrown at someone with sufficient force these could ruin a perfectly good white shirt.'

Meanwhile the Iraqi government said that Blix was 'a homosexual who went to Washington every two weeks to receive his instructions'. This is of course completely untrue. His office was in New York. Blix says that he used to laugh off all these various smears when he told his wife about them, but constant attacks can get to you eventually.

'Darling, did you find the TV remote control?'

'LISTEN, I HAVEN'T FOUND IT YET, ALL RIGHT!!' he snapped. 'It's not under the sofa cushions or behind the telly. I think it may have been destroyed or buried in the desert somewhere.'

With only a few weeks before he steps down, the United Nations has just set up a committee to organize Hans's leaving party and they are expected to publish a preliminary 500,000-word feasibility study in 2009. Bush is looking forward to Blix's retirement because he is planning to combine the event with a surprise leaving party for the rest of the UN staff as well.

'Leaving party? I didn't know we were leaving?'

'That's the surprise!' says George.

For 2003 is the year that the United Nations died. The most revealing thing about Blix's interview is his assertion that the Bush administration saw the UN as an alien power. There is no place for the UN in Dubya's new world order and henceforth the United Nations will be bypassed or disregarded. To get a sense of the crisis you only have to look at the last debate in that famous chamber: Motion 762/a – 'Is the United Nations being ignored?' Well, what does the American representative have to say about this?

'Er, he's not here, Mr Chair – he said he had some shopping to do.'

'Oh. All right, what about the British delegate?'

'Er, well, he's not here either. I think he's carrying the shopping . . .'

The last few remaining delegates never heard any of this anyway; they were trying to surpass their high scores on 'Snake' on their mobile phones.

With the UN being ignored to death, Dubya's secret plan will have worked and the organization will be formally wound up. Hundreds of unemployed translators will be cast onto the streets of New York, saying, 'Excuse me, can you spare some change please? Excusez-moi, avez vous de la monnaie? Scusi, posso avere dei soldi per favore?' And brash posters will be slapped all over the historic building that offered the world so much hope in 1945. 'United Nations – Closing Down Sale! Everything must go! International law, global security and US accountability! We've gone crazy! Third World aid – slashed! Development programmes, going fast! Hurry, hurry, hurry! It's the biggest sell-out in history!'

Open all hours

20 June 2003

A few months back a subcommittee of MPs was given the important job of researching the effects of twenty-four-hour drinking. Pretty soon it became apparent that they'd slightly misunderstood their brief, as they staggered back into the Culture Secretary's office singing 'Dancing Queen' by Abba and trying not to giggle when Tessa got all cross.

'I tell you what, Tess, you're a fit bird. No, seriously, if I wasn't already married, you and me . . . Hang on, I think I'm going to be sick.'

'You were supposed to be taking evidence. Didn't you talk to anyone?'

'Actually yeah, we talked to this bloke Brian in the Rose and Crown, and he reckoned that Hitler, right, well Hitler was working for MI5 all along. Have you got any beers in the fridge?'

Yesterday the Licensing Bill progressed to the House of Lords and very soon public houses will be able to stay open all hours of the day and night. Pubs will introduce the 'Breakfast Special': a can of Tuborg Extra Strong Lager in a brown paper bag for anyone with missing teeth and a gash on their forehead. No longer when the film ends at 10.55pm will you feel the urge to climb over that film buff who sits there watching all six minutes of credits.

The concern had been that the old hours brought problems of drunkenness and violence on the street at a particular time in the evening, but now this will be able to continue all night long. The bill also tightens up a loophole which had made it legal for under-eighteens to still buy alcohol on planes, which had often meant that there was none left for the pilot. The Licensing Bill is a pre-emptive step to stop all-out war breaking out between drinkers and bar staff at twenty past eleven. For years tension has been building as publicans adopted a new policy of 'shock and awe chucking-out time'. At one second past the legal drinking-up period, relaxed drinkers witnessed all the candles suddenly being extinguished and 4000-watt blinding arc lights being activated as all doors were wedged wide open and an arctic wind machine was turned on. Any hope of a last sip of your beer slipped away as weapons of mass disinfectant were sprayed over all the tables.

But this new bill should not just limit itself to the hours that bars are open; it should include a whole raft of reforms to Britain's public houses. Apart from the obviously annoying things like unfunny new pub names and tellies left permanently on in the corner of the bar, we should also demand the banning of novelty signs on the toilet doors saying 'Sires' and 'Wenches'. No more Motown's Greatest Hits end-lessly played on a tape loop and the abolition of the abbreviation 'n' instead of 'and' on pub menus. I always get a strange look from bar staff when I make a point of asking for the chicken pie AND chips, please. And names of British beers also need reforming; for some reason they always evoke Tolkein, the war and pre-decimal currency: 'Olde Baggins Bulldog Stout', 'Dragon's 80 Shilling Spitfire Ale', 'Olde Imperial Beardy Bitter', 'Big Fat Boring Bastard Ale'.

Of course, an increase in pub bores could well be the disastrous unforeseen consequence of this legislation. If we are going to have more drinking, publicans should be given the right to stop serving people when they have got too boring. In fact, it should be illegal to be 'drunk and uninteresting in a public place'. Police should be given powers to do random bore tests.

'Excuse me, sir, I saw you come out of that pub and you are talking very loudly. Can you say something into this machine please?'

'No, listen, like, Sir Alf Ramsey, right, he would have put Beckham up front, alongside Geoff Hurst . . .' An offence like this could result in a six-month court order, banning the offender from talking about the Kennedy assassination, classic cars or the greatest all-time England XI.

We have an immature attitude to drink in this country which needs urgent attention. People will describe their Saturday nights with the phrase, 'It was hilarious, we got completely pissed!' which I would propose is a highly subjective analysis. People drink to get drunk, and then make complete idiots of themselves. Not that this would ever have happened in the Palace of Westminster, of course, the one place where the bars were always open all hours. I suppose those bars will be closing earlier now that the Commons finishes at a civilized hour. And suddenly MPs are voting to have twenty-four-hour drinking in the pubs outside. Ah, now it all makes perfect sense.

Going for a song

27 June 2003

When the worldwide web first began to take off, no one had quite anticipated the degree to which this new resource would be used by millions of very sad men to access such appalling and depressing material.

When their family were all tucked up in bed, these middle-aged anoraks would furtively log on to the internet and then nervously click on the file entitled 'Phil Collins' Greatest Hits'. 'Can people at the other end tell my identity?' they fretted as they downloaded 'Lyin' Eyes' by The Eagles. 'What happens if I have to take my computer into PC World to be repaired – will they be able to tell that I've been accessing sites featuring the music of Gary Glitter?'

The swapping of music files on the internet has become so commonplace that this week the record industry announced it is going to sue individuals who download pirated tracks. It is a terrifying threat that has put fear into music lovers around the world: 'I know there are hundreds of millions of you and you're all impossible to identify, but you'd better watch out because one of you is going to get a lawsuit.'

The multi-nationals who run the music industry have obviously made this announcement in the hope that it will help turn public opinion against the digital music pirates. Imagine the scene outside the courtroom: with a blanket over his head the defendant is rushed between the crash barriers as he is jeered and spat at by the angry mob, who are filled with hatred at this flagrant breach of copyright laws.

'You bastard! You don't even care about Time Warner's profit margin! You should rot in hell!'

The trial itself will go on for months. First the jury will have to listen to all the music on the defendant's computer, doing their best to tap their feet cheerily and gently sway in unison to the DJ Hype remix of 'Smack My Bitch Up'. Then in order to verify a particular song's composers and its year of release, the judge will be passed a copy of the *Guinness Book of Hit Singles*. This is guaranteed to waste hundreds of hours of the court's time.

'Goodness, I never realized The Troggs had a number one hit with "Girl Like You".'

'Yes, if you could just turn back to the song in question, your honour . . .'

'Well I never – Smokie got to number five with "Living Next Door To Alice" . . .'

The greedy record industry only has itself to blame for the current situation. By forcing us to switch to CDs and buy our albums all over again, they laid the foundations for music's digital revolution, which they now find themselves unable to control. Did they care about the death of the vinyl LP and those millions of pounds of student grants that we spent in vain? Did they think about the dilemma of forty-somethings, faced with nowhere to store their old album collection now that the loft is being converted? And just what are young people supposed to roll their joints on these days?

Of course, music piracy has been happening ever since the very first teenager got out his crayons to try to recreate the cover of *Dark Side of the Moon* on a little piece of card to slot inside the plastic cassette case. So let he who is without a compilation tape throw the first stone. But the problem for the record companies is that now it's got so quick and easy. All you have to do is log on to the internet, go to one of the music-sharing sites and run a search on the track you want. Oh hang on, it's saying do I want to download kazaa media desktop v2.5 or v2.2 – what does that mean? 'Windows Media Player Not Configured' – well, how do I do that? I'll look in 'Help' – 'Ensure file extension is specified'? Good point. Er, what the bloody hell are they talking about?

The legality is a little easier to understand. The record industry are correct when they describe this practice as theft. And yet it's hard to feel even the mildest pang of sympathy. Perhaps it might be different if they'd ever shown any qualms about ripping off their customers or indeed any emerging musical talent.

If the record companies do win their first lawsuit they'll expect to be awarded millions of pounds of damages. But if there was any real justice they would then be handed a cheque for a mere hundred quid.

'What's this?' they'd say in astonishment.

'Ah, yeah, well, we had to deduct the money for your limos, publicity expenses, hotel bills, agents' fees and everything, and this is all that's left, honest. Now don't make a song and dance about it, guys. Because we held on to the copyright.'

The plane to Spain flies mainly over Staines

1 July 2003

After September 11th no planes flew over Britain's cities for three days. Nobody was woken up at five o'clock in the morning, and then again at 5.17am, finally drifting off only to be woken at six by their partner elbowing them in the ribs and saying, 'Listen to that one, that's the loudest one yet!' In all the theories about September 11th no one seemed to consider the possibility that maybe Osama Bin Laden lived in Hounslow and was just that desperate for a few nights' decent kip.

After a ruling this week in the European Court of Human Rights, the millions of Britons who live under the major flight paths will no longer be woken up by jumbo jets at 5.30 in the morning. This is because they won't have got to sleep in the first place; the planes are going to be allowed to roar overhead in the middle of the night. The court ruling agreed with the British government that to block the increased demand for all those businessmen who want to land at British airports would be detrimental to our national economic interest. Yup, it is simply vital to Britain's prosperity that there is no reduction in the number of blokes flying off to Dublin for stag week-ends, drinking too much and then puking up in O'Connell Street. Air travel is simply too important to our economy for us to limit the number of flights for lonely middle-aged men going to Bangkok.

It's only a hundred years since the Wright Brothers first got a rickety plane off the ground, while their sister wheeled the drinks trolley down the aisle and offered them the chance to purchase a duty-free teddy bear pilot and a giant Toblerone. Since then, air companies have become big business, with no government having the courage to clip their wings, as it were. Chris Mullin said that when he was at the Department of Transport he learned two things. Firstly that the airlines' demands are insatiable and, secondly, that they always get whatever they want. There was actually a third thing, but no one could hear him because a plane went overhead. When flight paths are drawn up they make sure that the planes go out of their way to disturb the maximum number of people possible. 'This is your captain speaking; time in London is 5.23am and we're just passing over Barnes. Unfortunately we did spot one or two homes where people didn't switch on their bedroom lights as we passed overhead, so we're going to have to go round again just to make sure.' Next there'll be a camp air steward ringing on every doorbell, waking us up with a little tray of congealed egg and two button mushrooms.

The skies have got so busy that now the radio traffic news has someone in a car looking up and reporting where the worst congestion is. The burning of aircraft fuel is a major contributor to greenhouse gases, but unlike petrol it remains untaxed. Next time you're in the duty-free shop trying to find a present for grandma that doesn't look like you got it at the airport on the way home, look out for that pilot buying a thousand gallons of duty-free aircraft fuel. Ever-increasing air travel means more noise, more pollution, more runways and, worst of all, more opportunities for Richard Branson to get his face on television.

The Minister for Transport should be meeting up with his opposite numbers across Europe to find ways to reduce the amount of traffic in the air. It'll mean dozens of ministers, with all their civil servants and translators, flying to Brussels on a regular basis – hang on, that's not going to work. If the government are not going to dampen down the demand for air travel then we will have to do it ourselves. Next time you are on a plane and the air hostess gives the safety demonstration, put your hand up and ask questions. 'Yeah, just going back to that bit about "in the event of an emergency landing on water . . ." How does that work exactly then? 'Cos you'd think the plane would just sink, wouldn't you?' Or when she demonstrates the oxygen masks dropping down, say, 'But what if we are all on fire? Wouldn't oxygen just make the flames worse?' Or before you get on the plane, when hordes of anxious travellers are lining up at the check-in desk, try walking along the queue shouting 'Anyone here flying to Marbella?' while dressed as the Grim Reaper.

Somebody has to stand up to the air companies. Whenever they look like they might not get everything they want, they either use 'Britain's economic interest' or, failing that, they'll play the 'safety' card. No wonder every passenger is supplied with a sick bag. They are interested in profit above all else, however much pollution or misery they cause to millions. I don't know how those airline bosses sleep at night. I suppose their answer would be simple: 'Well, we don't live under the flight path, obviously.'

Independence Day

4 July 2003

Among the brightly coloured bits of plastic at the bottom of a toy box in my house I recently came across a little plastic doll. It was a miniature Barbie that had been free at McDonald's, and in tiny writing on the back it said 'Made in Vietnam'. It sort of left me wondering who'd actually won the Vietnam War. One generation endured the heaviest bombardment in history and succeeded in driving out the world's most powerful army in order that their children could be free to sit in a sweatshop making little Aryan Barbie dolls to be given out free with a McDonald's Happy Meal.

Today is Independence Day in the United States, when Americans celebrate the day that they broke free from Britain. The final straw had been the enforcement of the Penal Acts, which had been passed so that two hundred years later teenage boys would giggle in history lessons. If today's British government had found themselves at war with the Americans they would have been very confused. 'Er, right, but can we still be on the same side as you anyway?' Re-reading the famous Declaration of Independence makes you realize what far-sighted men those first American politicians were: 'We hold these truths to be self-evident, that all men are created equal, that they are endowed by their Creator with certain unalienable Rights, that among these are Life, Liberty and the pursuit of Happiness. Oh and the right to put American bases in over a hundred independent countries, organize fascist coups to install pro-American puppet regimes, stifle free trade if it's not in US economic interests and force children everywhere to watch a schmaltzy purple dinosaur called Barney.'

But American imperialism is a lot more complex and subtle than the version that they themselves threw off a couple of centuries ago. For example, they have ruthlessly taken over our cinemas with the calculated and cynical trick known as 'making better films than we do'. And the British computer industry could never really compete with Microsoft; tragically, that abacus factory has closed down now. Sharing a language means our culture is even more open to colonization. My laptop tells me 'Your battery is running low' in an electronic Seattle accent. If French and German computers have their PCs talk to them in their own tongue, we should insist on no less. Computers sold in London should be programmed to talk like Cockneys: 'Do wot mate, yer bleedin' battery's running Barley Mow innit?' Dublin computers should say, 'I'd say the old battery's running out there, but I shouldn't worry about it.' And on the Isle of Wight, well, it's not an issue because they haven't got computers there yet.

The US fashion industry spotted a gap in the market and put a Gap in every high street, Nike have got a big tick against every country in the world, and if you have a coffee machine in your home, then expect Starbucks to open a branch in your kitchen any day now. Indeed, with coffee being the second most important trading commodity after oil, how long until anti-war protestors are chanting 'No Blood For Cappuccinos'?

American interests are advanced by NATO, the IMF, the WTO, the World Bank and dozens of multi-nationals whose turnover is greater than the GDP of most countries. Indeed it won't be long until an American company organizes the first leverage buy-out of a sovereign state. 'Ladies and gentlemen of the board, following a successful take-over bid, this company will now be known as Glaxo-Smith-Kline-Belgium. It gives us a seat in the European Union, a small army and an almost unlimited supply of yummy chocolates.'

There is a certain irony that today the American Empire is celebrating an essentially anti-imperialist event. But outside the

States, July 4th is now becoming the focus for a new campaign – a declaration of independence *from* America. Today at US bases in Britain, such as USAF Fairford in Gloucestershire or at Menwith Hill in Yorkshire, parties are being held to celebrate the idea that maybe one day we could live in a country that did not automatically assist in the star wars programme, did not send British troops in support of US foreign policy and were not forced to call Marathon bars 'Snickers'.

But being against US government policy should not be lazily extended to a general anti-Americanism. If you're a US citizen, please do not think I bear you any personal ill will (unless you yourself happen to be reading this, George W., which let's face it is unlikely given the absence of pictures). So Happy Independence Day, America; you did a fantastic job throwing off the hereditary monarchy of George III. But now would it be okay if we declared independence from the hereditary presidency of George II?

Acknowledgements

As ever I would like to thank Mark Burton and Pete Sinclair for permitting me to recycle the occasional line that we wrote together back in the golden age of the Home Service wireless and I am sure that they'll be particularly delighted that one of the old gang is being paid for their repetition (i.e. me). I'd also like to thank my agent Georgia Garrett, and Bill Scott-Kerr who edits my material so carefully and and glberdg

Although one or two pieces in this collection are published here for the first time in the UK, the vast majority of them originally appeared in the *Guardian*, for which I would like to thank Seumas Milne, Becky Gardiner, Stephen Moss, Joseph Harker and everyone else on the comment pages. Writing under the headline 'Comment and Analysis' has meant having to pretend to offer an opinion from time to time, so where I did not have the faintest idea what I thought about an issue I simply found out what Frederick Forsyth's angle was and then plumped for the opposite point of view.

But most of all, for warning me against the dangers of making an acknowledgements list a thinly disguised attempt at name-dropping, I would especially like to thank Philip Roth, Sting, Nicole Kidman, Bill and Hilary Clinton, the Dalai Lama and, of course, little Brooklyn Beckham.